Industrialization in
Sub-Saharan Africa

Industrialization in Sub-Saharan Africa

Seizing Opportunities in Global Value Chains

Kaleb G. Abreha, Woubet Kassa,
Emmanuel K. K. Lartey, Taye A. Mengistae,
Solomon Owusu, and Albert G. Zeufack

A copublication of the Agence française de développement and the World Bank

ISBN (paper): 978-1-4648-1673-4
ISBN (electronic): 978-1-4648-1721-2
DOI: 10.1596/978-1-4648-1673-4

Cover photo: A parts trolley drives through a vehicle assembly plant in Johannesburg, South Africa. © Wesley Poon / Shutterstock.com. Used with the permission of Wesley Poon / Shutterstock.com. Further permission required for reuse.
Cover design: Sergio Andres Moreno Tellez, World Bank

The Library of Congress Control Number has been requested.

Africa Development Forum Series

The **Africa Development Forum Series** was created in 2009 to focus on issues of significant relevance to Sub-Saharan Africa's social and economic development. Its aim is both to record the state of the art on a specific topic and to contribute to ongoing local, regional, and global policy debates. It is designed specifically to provide practitioners, scholars, and students with the most up-to-date research results while highlighting the promise, challenges, and opportunities that exist on the continent.

The series is sponsored by Agence française de développement and the World Bank. The manuscripts chosen for publication represent the highest quality in each institution and have been selected for their relevance to the development agenda. Working together with a shared sense of mission and interdisciplinary purpose, the two institutions are committed to a common search for new insights and new ways of analyzing the development realities of the Sub-Saharan Africa region.

Advisory Committee Members

Agence française de développement
Thomas Mélonio, Executive Director, Research and Knowledge Directorate
Hélène Djoufelkit, Director, Head of Economic Assessment and Public Policy Department
Marie-Pierre Nicollet, Director, Head of Knowledge Department on Sustainable Development
Sophie Chauvin, Head, Edition and Publication Division

World Bank
Albert G. Zeufack, Chief Economist, Africa Region
César Calderón, Lead Economist, Africa Region
Chorching Goh, Lead Economist, Africa Region

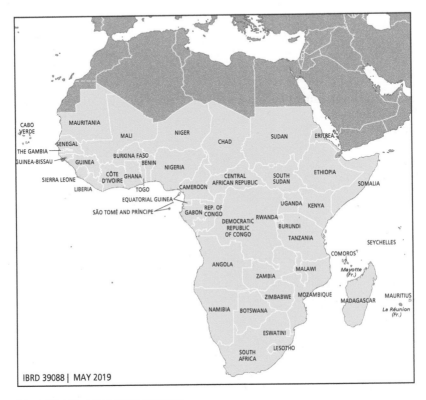

IBRD 39088 | MAY 2019

Source: World Bank (IBRD 39088, May 2019).

Titles in the Africa Development Forum Series

2021

Social Contracts for Development: Bargaining, Contention, and Social Inclusion in Sub-Saharan Africa (2021), Mathieu Clouthier, Bernard Harborne, Deborah Isser, Indhira Santos, Michael Watts

Industrialization in Sub-Saharan Africa: Seizing Opportunities in Global Value Chains (2021), Kaleb G. Abreha, Woubet Kassa, Emmanuel K. K. Lartey, Taye A. Mengistae, Solomon Owusu, Albert G. Zeufack

2020

*Les systèmes agroalimentaires en Afrique. Repenser le rôle des marchés (2020), *Food Systems in Africa: Rethinking the Role of Markets* (2021), Gaelle Balineau, Arthur Bauer, Martin Kessler, Nicole Madariaga

*The Future of Work in Africa: Harnessing the Potential of Digital Technologies for All (2020), *L'avenir du travail en Afrique : exploiter le potentiel des technologies numériques pour un monde du travail plus inclusif* (2021), Jieun Choi, Mark A. Dutz, Zainab Usman (eds.)

2019

All Hands on Deck: Reducing Stunting through Multisectoral Efforts in Sub-Saharan Africa (2019), Emmanuel Skoufias, Katja Vinha, Ryoko Sato

*The Skills Balancing Act in Sub-Saharan Africa: Investing in Skills for Productivity, Inclusivity, and Adaptability (2019), *Le développement des compétences en Afrique subsaharienne, un exercice d'équilibre : Investir dans les compétences pour la productivité, l'inclusion et l'adaptabilité* (2020), Omar Arias, David K. Evans, Indhira Santos

*Electricity Access in Sub-Saharan Africa: Uptake, Reliability, and Complementary Factors for Economic Impact (2019), *Accès à l'électricité en Afrique subsaharienne : adoption, fiabilité et facteurs complémentaires d'impact économique* (2020), Moussa P. Blimpo, Malcolm Cosgrove-Davies

2018

*Facing Forward: Schooling for Learning in Africa (2018), *Perspectives : l'école au service de l'apprentissage en Afrique* (2019), Sajitha Bashir, Marlaine Lockheed, Elizabeth Ninan, Jee-Peng Tan

Realizing the Full Potential of Social Safety Nets in Africa (2018), Kathleen Beegle, Aline Coudouel, Emma Monsalve (eds.)

2017

*Mining in Africa: Are Local Communities Better Off? (2017), *L'exploitation minière en Afrique : les communautés locales en tirent-elles parti?* (2020), Punam Chuhan-Pole, Andrew L. Dabalen, Bryan Christopher Land

*Reaping Richer Returns: Public Spending Priorities for African Agriculture Productivity Growth (2017), *Obtenir de meilleurs résultats : priorités en matière de dépenses publiques pour les gains de productivité de l'agriculture africaine* (2020), Aparajita Goyal, John Nash

2016

Confronting Drought in Africa's Drylands: Opportunities for Enhancing Resilience (2016), Raffaello Cervigni, Michael Morris (eds.)

2015

*Africa's Demographic Transition: Dividend or Disaster? (2015), *La transition démographique de l'Afrique : dividende ou catastrophe ?* (2016), David Canning, Sangeeta Raja, Abdo Yazbech

Highways to Success or Byways to Waste: Estimating the Economic Benefits of Roads in Africa (2015), Ali A. Rubaba, Federico Barra, Claudia Berg, Richard Damania, John Nash, Jason Russ

Enhancing the Climate Resilience of Africa's Infrastructure: The Power and Water Sectors (2015), Raffaello Cervigni, Rikard Liden, James E. Neumann, Kenneth M. Strzepek (eds.)

The Challenge of Stability and Security in West Africa (2015), Alexandre Marc, Neelam Verjee, Stephen Mogaka

*Land Delivery Systems in West African Cities: The Example of Bamako, Mali (2015), *Le système d'approvisionnement en terres dans les villes d'Afrique de l'Ouest : L'exemple de Bamako* (2015), Alain Durand-Lasserve, Maÿlis Durand- Lasserve, Harris Selod

*Safety Nets in Africa: Effective Mechanisms to Reach the Poor and Most Vulnerable (2015), *Les filets sociaux en Afrique : méthodes efficaces pour cibler les populations pauvres et vulnérables en Afrique subsaharienne* (2015), Carlo del Ninno, Bradford Mills (eds.)

2014

Tourism in Africa: Harnessing Tourism for Growth and Improved Livelihoods (2014), Iain Christie, Eneida Fernandes, Hannah Messerli, Louise Twining-Ward

Youth Employment in Sub-Saharan Africa (2014), *L'emploi des jeunes en Afrique subsaharienne* (2014), Deon Filmer, Louise Fox

2013

Les marchés urbains du travail en Afrique subsaharienne (2013), *Urban Labor Markets in Sub-Saharan Africa* (2013), Philippe De Vreyer, François Roubaud (eds.).

Enterprising Women: Expanding Economic Opportunities in Africa (2013), Mary Hallward-Driemeier

Securing Africa's Land for Shared Prosperity: A Program to Scale Up Reforms and Investments (2013), Frank F. K. Byamugisha

The Political Economy of Decentralization in Sub-Saharan Africa: A New Implementation Model (2013), Bernard Dafflon, Thierry Madiès (eds.)

2012

Empowering Women: Legal Rights and Economic Opportunities in Africa (2012), Mary Hallward-Driemeier, Tazeen Hasan

Financing Africa's Cities: The Imperative of Local Investment (2012), *Financer les villes d'Afrique : l'enjeu de l'investissement local* (2012), Thierry Paulais

Structural Transformation and Rural Change Revisited: Challenges for Late Developing Countries in a Globalizing World (2012), Transformations rurales et développement : les défis du changement structurel dans un monde globalisé (2013), Bruno Losch, Sandrine Fréguin-Gresh, Eric Thomas White

Light Manufacturing in Africa: Targeted Policies to Enhance Private Investment and Create Jobs (2012), L'Industrie légère en Afrique : politiques ciblées pour susciter l'investissement privé et créer des emplois (2012), Hinh T. Dinh, Vincent Palmade, Vandana Chandra, Frances Cossar

Informal Sector in Francophone Africa: Firm Size, Productivity, and Institutions (2012), Les entreprises informelles de l'Afrique de l'ouest francophone : taille, productivité et institutions (2012), Nancy Benjamin, Ahmadou Aly Mbaye

2011

Contemporary Migration to South Africa: A Regional Development Issue (2011), Aurelia Segatti, Loren Landau (eds.)

Challenges for African Agriculture (2011), Jean-Claude Deveze (ed.)

L'Économie politique de la décentralisation dans quatre pays d'Afrique subsaharienne : Burkina Faso, Sénégal, Ghana et Kenya (2011), Bernard Dafflon, Thierry Madiès (eds.)

2010

Gender Disparities in Africa's Labor Market (2010), Jorge Saba Arbache, Alexandre Kolev, Ewa Filipiak (eds.)

*Africa's Infrastructure: A Time for Transformation (2010), *Infrastructures africaines, une transformation impérative* (2010), Vivien Foster, Cecilia Briceño-Garmendia (eds.)

Challenges for African Agriculture (2011), Jean-Claude Deveze (ed.)

*Available in French

All books in the Africa Development Forum series that were copublished by Agence française de développement and the World Bank are available for free at https://openknowledge.worldbank.org/handle/10986/2150

Contents

Figures

Tables

Foreword

Industrialization has been the driving force behind structural transformation in both developed and newly industrializing countries. For countries in Sub-Saharan Africa, however, the messages on whether manufacturing can play a similar role in promoting sustainable growth have been mixed. The nature of emerging technologies, in particular, has contributed to the narrative that the opportunities to industrialize economies in Sub-Saharan Africa may be limited. However, the COVID-19 (coronavirus) global pandemic that brought world trade to a standstill and disrupted global supply chains has brought the issue of Africa's industrialization back to center stage.

This report provides a comprehensive assessment of the issue and shows that the prospects for industrialization are bound to differ across countries in Sub-Saharan Africa, depending on resource endowments and initial policy configurations related to industrial development. Furthermore, it argues that these prospects must be assessed in specific countries in the context of emerging technologies, the evolution of regional and global value chains (GVCs), and the implications of regional trade agreements for these developments. The report underscores the need to seize opportunities and integrate into GVCs by exploiting current comparative advantages in low-skill tasks, promoting value addition, and upgrading into high-skill tasks as a way to increase the scale and speed of industrialization.

Industrialization offers a viable path to structural transformation and job creation, but policy makers must reorient policy strategies to provide support for integration into GVCs. While the fragmentation of manufacturing activities across countries has created opportunities to industrialize, long term success will depend on investments in skills and technologies. These investments will be critical to enhance production capabilities, build comparative advantages in higher-value-added tasks to promote more and better jobs, raise productivity, and foster structural transformation.

Rising wages in recent years, coupled with low levels of productivity in manufacturing, pose potential challenges to the prospects for job growth in the short term. It would, therefore, be imperative for policies to be directed at boosting productivity growth to enable competitiveness and bolster robust job creation in manufacturing over the foreseeable future. The report proposes reforming state-owned enterprises and promoting a competitive environment that facilitates the allocation of resources toward more productive firms. Easing licensing requirements and other requirements for the establishment of new firms, and supporting young firms—the group of firms that have been the primary drivers of job creation—as well as promoting access to finance, should go a long way toward helping countries enhance market competitiveness. These policies must be combined with investment in enabling sectors, including digital and physical infrastructure and energy, and investment in industry-specific skills-development programs that incorporate the adoption of emerging technologies. The savvy mix of these ingredients, accounting for countries' endowment, should produce the much needed catalyst to productivity growth, key to job creation in Sub-Saharan Africa.

Industrial development must be an integral component of the economic transformation agenda in Sub-Saharan Africa, but to be successful, policies should foster integration into GVCs and aim to develop regional value chains. Thus, the quest to industrialize countries in Sub-Saharan Africa will require collaboration. A promising start is the African Continental Free Trade Area (AfCFTA), which provides a significant avenue for promoting intraregional trade to increase the processing of raw materials for export to external markets, adding value to imported raw materials from within the region, and expanding access to markets in the region for these products.

The World Bank is currently engaged in several initiatives to further this agenda, including support for investment in critical infrastructure to facilitate communication and transportation and overall connectivity between economies. Projects have also been launched to encourage regional trade and integrate markets. These steps all support policy strategies designed to promote the development of manufacturing regional value chains and integration into GVCs. We urge policy makers in Sub-Saharan Africa to capitalize on current opportunities for value addition and create a conducive environment for the emergence of new activities. Let's together seize the unprecedented opportunities offered by the digital revolution, an African single market, and adaptation to climate change to transform the African economy and create jobs.

Ousmane Diagana
Vice President
Western and Central Africa Region
World Bank
Washington, DC

Hafez M. H. Ghanem
Vice President
Eastern and Southern Africa Region
World Bank
Washington, DC

Acknowledgments

This volume is part of the African Regional Studies Program, an initiative of the Africa Region Vice Presidency at the World Bank. This series of studies aims to combine high levels of analytical rigor and policy relevance, and to apply them to various topics important for the social and economic development of Sub-Saharan Africa. Quality control and oversight are provided by the Office of the Chief Economist of the Africa Region.

This regional study was prepared by the following core team members: Kaleb G. Abreha, Woubet Kassa, Emmanuel K. K. Lartey, Taye A. Mengistae, Solomon Owusu, and Albert G. Zeufack.

Authors of the technical papers for the report include Derrick Abudu, Stefano Caria, Jieun Choi, Garth Frazer, Emiko Fukase, Reitze Gouma, Kebba Jammeh, Patricia Jones, Andrew Kerr, Emmanuel B. Mensah, Bruce McDougall, Wim Naude, Pierre Nguimkeu, Stefan Pahl, Marcel P. Timmer, Johannes Van Biesebroeck, Pieter J. Woltjer, Nadege Yameogo, and Elena Zaurino.

The report incorporated insightful comments and useful guidance received at the concept note review and decision meetings. In this regard, the team is grateful to peer reviewers at the decision meeting—Ndiamé Diop, Gaurav Nayyar, Mans Söderbom, and an anonymous referee. Additional comments were received from Caroline Freund, Caren Grown, Hans Peter Lankes, Maura K. Leary, Martha Martinez Licetti, Michal Rutkowski, Mathew A. Verghis, and Fan Yang. The report also benefited from discussion and feedback at the concept note review meeting, including from Paulo Bastos, Ted H. Chu, Ana Fernandes, Deon Filmer, Ejaz Ghani, Hiau Looi Kee, Daniel Lederman, Hibret Maemir, Aaditya Mattoo, Nataliya Mylenko, and Yutaka Yoshino. These comments improved the overall quality of the report.

The team thanks Moussa P. Blimpo for his extensive advisory role and feedback at various stages. The report also benefited from discussions by

Cesar Calderon, Jim Cust, and Mark Dutz and other participants at the authors' workshop. A useful set of comments was also received from Margaret McMillian. Beatrice A. Berman, Nora FitzGerald, and Maura Leary provided excellent communications support for the dissemination of the report. Sandra Gain and Amy Lynn Grossman provided valuable editorial assistance.

About the Authors

Kaleb G. Abreha is an economist in the Office of the Chief Economist for the Africa Region at the World Bank. He was also a World Bank Africa fellow. Before joining the World Bank, he was a postdoctoral research fellow at the Department of Economics and Business Economics and the Department of Management, Aarhus University (Denmark). Kaleb's research focuses on industrialization, international trade and investment, global value chains, productivity, exchange rates, and CEOs and firm performance. His research has been published in peer-reviewed journals such as the *World Bank Economic Review* and the *World Economy*. He has a PhD in economics from Aarhus University (Denmark), an MSc in agricultural economics from the University of Copenhagen (Denmark), and a BA in economics from Addis Ababa University (Ethiopia).

Woubet Kassa is an economist in the Office of the Chief Economist for the Africa Region at the World Bank. Before joining the Africa Region, he worked with the Trade and International Integration Unit of the Development Research Group at the World Bank. He is currently working on topics including international trade, global value chains, regional integration, and industrialization. Woubet is from Ethiopia, where he was a lecturer at Addis Ababa University and worked with the Ethiopian Policy Research Institute. He received his PhD in economics from American University where he is currently an adjunct professorial lecturer.

Emmanuel K. K. Lartey is a professor of economics at California State University, Fullerton. He has also worked as an economist in the Office of the Chief Economist for the Africa Region at the World Bank. His research focuses on policy-relevant issues in international macroeconomics in the context of developing economies and covers manufacturing productivity and global value chains. He has published extensively and holds a PhD in economics from Boston College.

Taye A. Mengistae is a former senior economist at the World Bank. He holds a PhD in economics from the University of Oxford.

Solomon Owusu is a research economist at the German Development Institute (DIE) in Bonn, Germany, and also serves as a coordinator of the Complexity Economics Working Group of the Young Scholars' Initiative, Institute for New Economic Thinking (New York). He is a former World Bank Africa fellow. Solomon has experience in economic research, teaching, and policy from working with and on projects for organizations including the World Bank (Washington, DC), United Nations Industrial Development Organization (Vienna), European Commission (EU-JRC, Belgium), Asian Development Bank, United Nations University–MERIT (the Netherlands), and Ghana Statistical Service. Solomon's research focuses broadly on development economics in areas such as the measurement and analysis of structural transformation, jobs and inclusive growth, global and regional value chains, international trade, and issues at the intersection of technology and productivity in developing countries with particular focus on Africa. Solomon's research has been published in peer-reviewed journals such as the *World Economy* and *Journal of Economic Behavior & Organization*. He is finalizing his PhD in economics at the Maastricht University in the Netherlands.

Albert G. Zeufack is the World Bank's chief economist for Africa. Before his appointment in May 2016, he was practice manager in the Macroeconomics and Fiscal Management Global Practice and leader of the World Bank–wide Community of Practice for the Management of Natural Resources Rents. His main research interest is in the microfoundations of macroeconomics. He joined the World Bank in 1997 as a Young Professional and started his career as a research economist in the Macroeconomics Division of the Research Department. Since then, he has held several positions in the Africa, East Asia and Pacific, and Europe and Central Asia Regions. Between 2008 and 2012, on leave from the World Bank, he was the director of research and investment strategy / chief economist for Khazanah Nasional Berhad, a Malaysian sovereign wealth fund. He is a member of the Technical Advisory Committee of the Natural Resource Charter at the University of Oxford, the Advisory Board of the Natural Resource Governance Institute, the United Nations Sustainable Development Solutions Network, and the board of the African Economic Research Consortium. He received his PhD in economics from CERDI, the University of Clermont-Ferrand (France), where he taught before joining the World Bank. He holds a master's degree in economic analysis and policy from the University of Yaoundé (Cameroon) and has received executive education from Harvard University and Stanford University.

Abbreviations

AfCFTA	African Continental Free Trade Area
AGOA	African Growth and Opportunity Act
DVA	domestic value added
DVX	indirect value added
EBA	Everything But Arms
EU	European Union
FDI	foreign direct investment
FVA	foreign value added
GDP	gross domestic product
GSP	Generalized System of Preferences
GVC	global value chain
ICT	information and communication technology
ICUE	Integrate, Compete, Upgrade, and Enable
NTBs	nontariff barriers
SOE	state-owned enterprise
TFP	total factor productivity
UNDP	United Nations Development Programme
UNIDO	United Nations Industrial Development Organization

UNCTAD   United Nations Conference on Trade and Development

US$ United States dollar

For a list of the 3-letter country codes used by the World Bank, please go to https://datahelpdesk.worldbank.org/knowledgebase/articles/906519-world -bank-country-and-lending-groups.

All dollar amounts are US dollars unless otherwise indicated.

Overview

Industrialization drives the sustained growth in jobs and productivity that marks the social and economic take-off of most developed economies. However, with emerging trends in technology and international trade, there are concerns that the prospects of manufacturing in Sub-Saharan Africa is limited. There are strong claims that economies in the region have experienced "premature deindustrialization," which may have reduced the viability of policies and strategies to promote manufacturing as a driver of sustainable growth.

Despite this narrative, industrialization and structural transformation are currently integral components of the African Union's Agenda 2063. In fact, industrialization features prominently in several African countries' development strategies, and some are currently implementing policies to promote the capacity of the manufacturing sector to engage in value-addition processes and create jobs. To the extent that there is renewed interest in industrialization across the continent, and certain countries have had some success in creating jobs in manufacturing, the central question is not whether countries in Sub-Saharan Africa should pursue industrialization as a potential path to sustainable growth but how to support their industrialization efforts.

The case for encouraging industrialization partly rests on the fact that manufacturing has strong links and spillover effects with other key sectors such as agriculture and services. In addition, manufacturing produces tradable goods that are subject to economies of scale and scope. It is also a conduit for international technology transfer and local knowledge spillovers. The scale and quality of job growth in manufacturing, therefore, can be driven as much by the growth of exports as by the expansion of domestic demand. Thus, a critical factor in the scale and speed of industrialization is the ability of local manufacturers to seize opportunities from the international production network and compete across value chains in local, regional, and global markets.

Indeed, most manufacturing activities now occur across global value chains (GVCs), such that many firms in different countries are involved in tasks ranging from the design of products, to the procurement of parts and components, to the final delivery of products to end users in the global market. This breakdown of the manufacturing process across GVCs, straddling international borders, has made it possible for developing countries to industrialize. It has created opportunities for countries to kick-start industrialization by initially specializing in lower-value-added tasks in which they have a comparative advantage along a given GVC, while at the same time actively investing in activities that culminate in building a comparative advantage in higher-value-added tasks. These developments offer opportunities that policy makers could capitalize on and strategize around to make industrialization work in the context of GVCs.

This report reassesses the prospects for industrialization in Sub-Saharan African countries via integration into GVCs and discusses the role of policy in enhancing these prospects. Industrialization stands to be a key precursor for jobs growth in Sub-Saharan Africa, with transformative potential in many parts of the continent. Thus, the focus should turn to creating the right policy environment to enable countries to integrate into manufacturing GVCs as a path to industrial development. However, not all countries in the region may be able to seize these opportunities, which gives rise to two interrelated questions. First, what are the prospects for countries in the region participating in specific manufacturing GVCs to generate significant and sustained gains in jobs and productivity? Second, what role, if any, can industrial policy play in promoting such prospects? The answers to these questions should be sought against the backdrop of the Fourth Industrial Revolution (the ongoing automation of traditional manufacturing and industrial practices using modern technology) and growing protectionism in developed countries.

The prospects for industrialization are bound to differ across countries, depending on resource endowments and initial policy configurations. Thus, an assessment of the region should account for the heterogeneity across the continent. Such prospects must also be assessed in specific countries in the context of new and emerging digital technologies, the evolution of regional and global value chains, and the implications of these developments for regional trade agreements and the broader international trading system.

Despite considerable heterogeneity across countries in the region, the evidence shows that Africa has not experienced premature deindustrialization. Moreover, manufacturing employment is driven primarily by the formation of new establishments and the growth of younger ones, similar to what is observed in advanced economies. This pattern is most evident in the earliest phase of the job growth process, when employers benefit from an environment of "unlimited labor supply" by hiring more workers at roughly constant wages. However, based on specific country cases, this phase of job growth is not sustainable, given that wages have been rising in recent years. This rising wage trend implies that robust job creation in manufacturing will rely more on sustained productivity growth.

Analyses of the dynamics of productivity at the establishment level show that participation in international trade increases productivity and generates more and better jobs in manufacturing as well as in the rest of the economy (through backward and forward links). More importantly, the integration of local enterprises into GVCs facilitates the industrialization process because global trade and regional integration are essential outlets for domestic production (exports) and sources of inputs (imports).

Although GVC links are associated with manufacturing employment and productivity growth, and countries have been industrializing across value chains, current GVC activities in the region are predominantly via forward links. In addition, the extent to which countries participate in GVCs depends on their resource endowments and geography, among other factors. For resource-rich economies, policy reforms especially aimed at value upgrading along GVCs provide opportunities to industrialize.

Policies to promote industrialization should aim to enhance integration into global value chains by building up from regional ones. Such policies should focus on facilitating the entry and survival of new establishments by maintaining a competitive market environment. However, with rising wages, policies should also aim to accelerate productivity growth via GVC upgrading combined with investment in critical enabling sectors such as infrastructure (physical and digital), finance, energy, and the type of skills development that incorporates entrepreneurship and the adoption of digital technologies.

Key Messages

Contrary to the predominant narrative, manufacturing represents a viable path to structural transformation in Africa

Sub-Saharan Africa, as a region, has not been prematurely deindustrializing. On the contrary, the region has continued to industrialize given that the share of manufacturing employment and value added in total output has either increased or at worst remained flat in most regions of the continent. Manufacturing value added as a share of gross domestic product (GDP), in particular, has been rising with income level in non-oil economies,[1] underscoring the key role of resource endowments in the industrialization experiences of Sub-Saharan African countries (figure O.1).

The employment share of the manufacturing sector also exhibits a steady upward trend with rising income during the period 1970–2015 (figure O.2). The region experienced a 148 percent increase in manufacturing jobs, from a total of 8.6 million in 1990 to 21.3 million in 2018.[2] Moreover, trends in alternative

Figure O.1 Trends in Manufacturing Value-Added Shares in GDP and Non-Oil GDP in Sub-Saharan Africa

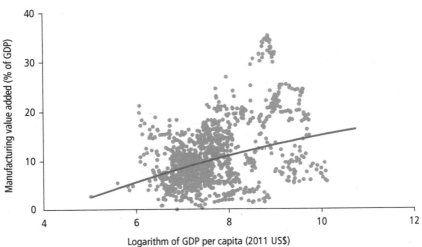

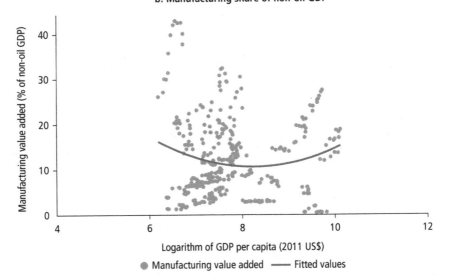

Source: Nguimkeu and Zeufack 2019.
Note: GDP = gross domestic product.

Figure O.2 Manufacturing Employment Share versus GDP per Capita in Sub-Saharan Africa, 1970–2015

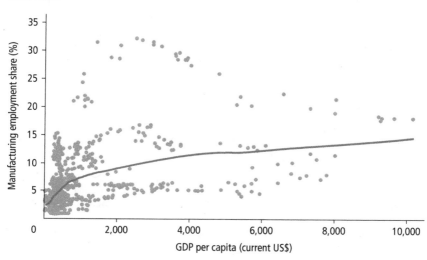

Source: World Bank calculation based on Expanded Africa Sector Database (1970–2015); Mensah and Szirmai 2018; Mensah et al. 2018.
Note: GDP = gross domestic product.

indicators of industrialization, such as the absolute size of manufacturing value added, show that the region is industrializing.

The industrialization trends and patterns vary across the region, with significant subregional differences in the evolution of manufacturing output shares across income levels. The contribution of manufacturing to value added has picked up moderately in eastern and central Africa, has remained flat in West Africa, and has declined in southern Africa.[3] These differences illustrate that the potential to industrialize will be different across the region, and, based on the evolution of manufacturing value added and employment over the past two decades, the sector cannot be ruled out as a viable path to structural transformation, at least for some countries in Africa.

Still, the increase in shares of manufacturing value added and employment has not been on the scale of what happened in emerging market economies in East Asia. Even when economic growth was relatively high, it was not characterized by a shift in the production structure from relatively low-productivity enterprises in agriculture to high-productivity enterprises in manufacturing, and significant job growth.

Thus, there seems to be scope for job growth through further industrialization in the region on a large scale. The challenge is to come up with innovative industrial policy tools to address issues peculiar to the current global setting, including rising protectionism and rapid advances in labor-saving technologies that can limit the traditional mass job creation associated with industrialization.

Industrial policies must be designed to address the challenges of industrialization in Sub-Saharan African countries. To the extent that modern manufacturing activity occurs within GVCs, such policies should facilitate and reinforce integration into manufacturing GVCs.

African countries are relatively well integrated into GVCs, but links need to be strengthened by increasing value added to current exports and strategizing to upgrade into knowledge-intensive industries

The participation rate of manufacturing firms in GVCs is greater than 40 percent in Sub-Saharan Africa (figure O.3), indicating that a significant share of the region's trade occurs along value chains. GVC participation rates are reasonably high compared with a benchmark group of countries comprising Bangladesh, Cambodia, Indonesia, and Vietnam. GVC participation rates are particularly high for oil exporters (oil-resource-rich countries) and minerals and metals exporters (non-oil-resource-rich countries). Participation rates range from 59 percent for oil exporters to 45 percent for the group of minerals exporters to 37 percent for the non-resource-rich group of countries. These participation rates are comparable to the average for the benchmark group of countries, which is about 55 percent (figure O.4).

Sub-Saharan Africa's participation in GVCs, however, is dominated by exports of primary products rather than imports of intermediate goods for further upgrading and export. The dependence on commodity exports has likely discouraged the development of manufacturing activities, with limited imported content in their exports. Imported intermediate goods are essential for quality upgrading and productivity enhancement. Thus, countries in Sub-Saharan Africa should pursue policies that create an environment conducive to the manufacturing activities that facilitate such activities, to foster transfer of knowledge and technology. Nevertheless, the differences in backward and forward participation rates suggest that there should be some variation in the economic policies adopted across countries, aimed at promoting integration into manufacturing GVCs at the national and subregional levels.

Manufacturers in Sub-Saharan Africa have relied on domestic intermediate goods in their production processes, with significant variation across countries, accounting for 77 percent in Djibouti, 66 percent in Rwanda, and more than

Figure O.3 Trends in Sub-Saharan Africa's Participation in GVCs, 1990–2015

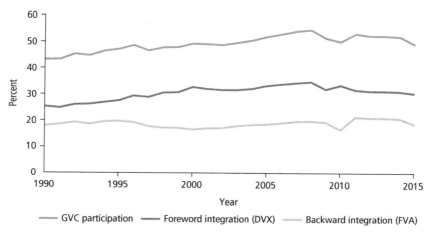

Source: Based on data from the UNCTAD Eora database.
Note: DVX = indirect value added; FVA = foreign value added; GVC = global value chain.

Figure O.4 Links to All Manufacturing GVCs, by Country Group

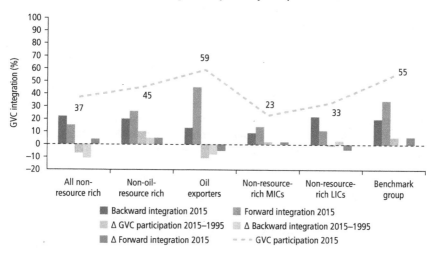

Source: Abreha et al. 2019.
Note: GVC = global value chain; LICs = low-income countries; MICs = middle-income countries.

50 percent in countries such as Cameroon, Guinea, Madagascar, Mali, and Mauritania (figure O.5). Overall, the share of inputs purchased domestically is 48 percent, on average, whereas the share of imported intermediate inputs is 14 percent and the share of value added created domestically is 38 percent.

Imported intermediate goods, although not prevalent, predominantly originated from the European Union and the United States during the period 1995–2015. However, imports of intermediate goods from China are growing rapidly. Furthermore, there is limited intraregional value-added trade activity within Sub-Saharan Africa, with intermediate inputs from within the region cumulatively accounting for an average of 0.7 percent of the total value of manufacturing output.

The rising shares of China and East Asia in the import content of Sub-Saharan African exports and the declining shares of the European Union and the United States suggest an important shift in global trade and underscore the need to consider reorienting some of the region's trade and industrialization strategies toward East Asia. In addition, to the extent possible, intraregional trade in intermediate goods will need to pick up significantly.

In current settings, efforts to promote job growth through industrialization would succeed to the extent that such policies are consistent with domestic firms' participation in manufacturing GVCs at links that maximize gains in jobs and productivity. Although the current rates of participation in manufacturing GVCs are comparable to those in South Asia and East Asia, tasks are mostly in labor-intensive industries and predominantly in natural resource–intensive sectors. It is therefore imperative that countries exploit their current comparative advantages to create jobs while strategically repositioning to upgrade into high-value-added tasks and industries where opportunities exist by promoting competitiveness along those dimensions. Dynamic comparative advantages, therefore, will be critical to industrialization efforts as countries confront emerging technologies and strive to remain competitive to seize opportunities along GVCs. An equally significant factor is skills enhancement, which should be an integral part of policy configurations aimed at promoting participation and upgrading in GVCs.

Africa has the potential to exploit opportunities in manufacturing GVCs for job creation and structural transformation by facilitating productivity growth and promoting competitiveness

Although the potential to industrialize through GVC integration is quite promising for Sub-Saharan African countries, a number of key policy priorities are needed to bolster these efforts' chances of success.

Promoting competitiveness through dynamic comparative advantage

Participation in manufacturing GVCs has led to job growth in Sub-Saharan Africa, mainly because of expanding global demand for manufacturing goods in

Figure O.5 Sources of Intermediate Inputs in Manufacturing, 2015

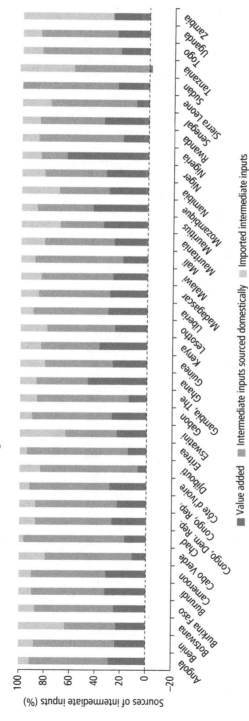

■ Value added   ■ Intermediate inputs sourced domestically   ▦ Imported intermediate inputs

Source: World Bank illustration based on data from Van Biesebroeck and Mensah 2019.

the world economy. Expanding global demand added 1.69 log points to manufacturing GVC job growth in Ethiopia.[4] In Kenya, Senegal, and South Africa, it added 0.89 log points, 0.63 log points, and 0.46 log points, respectively, to GVC job growth between 2000 and 2014. These gains notwithstanding, the region still has the lowest average share of formal manufacturing jobs in GVCs, at about 15 percent (figure O.6). The share of formal manufacturing jobs in GVCs is well above 35 percent in comparator countries such as Bangladesh, Brazil, China, India, and Malaysia.

Although job growth through GVC participation was bolstered by global demand, it has been weakened by two proximate factors: a decline in competitiveness and a decline in the labor requirements needed per unit of output arising from the adoption of labor-saving technologies to replace routine jobs in production along GVCs (Pahl et al. 2019). The decline in labor demand in the execution of activities along GVCs reduced job growth by 0.35 log points, 0.22 log points, and 0.10 log points in South Africa, Senegal, and

Figure O.6 **Share of Workers in GVCs, by Sector of Employment in Sub-Saharan Africa and Benchmark Countries, 2014**

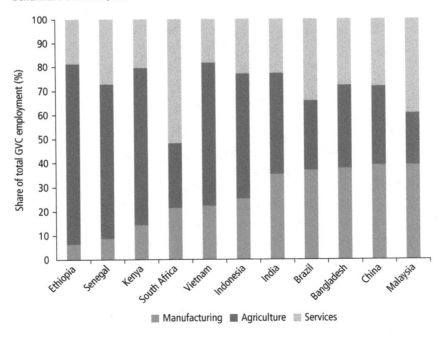

Source: Pahl et al. 2019.
Note: Services include other industry. Countries are ranked by share of manufacturing global value chain (GVC) employment.

Kenya, respectively (figure O.7). Even so, labor requirements in manufacturing went up in some countries, such as by 0.34 log points in Ethiopia. Loss of competitiveness also depressed the creation of jobs within GVCs in Ethiopia, Kenya, Senegal, and South Africa.

An overwhelming majority of the share of the labor force in the manufacturing sector in Sub-Saharan African countries is employed in low-value-added industries. Still, there is evidence that integrating into manufacturing GVCs has had positive effects on productivity growth (with some variation across the region), which is contrary to the notion that developing countries could be locked into unproductive activities in low-value-added stages of the value chain (Dalle, Fossati, and Lavopa 2013).

These developments notwithstanding, exploiting comparative advantages to upgrade in tasks along GVCs should remain a policy priority given that upgrading along GVCs generates manufacturing jobs.[5] These employment effects tend to occur through export upgrading in GVCs, with the export upgrading predominantly occurring through exporting products with imported intermediate inputs, which enhances the quality of exports. Thus, policies to facilitate imports of intermediates will be essential to upgrading in GVCs. In addition,

Figure O.7 GVC Participation and Manufacturing Job Growth: The Roles of Technology, Competitiveness, and Demand in Sub-Saharan Africa and Benchmark Countries, 2000–14

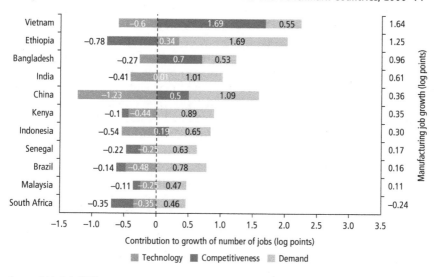

Contribution to growth of number of jobs (log points)

■ Technology   ■ Competitiveness   ▨ Demand

Source: Pahl et al. 2019.
Note: Countries are ordered by growth in number of manufacturing jobs (workers), indicated on the right-hand side (ignoring approximation error). *Technology* measures the effect of the change in labor requirement per value added. *Competitiveness* captures the effect attributed to the change in a country's income share in the GVCs; *Demand* refers to the effect of growth in world expenditure on final goods completed in the GVCs. GVC = global value chain.

ugrading would require targeted programs to develop the skills necessary to engage in high-skill tasks in GVCs.

Although upgrading in GVCs is essential for jobs and productivity growth, it tends to be biased toward skilled manufacturing and functional business-related jobs. It is, therefore, equally essential to ensure that there are job opportunities in low-skill tasks in the value chains for the large unskilled workforce in the region to ensure that integration into manufacturing GVCs leads to more inclusive growth. This requirement further underscores the need to adopt a policy configuration that incorporates dynamic comparative advantages.

Reducing market barriers and constraints to facilitate the establishment of new and growth of young firms

Manufacturing job growth in the region has been driven mainly by new and young firms over the past two decades. For example, firms in Côte d'Ivoire contributed to the creation of more than 25,000 jobs between 2003 and 2014, fueled primarily by young firms. Similarly, an estimated 128,000 manufacturing jobs were created in Ethiopia between 1996 and 2016 in establishments employing 10 workers or more, with the new jobs being concentrated in new and young firms (figure O.8).

Although the pace of job growth was uniformly high among small and large firms in both countries, new firms played a lesser role in job growth in Côte d'Ivoire than in Ethiopia, which is likely due to the lower rates of entry and exit in Côte d'Ivoire.

Manufacturing job growth in Ethiopia has been fueled by relatively low wages, an opportunity that was seized primarily by new and young firms. Gross profit margin per worker also rose steadily in new and young firms, reflecting a constant rise in average labor productivity. In addition, in Côte d'Ivoire, manufacturing job growth has been enabled by low wages, and firms appear to have taken advantage of low wages to invest in labor-intensive activities and techniques.

However, there is clear evidence that the scope for job growth at low wages has diminished: average wages have been rising with job growth in recent years, indicating that the potential for industrialization over the long term would depend on productivity growth. Thus, wages relative to productivity, and hence unit labor costs, will be critical to job growth in manufacturing.

The broader policy implication of the concentration of job growth in new and young firms is that public interventions to stimulate job growth should avoid size-based support schemes and aim to lower barriers to entry, enabling the growth of new and young firms and promoting productivity growth within firms. Such policies should also encompass investments in energy and infrastructure as well as digital technologies.

Figure O.8 **Number of Manufacturing Workers, by Age of Firms, Côte d'Ivoire and Ethiopia**

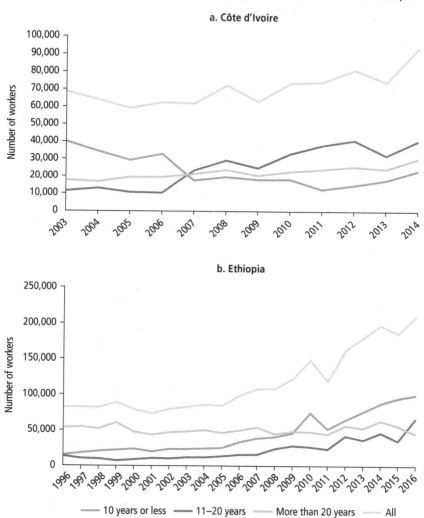

a. Côte d'Ivoire

b. Ethiopia

Source: Abreha et al. 2019.

Promoting innovation in processes and products along with addressing the severe misallocations within and across firms and industries
Across the region, the growth rate of total factor productivity in manufacturing has been consistently higher in countries where manufacturing job growth

rates have been higher, and a large share of the observed productivity growth has also been driven by the reallocation of market share. Reallocation of market share from less productive firms to more productive ones has provided a significant boost to productivity growth in Côte d'Ivoire and Ethiopia, and has occurred through the expansion and contraction of incumbent producers as well as new plant openings and plant closures, eliminating the least productive plants through exposure to greater competition from new firms.

A study of Ugandan firms also illustrates the extent of misallocation of resources, that is, failure to allocate resources to their most productive uses, and its impact in Sub-Saharan African manufacturing. Between 2002 and 2009, labor productivity in Uganda grew, on average, by 13 percent annually (Dennis et al. 2016). The productivity gains were due to improvements in the technical efficiency of operating firms and the movement of labor and capital across industries and firms within industries. About 20 percent of the growth was a result of labor movement to more productive sectors and industries, and reallocation of labor across firms explains 55 percent to 90 percent of growth at the industry level.

The current trend of rising wages suggests that aggregate productivity will have to be driven by productivity growth within firms, which tends to occur through three fundamental channels: international trade, foreign direct investment (FDI), and clustering.

The impact of trade on productivity occurs through exposure to foreign demand, better technology, a variety of inputs, intense competition in the goods markets and associated gains in market share, and resource reallocation toward productive firms (Harrison and Rodriguez-Clare 2010). Exporters and importers in Sub-Saharan African manufacturing outperform their domestic counterparts in productivity (see, for example, Bigsten et al. 2004; Mengistae and Pattillo 2004; Van Biesebroeck 2005), which aligns with the generally accepted view that firms with superior performance tend to engage in exporting and importing activities and, therefore, are more productive (Abreha 2019; Bigsten and Gebreeyesus 2009). Relatedly, enterprises experience significant productivity improvement after becoming exporters and importers.[6]

Foreign capital (FDI) provides incentives for innovation, and innovation attracts foreign ownership. Foreign-owned enterprises drive productivity growth via enhanced access to credit, adoption of better organizational and management practices, and diffusion of technical and business skills as well as technology to domestic firms. The benefits of foreign investment are not limited to foreign-owned firms but are shared by domestic firms through technology spillovers and other pecuniary externalities and competition effects.[7] In Ghana, firms managed by entrepreneurs with previous experience in foreign-owned enterprises enjoy a productivity premium over other domestic firms (Gorg and Strobl 2005). Moreover, total factor productivity is found to be 8 percent higher among domestic firms in Ethiopia that are located in districts that attracted significant greenfield FDI (Abebe, McMillan, and Serafinelli 2018).

Economic clusters improve innovation by enhancing innovation capability through the sharing of resources, such as infrastructure and goods with scale economies; better matching between producers and inputs; and learning from exchange and transfer of knowledge and skills. Urbanization, via clustering, provides a platform for interactions between firms and workers in markets for final goods and services, intermediate inputs, and knowledge. These interactions constitute agglomeration economies and usually translate into a competitive environment that stimulates innovation, productivity growth, and ultimately more and better jobs. For example, in Ethiopia, the agglomeration drives up productivity in firms that produce the same product (Bigsten et al. 2012).

More generally, agglomeration effects are rather weaker than expected in Sub-Saharan African countries (Siba and Söderbom 2015). In Côte d'Ivoire and Ghana, for instance, although urbanization has been driven by the formation of consumption cities because of discovery, production, and export of resource commodities, it is unlikely to result in agglomeration economies. However, there is still potential for agglomeration as a key driver of productivity growth and job generation.

Policy measures, therefore, should focus on accelerating productivity growth by increasing trade openness and integration into regional and global value chains, promoting innovation in production processes and products, adopting new technology and better management practices, enforcing effective entry and competition regulations, and leveraging urbanization as well as establishing and bolstering economic clusters.

Leveraging the African Continental Free Trade Area and other trade agreements to expand access to external markets

One strategy for Sub-Saharan African countries to create jobs through GVCs would be to facilitate an increase in the global share of value added in various GVCs across a more diversified array of manufacturing industries. Another approach would be to enter and expand activities in high-growth end markets and improve their share in serving those markets. For this strategy, fast-growing end markets are as important as domestic demand. Equally important would be leveraging trade policy using the African Continental Free Trade Area to promote intracontinental trade in manufactures, which should boost job growth through economies of scale and scope.

Countries in Sub-Saharan Africa impose high barriers to trade with each other, which raises production costs, erodes potential comparative advantages, and hinders integration into GVCs. Tariffs on inputs imported into the region, although declining, are also high, especially for transport equipment and parts and accessories. The growing fragmentation of production across borders highlights the need for the region to negotiate and implement policies on tariffs, nontariff barriers, and competitive exchange rate regimes. Such policies would facilitate more open, predictable, and transparent trade relations; expand market access with trading partners; and build and strengthen existing links to GVCs. Reducing trade barriers is a necessary condition for integrating into GVCs and strengthening links, particularly for resource-rich countries that need to import production equipment and intermediate inputs at lower costs to add value to natural resources for export, because high import barriers directly influence firms' costs of importing or exporting and, hence, participation in GVCs.

Furthermore, external trade policies that facilitate access to export markets would be beneficial to firms in manufacturing GVCs that engage in textiles and apparel exports, agro-processing, and processing of natural resources before export, activities in which Sub-Saharan African countries have a natural comparative advantage and where they can leverage the most gains.

A regional industrial policy in the context of the African Continental Free Trade Area could bolster scale economies and complementarities to drive more production, processing, and higher-value exports from the region, and facilitate industrialization through GVCs. In addition, the agreement should be designed to promote, produce, and export specific manufactured products within the regional market based on country-specific comparative advantages (Odijie 2018). In this respect, countries in the region are heterogeneous and have different comparative advantages that can be exploited to develop regional value chains in manufacturing.

A Policy Framework for Industrializing along Global Value Chains: Integrate, Compete, Upgrade, Enable

The prospects for industrialization in African countries depend on their capacity to participate and upgrade in manufacturing GVCs and are bound to vary across countries based on resource endowments, geography, and level of development. Building that capacity, however, requires an appropriate industrial policy package that combines soft policies and hard policies.

Soft industrial policies aim to support the growth and productivity of all sectors in the economy, whereas hard policies focus on developing traditional manufacturing, building sectors with some characteristics of manufacturing, and promoting indigenous entrepreneurship in small-scale manufacturing. The design of such policy configurations must factor in, and be consistent with, country-specific characteristics, given the wide variation in resources, income, size, and level of industrialization across countries in Sub-Saharan Africa.

Thus, industrial policies and strategies in Sub-Saharan African countries must exploit current comparative advantages while developing capabilities to compete in high-skill and knowledge-intensive industries. In essence, dynamic comparative advantages must be at the core of policy packages for industrializing along manufacturing GVCs.

Furthermore, emerging megatrends, such as changing technologies, shifting globalization patterns, climate change, and global pandemics, need to be accounted for in the design of policies to promote industrialization.[8]

A set of overarching policy implications that emerge from the analysis can be summarized within a policy framework that consists of four pillars: Integrate, Compete, Upgrade, and Enable, or ICUE (figure O.9).

- *Integrate.* The integration pillar captures policies that promote GVC participation as well as overall integration into regional and global economies through trade and FDI. These policies include trade liberalization, trade diversification toward emerging market economies, and regional trade agreements.

- *Compete.* The competition pillar is the set of policies that aim to reduce market distortions through reforms of state-owned enterprises and credit markets and improvement of the investment climate, and that aim to ease licensing requirements to facilitate the entry, survival, and growth of new and young establishments.

- *Upgrade.* The upgrading pillar encompasses policies that promote both industrial and GVC upgrading and that facilitate industrial shifts in employment shares and value added creation. Industrial upgrading is the rapid growth (in relative terms) and redistribution of employment and value added toward knowledge-intensive industries (for example, electrical and machinery and transport equipment) and away from agriculture-based, labor-intensive industries (food and beverages, textiles and apparel, and wood and paper) and mining-based, capital-intensive industries (chemicals and nonmetals and metals). GVC upgrading denotes the movement of workers into more sophisticated business functions in GVCs, such as when firms in an industry move from performing assembly activities to product design and redesign, logistics, after-sales services, and repairs. Policies that promote upgrading include subsidizing research and development and innovation, supporting human resource management practices, and leveraging urbanizing and developing economic clusters.

- *Enable.* The enabling pillar is the set of policies that support and promote investment in enabling sectors, including digital infrastructure, energy, finance, transportation and logistics, and skills development. These sectors are cross-cutting and capable of improving productive and absorptive capacity in agriculture and services, strengthening their links with manufacturing, and supporting inclusive and better job creation.

Figure O.9 Policy Framework: Integrate, Compete, Upgrade, and Enable

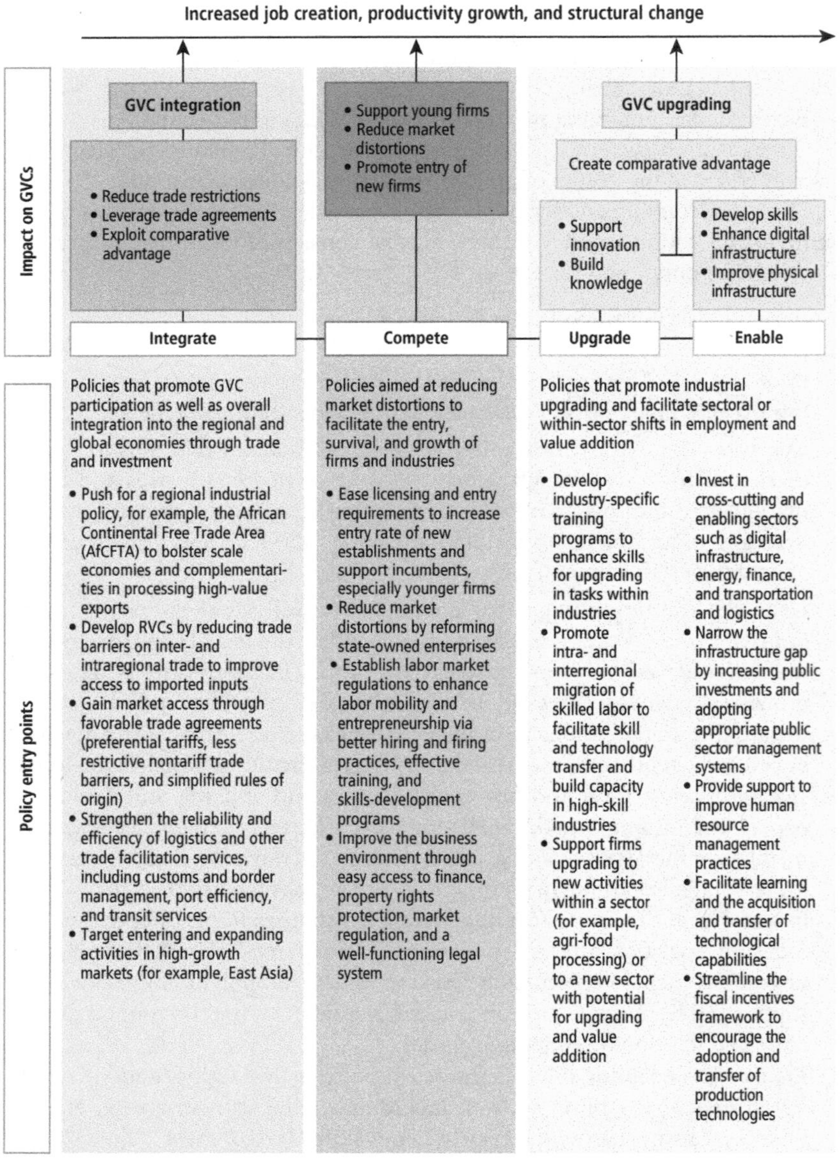

Increased job creation, productivity growth, and structural change

Impact on GVCs

GVC integration
• Reduce trade restrictions • Leverage trade agreements • Exploit comparative advantage

• Support young firms
• Reduce market distortions
• Promote entry of new firms

GVC upgrading
Create comparative advantage

• Support innovation • Build knowledge	• Develop skills • Enhance digital infrastructure • Improve physical infrastructure

Integrate	Compete	Upgrade	Enable

Policy entry points

Policies that promote GVC participation as well as overall integration into the regional and global economies through trade and investment

• Push for a regional industrial policy, for example, the African Continental Free Trade Area (AfCFTA) to bolster scale economies and complementarities in processing high-value exports
• Develop RVCs by reducing trade barriers on inter- and intraregional trade to improve access to imported inputs
• Gain market access through favorable trade agreements (preferential tariffs, less restrictive nontariff trade barriers, and simplified rules of origin)
• Strengthen the reliability and efficiency of logistics and other trade facilitation services, including customs and border management, port efficiency, and transit services
• Target entering and expanding activities in high-growth markets (for example, East Asia)

Policies aimed at reducing market distortions to facilitate the entry, survival, and growth of firms and industries

• Ease licensing and entry requirements to increase entry rate of new establishments and support incumbents, especially younger firms
• Reduce market distortions by reforming state-owned enterprises
• Establish labor market regulations to enhance labor mobility and entrepreneurship via better hiring and firing practices, effective training, and skills-development programs
• Improve the business environment through easy access to finance, property rights protection, market regulation, and a well-functioning legal system

Policies that promote industrial upgrading and facilitate sectoral or within-sector shifts in employment and value addition

• Develop industry-specific training programs to enhance skills for upgrading in tasks within industries
• Promote intra- and interregional migration of skilled labor to facilitate skill and technology transfer and build capacity in high-skill industries
• Support firms upgrading to new activities within a sector (for example, agri-food processing) or to a new sector with potential for upgrading and value addition

• Invest in cross-cutting and enabling sectors such as digital infrastructure, energy, finance, and transportation and logistics
• Narrow the infrastructure gap by increasing public investments and adopting appropriate public sector management systems
• Provide support to improve human resource management practices
• Facilitate learning and the acquisition and transfer of technological capabilities
• Streamline the fiscal incentives framework to encourage the adoption and transfer of production technologies

Source: Original figure for this publication.
Note: GVC = global value chain; RVC = regional value chain.

Notes

1. Given that challenges to industrialization are likely to vary between resource-rich economies, particularly oil exporters, and non-resource-rich economies, the appropriate measure of industrialization is the share of manufacturing in non-oil GDP.
2. World Bank calculation based on the Expanded Africa Sector Database (1970–2015).
3. See Nguimkeu and Zeufack (2019).
4. Multiplying log point growth by 100 yields percentage growth rate.
5. Except in the food and beverages industry, although the correlation is weak and not significantly different from zero.
6. See Abreha (2019) and Bigsten and Gebreeyesus (2009) for Ethiopia; Bigsten et al. (2004) for selected countries in Sub-Saharan Africa; Halpern, Koren, and Szeidl (2015) for Hungary; Kasahara and Lapham (2013) and Kasahara and Rodrigue (2008) for Chile; and Van Biesebroeck (2005) for selected countries in Sub-Saharan Africa.
7. There is a distinction between inward and outward FDI spillovers. Inward FDI spillovers refer to effects in the host country, whereas outward FDI spillovers denote their counterparts in the source country. Because almost all Sub-Saharan African countries are recipients of foreign direct investment, and they are the focus of the analysis, the discussion on FDI in this report is entirely about inward FDI and Sub-Saharan African countries as hosts.
8. The potential for an event like COVID-19 (coronavirus) to disrupt supply chains, thereby hindering integration into GVCs, has recently been at the forefront of policy discussions. Preliminary evidence, however, suggests that the impact in Kenya, for example, has been minimal. In particular, Kenyan exports have been found to be particularly resilient during the pandemic (Mold and Mveyange 2020).

References

Abebe, G., M. S. McMillan, and M. Serafinelli. 2018. "Foreign Direct Investment and Knowledge Diffusion in Poor Locations: Evidence from Ethiopia." NBER Working Paper 24461, National Bureau of Economic Research, Cambridge, MA.

Abreha, K. G. 2019. "Importing and Firm Productivity in Ethiopian Manufacturing." *World Bank Economic Review* 33 (3): 772–92.

Abreha, K. G., P. Jones, E. Lartey, T. Mengistae, and A. Zeufack. 2019. "Manufacturing Job Growth in Africa: What Is Driving It? The Cases of Côte d'Ivoire and Ethiopia." World Bank, Washington, DC.

Bigsten, A., P. Collier, S. Dercon, M. Fafchamps, B. Gauthier, J. W. Gunning, A. Oduro, et al. 2004. "Do African Manufacturing Firms Learn from Exporting?" *Journal of Development Studies* 40 (3): 115–41.

Bigsten, A., and M. Gebreeyesus. 2009. "Firm Productivity and Exports: Evidence from Ethiopian Manufacturing." *Journal of Development Studies* 45 (10): 1594–614.

Bigsten, A., M. Gebreeyesus, E. Siba, and M. Söderbom. 2012. "Enterprise Agglomeration, Output Prices, and Physical Productivity: Firm-Level Evidence from Ethiopia." UNU-WIDER Working Paper 2012/85, United Nations University–World Institute for Development Economics Research, Helsinki, Finland.

Dalle, D., V. Fossati, and F. Lavopa. 2013. "Industrial Policy and Developmental Space: The Missing Piece in the GVCs Debate." *Revista Argentina de Economía Internacional* 2.

Dennis, A., T. Mengistae, Y. Yoshino, and A. Zeufack. 2016. "Sources of Productivity Growth in Uganda: The Role of Interindustry and Intra-Industry Misallocation in the 2000s." Policy Research Working Paper 7909, World Bank, Washington, DC.

Gorg, H., and E. Strobl. 2005. "Spillovers from Foreign Firms through Worker Mobility: An Empirical Investigation." *Scandinavian Journal of Economics* 107 (4): 693–709.

Halpern, L., M. Koren, and A. Szeidl. 2015. "Imported Inputs and Productivity." *American Economic Review* 105 (12): 3660–703.

Harrison, A., and A. Rodríguez-Clare. 2010. "Trade, Foreign Investment, and Industrial Policy for Developing Countries." In *Handbook of Development Economics,* vol. 5, edited by D. Rodrik and M. Rosenzweig, 4039–14. Amsterdam: North-Holland.

Kasahara, H., and B. Lapham. 2013. "Productivity and the Decision to Import and Export: Theory and Evidence." *Journal of International Economics* 89 (2): 297–316.

Kasahara, H., and J. Rodrigue. 2008. "Does the Use of Imported Intermediates Increase Productivity? Plant-Level Evidence." *Journal of Development Economics* 87 (1): 106–18.

Mengistae, T., and C. Pattillo. 2004. "Export Orientation and Productivity in Sub-Saharan Africa." *IMF Staff Papers* 51 (2): 327–53.

Mensah, E. B., S. Owusu, N. Foster-McGregor, and A. Szirmai. 2018. "Structural Change, Productivity Growth and Labor Market Turbulence in Africa." UNU-MERIT Working Paper Series 2018-025, United Nations University–Maastricht Economic and Social Research Institute on Innovation and Technology, Maastricht, Netherlands.

Mensah, E. B., and A. Szirmai. 2018. "Africa Sector Database: Expansion and Update." UNU-MERIT Working Paper Series 2018-020, United Nations University–Maastricht Economic and Social Research Institute on Innovation and Technology, Maastricht, Netherlands.

Mold, A., and A. Mveyange. 2020. "Crisis? What Crisis? Covid-19 and the Unexpected Recovery of Regional Trade in East Africa." Brookings Institution, *Africa in Focus* (blog), September 28, 2020. https://www.brookings.edu/blog/africa-in-focus/2020/09/28/crisis-what-crisis-covid-19-and-the-unexpected-recovery-of-regional-trade-in-east-africa/.

Nguimkeu, P., and A. G. Zeufack. 2019. "Manufacturing in Structural Change in Africa." Policy Research Working Paper 8992, World Bank, Washington, DC.

Odijie, E. M. 2018. "The Need for Industrial Policy Coordination in the African Continental Free Trade Area." *African Affairs* 118 (470): 182–93.

Pahl, S., M. Timmer, R. Gouma, and P. Woltjer. 2019. "Jobs in Global Value Chains: New Evidence for Four African Countries in International Perspective." Policy Research Working Paper 8953, World Bank, Washington, DC.

Siba, E., and M. Söderbom. 2015. "Enterprise Agglomeration and Firm Performance in Sub-Saharan Africa." In *Handbook on Trade and Development,* edited by O. Morrissey, R. Lopez, and K. Sharma, 169–78. Cheltenham, U.K.: Edward Elgar Publishing.

Van Biesebroeck, J. 2005. "Exporting Raises Productivity in Sub-Saharan African Manufacturing Firms." *Journal of International Economics* 67 (2): 373–91.

Van Biesebroeck, J., and E. B. Mensah. 2019. "The Extent of GVC Engagement in Sub-Saharan Africa." Policy Research Working Paper 8937, World Bank, Washington, DC.

Chapter 1

Manufacturing in Structural Change in Africa: Assessing the Record and Redefining Prospects for Industrialization

Structural change has historically been the force behind sustained economic growth, driving large-scale job creation and productivity growth. It is well established in theory and practice that industrialization, defined in this report as the rapid transformation of the significance of manufacturing in relation to other sectors, has been the mainstay of structural transformation and the resulting economic growth and development. Going back to the first industrialization in Western Europe and then in the United States, and Japan, followed more recently by China and the Republic of Korea, manufacturing has been the engine of economic transformation. Relative to other sectors, manufacturing presents greater opportunities to accumulate capital, exploit economies of scale, acquire new technologies, and more fundamentally foster embodied and disembodied technological change (UNIDO 2013). It is the only sector for which the further from the frontier an economy is, the faster is the growth in labor productivity, regardless of geography, policies, or other conditioning country characteristics (Rodrik 2013). Thus, the evidence points to industrialization as a reliable path to fast-tracking countries into becoming middle- and high-income economies. Manufacturing and exports of manufacturing goods have played a predominant role in countries that have registered the largest reductions in poverty.

It follows that efforts to create jobs and reduce poverty on a large scale in Sub-Saharan Africa would benefit from an expansion of the manufacturing sector. Industrialization-driven structural transformation should therefore be at the forefront of policy strategies for Sub-Saharan African countries as they pursue the goals of job creation, poverty reduction, and sustainable growth. Manufacturing-based industrialization is also at the center of the African Union's Agenda 2063, a document that provides the blueprint for transforming the continent.

Recently, the role of manufacturing in growth and structural change has been further bolstered by the rapid pace of globalization, increased trade, and significant changes in global production processes. Yet new technology and changing production processes, accompanied by shifts in the political economy of developed economies, are changing the landscape of global manufacturing, posing new risks to the prospects for developing economies to use manufacturing as an engine of growth and job creation on a large scale (Hallward-Driemeier and Nayyar 2017).

Sustainable Growth and Structural Transformation in Africa

A key stylized fact observed over the previous two centuries is that income increases have been accompanied by a fall in the value-added and employment shares of agriculture and an increase in the employment and value-added shares in services. However, the dynamics in the manufacturing sector have been different, in that value-added and employment shares follow an inverted-U shape, rising at low levels of income, reaching a peak, and falling at higher levels of income. Globalization and international trade have facilitated structural transformation with rapid growth of the manufacturing sector in emerging market economies, as in East Asia. In Sub-Saharan Africa, however, the structural transformation powered by industrialization has not been sufficiently robust to enable countries to move from low-income to middle- and high-income status.

In the decade following 2000, Africa enjoyed relatively robust economic growth, exceeding an annual rate of 5 percent, higher than the sluggish growth during 1991–2000, which averaged about 2 percent. In more recent years, economic growth has remained at about half the pace experienced during 2000–11. However, during the period of relatively robust economic growth, the rate of job growth was generally negligible. Except for a few countries, the growth experiences in much of Sub-Saharan Africa were not accompanied by robust job growth or structural transformation of the nature historically observed in today's developed economies.

With few exceptions, the main trends underlying the region's growth episodes during the 2000s were rising exports of key natural resources and growth of the services sector, driven by construction and other nontradable services. Even when relatively high, economic growth has not been associated with structural transformation. Such transformation would reflect a shift in the production structure from relatively low-productivity enterprises in agriculture to high-productivity enterprises in manufacturing. Sub-Saharan Africa's growth episodes have been short-lived, with limited implications for poverty reduction through mass job creation.

Between 1965 and 2000, minimal changes occurred in the average sectoral output shares in Sub-Saharan Africa. There were striking disparities, however, in the sectoral shares of employment and output, even at the same level of income across countries in the region. Structural change in Sub-Saharan Africa has been characterized by high shares of employment and value added in the services sector, even at very low levels of income. This situation is a significant departure from the structural change associated with the experience of developed economies. The observed trends in the region suggest that there has been very little change in the sectoral shares of manufacturing value added, whereas the shares of agriculture have been falling. Still, the region has registered a continuous rise in the share of manufacturing employment with income (figure 1.1).

The contribution of structural transformation to job creation has been far from satisfactory. The average unemployment rate in Sub-Saharan Africa during 2001–12 was only half a percentage point less than the rate in 1991–2000. This has raised concerns about the prospects for reducing poverty and promoting shared prosperity where growth experiences are nontransformational and unsustainable. Moreover, the need for job creation has become an economic imperative given that the supply of labor in the region is expected to increase by 198 million persons between 2017 and 2030 (ILO 2018).

Industrialization in Africa: No Strong Evidence of Premature Deindustrialization

An emerging narrative pertaining to the state of structural transformation in Africa is that economies in the region have experienced premature deindustrialization (Rodrik 2016). The shares of manufacturing in economy-wide output and employment, which are conventional measures of the level of industrialization of an economy, typically follow an inverted U-shaped path over the course of development. That is, manufacturing activities hit a maximum threshold as the main driver of economic growth and decline thereafter, signaling a decline of that role in the economy. This decline in manufacturing is referred to as *deindustrialization*. Recent studies document that, in some developing countries, the threshold level of manufacturing output and employment shares has occurred earlier in the development process than has been observed historically. Deindustrialization is said to have occurred prematurely if manufacturing shrinks at levels of income that are much lower than those at which the developed economies began to deindustrialize. The claim is that Sub-Saharan Africa and Latin America experienced premature deindustrialization, and the share of manufacturing

Figure 1.1 Structural Transformation in Africa: Employment and Value Added Shares, 1970–2015

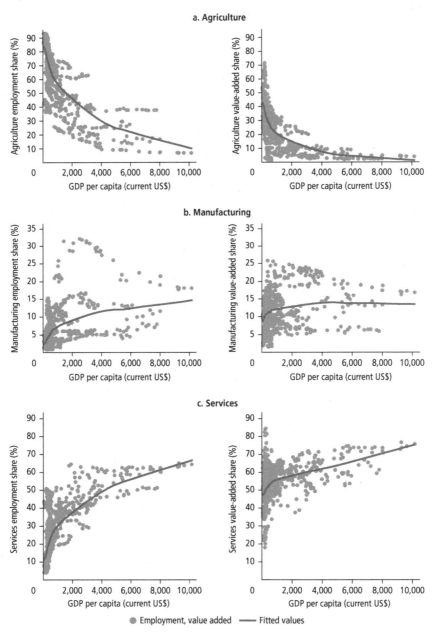

Source: World Bank calculation based on the Extended Africa Sector Database (1970–2015).

in gross domestic product (GDP) has peaked at very low levels of income. The subsequent policy implications provide a dismal prediction for the regions' prospects for industrialization.

An analysis of the performance of the manufacturing sector reveals no strong evidence that, as a region, Africa has experienced premature deindustrialization (Mensah 2020; Nguimkeu and Zeufack 2019). On the contrary, the region has continued to industrialize, given that the employment share of the manufacturing sector has been on a steady upward trend over the period 1970–2015 (figure 1.1, panel b). However, the evidence on the share of manufacturing value added does not follow the observed trend in manufacturing employment shares. Although there is evidence that Sub-Saharan Africa has deindustrialized on the basis of manufacturing value added shares, this outcome may be driven by a small subset of countries (Nguimkeu and Zeufack 2019). Excluding high-exporting countries weakens the evidence for the inverted U-shaped relationship. The value added in the manufacturing sector has been growing over the years, albeit fairly slowly. The decline in the value-added share of manufacturing and the increase in the employment share of manufacturing have contributed to stagnation and sometimes a decline in manufacturing labor productivity in the region.

Heterogeneity of Sub-Saharan Africa's Industrialization Experience

Higher Share of Manufacturing Value Added in Non-Oil GDP at Higher Levels of Income

The trends and patterns of industrialization are strikingly heterogeneous across Sub-Saharan Africa. Different trajectories emerge when the evolution of one of the measures of industrialization—the share of manufacturing value added—is expressed in terms of overall GDP compared with non-oil GDP (figure 1.2). This distinction is important, given that the challenges to industrialization are likely to vary between resource-rich economies, especially oil exporters, and non-resource-rich economies. When industrialization is measured by the share of manufacturing value added in non-oil GDP, there is a U-shaped relationship between manufacturing and the level of income, indicating that manufacturing value added as a share of GDP has been rising in non-oil economies. When expressed as a share of overall GDP, there is a weak semblance of an inverted U-shaped relationship between manufacturing value added and the level of income, indicating that, even as a share of GDP, manufacturing value added has increased steadily in non-oil economies. As shown in figure 1.1, for the entire sample of countries, there has been an upward trend in the share of manufacturing employment.

Figure 1.2 Manufacturing Value-Added Shares in GDP and Non-Oil GDP in Sub-Saharan Africa

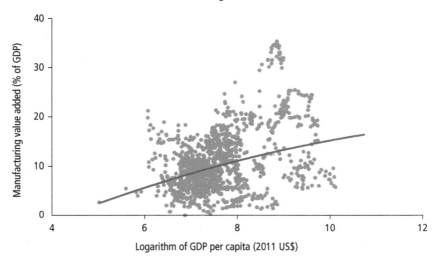

a. Manufacturing share of overall GDP

b. Manufacturing share of non-oil GDP

These two observations suggest that the premise of premature deindustrialization does not have solid empirical backing in the region.

Subregional Patterns of Increased Manufacturing Value Added Shares with Increased Level of Income

The majority of countries in the region show a relatively stable trend in the share of manufacturing value added in GDP: 10 countries reveal a declining trend, and 7 show an increasing trend. Only 5 of 41 countries in Sub-Saharan Africa show evidence consistent with an inverted U-shape in real manufacturing value added.

The single story of premature deindustrialization is not a defining feature of the industrialization experience in the region. In figure 1.3, panel a depicts significant variation in the trends and patterns of industrialization across subregions, based on the share of manufacturing value added highlighting the heterogeneity in industrialization experiences along a geographical dimension, with the share of manufacturing value added being higher at higher income levels in East Africa and Southern Africa.

Moreover, figure 1.3, panel b, which presents the predicted shares of manufacturing, depicts significant subregional differences in the evolution of manufacturing value added shares across income levels. Southern Africa is the only subregion that appears to have experienced deindustrialization, demonstrating an inverted U-shape for manufacturing value added shares, an observation that is confirmed by other studies (Lind and Mehlum 2010).

In contrast, the share of manufacturing is flat for West Africa and Central Africa whereas it rises with the level of income in East Africa, indicating that deindustrialization, measured by manufacturing value added shares, is not the experience of the vast majority of countries in the region. Furthermore, although Southern Africa has deindustrialized, this phenomenon is not occurring at lower levels of per capita income. Thus, there is no evidence of premature deindustrialization, even in Southern Africa. Additional evidence shows that in Ethiopia, Kenya, Malawi, Senegal, and Tanzania the share of employment in manufacturing is steadily growing. Mauritius appears to have followed a path similar to the East Asian economies in the shares of manufacturing employment and value added. Thus, industrialization in Sub-Saharan Africa, as measured by trends in manufacturing employment shares, seems to fit the experiences of structural change in other economies.

Debunking the Deindustrialization Label

More recently, growth-promoting structural change has been significant in some Sub-Saharan Africa economies, especially Ethiopia, Malawi, Rwanda, Senegal, and Tanzania. An evaluation of the trends in alternative indicators of industrialization—including the absolute size of manufacturing value added, share of manufacturing exports, absolute size of manufacturing employment, and share of manufacturing employment—shows that the Africa region is industrializing. The region experienced an increase of 148 percent in manufacturing employment, from a total of 8.6 million in 1990 to 21.3 million in 2018. Hence, manufacturing jobs in the region have been increasing, adding millions of jobs to the sector. Except for Botswana and South Africa, more recent patterns of

Figure 1.3 Subregional Variation in Manufacturing Value-Added Shares

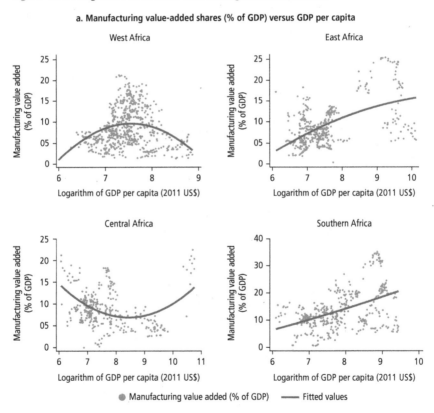

a. Manufacturing value-added shares (% of GDP) versus GDP per capita

(continued next page)

Figure 1.3 Subregional Variation in Manufacturing Value-Added Shares (continued)

b. Predicted manufacturing value added (% of GDP) versus GDP per capita

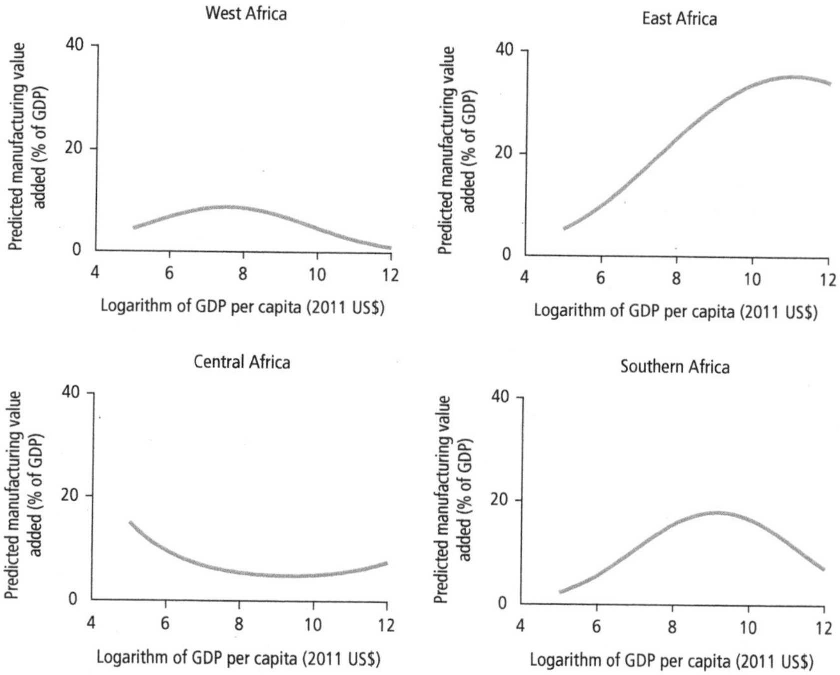

Source: Nguimkeu and Zeufack 2019.

employment shares appear to fit the stylized facts of historical development in other regions (Diao, Harttgen, and McMillan 2017).

The notion that African countries have undergone premature deindustrialization lacks merit for two reasons. First, it derives from limited evidence based on 10 countries in the region (Rodrik 2016); therefore, the implications may not apply to other countries in the region. Second, there is a possible mistaking of early failures and false starts in industrialization efforts in the region as peaks in the process of industrialization. Claims that Africa's prospects for industrialization are doomed rely largely on the hypothesis of premature deindustrialization. However, the hypothesis is not well-founded and overlooks some important developments in the region's economies as well as in global trade, which suggest significant optimism for industrialization in the region. In addition, even for a country that may have potentially experienced premature deindustrialization, the argument could be made that the early failures may not necessarily define its future prospects for industrialization.

Lack of industries is a defining characteristic of many developing economies at low levels of income. Hence, the industrialization peaks identified in Rodrik (2016) for a few countries may be false starts or unsuccessful attempts at industrialization caused by well-known factors, including political economy constraints, poor investment climate, low productivity, and lack of effective industrial policies and partnerships between governments and the private sector. Thus, to the extent that a strong industrial base has not yet been developed in the region, any suggestion of premature deindustrialization is misleading. The case remains, however, that Sub-Saharan Africa is the least industrialized region in the world. Only a few countries, including Mauritius and South Africa, have successfully developed strong industrial economies.

Failure has often characterized the efforts of developing economies before their successful industrialization. Still, the predominant pessimism about industrialization prospects in the region highlights important challenges that Sub-Saharan African countries face in their industrialization efforts, including technical progress in manufacturing that is making it increasingly labor saving, which limits the traditional mass job creation prospects associated with industrialization. It is therefore important to distinguish between early failures in industrialization efforts and premature deindustrialization, given that the policy implications of this distinction are especially important for the prospects for industrialization in the region.

In summary, countries in Sub-Saharan Africa have had different experiences in industrializing their economies, and clear evidence of premature deindustrialization in the region as a whole is lacking. Yet many countries have not undergone the kind of successful structural transformations associated with sustained economic growth and job creation on a large enough scale to have an impact on poverty reduction. Emerging trends in international trade policies; changes in global production processes, mainly caused by the emergence of global value chains; and unprecedentedly rapid technological advances biased toward labor-saving technologies present significant challenges for the region in its efforts to follow traditional models of structural transformation through industrialization. However, much of the pessimism about the prospects for industrialization in Africa is overstated because the debate has been dominated by the consideration of past failures as signals of poor prospects for the future.

The Future of Industrialization in Africa

Given the uncertainty that has emerged about the path of industrialization that countries should follow, there is no guarantee that all countries in the

Africa region will successfully industrialize (Hallward-Driemeier and Nayyar 2017). This uncertainty is partly due to emerging technologies, including automation, artificial intelligence, the Internet of Things, and 3D printing, that are radically changing the nature of manufacturing. Changing technologies and shifting globalization patterns have raised questions about the prospects for manufacturing-led development. The emergence and impact of the Fourth Industrial Evolution such as automation are phenomena that present opportunities and challenges.

Consequently, there is a need to rethink industrial policy for the new age of global trade and technological development. Industrial policy should not be restricted to the idea that countries should focus on specific industries that provide the greatest welfare and outcome in resource allocation. Instead, industrial policy should be considered within the framework of dynamic comparative advantage or a path of economic transformation that promotes increased growth and job creation.

The failures of industrialization in many African countries since the 1970s are cause for legitimate concern. Moreover, rapid urbanization and growth in the services economy have yielded productivity-reducing structural change (McMillan and Rodrik 2011) and resulted in static gains but dynamic losses for African economies (de Vries, Timmer, and de Vries 2013). Some of the key challenges for late industrializers include the lock-in effects of first movers, the growing sophistication of markets and consumer demand, the slicing up of production into global value chains (GVCs) dominated by buyers, and the greater complexity of manufacturing. These challenges are compounded by recent shifts in the political economy of developed economies toward greater protectionism in international trade.

In addition, the recent COVID-19 (coronavirus) pandemic is expected to have significant implications for industrialization prospects in the region. The combination of trade policy shocks and the enduring public health concerns from COVID-19 has created uncertainty about the future of international trade, resulting in a rethinking of GVCs in manufacturing (Kassa 2020). Because of COVID-19 and emerging geopolitical trends in advanced economies, there is a growing preference for resilience or a "de-risking" strategy. COVID-19 is expected to reinforce an ongoing change in GVCs with respect to geographic rebalancing. The change in heavily traded labor-intensive manufacturing GVCs, where many African countries' comparative advantages lie, is expected to be significant. On the basis of their comparative advantages, African countries could be viable alternatives for attracting some of these potentially shifting investments. Countries with relatively higher backward linkages in manufacturing GVCs may need to reposition themselves to reap any gains that may arise from fundamental changes in GVCs due to global shocks, including the current pandemic.

More generally, the nature of industrialization keeps shifting such that the desire for African countries to industrialize is akin to chasing a moving target. The argument is that industrialization is not impossible but is more difficult. It is, however, nearly impossible for industrially lagging countries to catch up to the existing developed economies by following the traditional approaches. In essence, to industrialize on the basis of the traditional understanding would be tantamount to chasing a mirage.

Rethinking Industrial Policy for Africa

The concept and the practice of industrial policy are continuously evolving, and there is no single widely accepted definition. The discussion of industrial policy in this report refers to government activities in reorienting production, technologies, and trade, aimed at achieving structural transformation. Industrial policies underpin guiding principles on the "best" way for any society to move its human, capital, and financial resources from low- to high-productivity sectors (Stiglitz, Lin, and Monga 2013). In countries that have managed to transform their economies from low income to middle and high income—including European Union countries, Japan, and the United States, and more recently China, Korea, and Taiwan, China—active government interventions that promoted structural transformation, industrialization, and trade, including active pursuit of selected sectors and markets, are key defining features.

There is now an almost complete consensus on the need for a modern industrial policy for Africa. Industrial policies can "tilt" the playing field toward sectors or technologies with positive spillovers or externalities and away from those with negative spillovers or externalities (Stiglitz et al. 2013). Still, for every successful case of industrial policy in East Asia, North America, or Western Europe, there are cases in which industrial policy has failed or may have even restricted the prospects for industrialization and growth, reinforcing the notion that there is no one-size-fits-all policy, and risks of capture by vested interests remain.[1] The question is how to implement industrial policy in the current setting in Africa. Pursuing an answer to this question requires a rethinking of industrial policies beyond correcting externalities, market imperfections, and distortions. In this framework, this report adopts two broad classifications of industrial policy—*soft industrial policies* and *hard industrial policies*—to address the challenge of providing guidance on industrial policy frameworks for African countries. The distinction is based on scope rather than priorities, and both types of policies are equally important.

Soft Industrial Policies: Building a System of Capabilities and Technologies That Are Conducive to Industrialization

Soft industrial policies refer to policies aimed at supporting the growth and productivity of all sectors in the economy; they are not exclusive to manufacturing. In this respect, every country has an industrial policy, whether explicit or implicit. The traditional approach of "good policy" recommendations may not be relevant in an African context, where efforts to promote "East Asian–like" industrialization have often failed. Soft industrial policies largely reflect a commitment to building competitive advantages across the entire spectrum of the economy, reinforcing the learning capacity of private and public enterprises. These policies should focus on factors that drive the productivity and growth of firms and boost their capacity to adapt to emerging challenges. This approach requires strong synergies across multiple sets of policies in building skills, promoting competition by promoting new entry, easing labor market rigidities, improving trade facilitation, developing physical infrastructure, and ensuring easy access to credit. As latecomers, African countries may have an even greater need for industrial policy, which may require a more robust role for the state compared with their developed counterparts, which, in turn, requires the state mechanism to work effectively to craft and implement policies. Thus, the study of the state policy process is at least as important as the policies themselves (Jordan, Turban, and Wilse-Samson 2013). Four dimensions are critical for the success of such policies (Cusolito and Maloney 2018): the rationale and design of the policy, the efficacy of implementation, the coherence of policies across actors, and policy consistency and predictability over time.

In addition, the country and context matter for industrial policy design and practice. There is no one-size-fits-all industrial strategy. The heterogeneity across countries and time in context, resource base, and level of development, and the likelihood that countries will experience different varieties of industries simultaneously, mean that a one-size-fits-all approach would be suboptimal. Each country will benefit by deliberating on and designing its response to create an environment wherein multiple industrial futures can thrive. However, some fundamental capabilities are needed to support the birth and growth of firms and industries across all countries. Industrialization is primarily a process of capacity building with more and better-quality physical infrastructure, including better and more reliable energy and electricity, low costs of transport and communications, accumulation of workers' skills and continuous skill upgrading, and technical progress.

If Africa is to capture the emerging opportunities associated with changes in the global economy—including the China's rebalancing, increasingly lower costs of transport and communications, and the ease of relocating production clusters—countries need to invest strategically in these key capabilities.

The design of industrial policy should consider the industrial firm as the key determinant of successful industrialization and address problems arising from firm and industry capabilities (table 1.1) (UNIDO 2013). Policy needs to work toward improving the operating environment, human capital, and firm capabilities, which are essential and complementary ingredients that cut across all components (Cusolito and Maloney 2018).

The following represents a taxonomy of key firm capabilities (table 1.1):

- *Production capabilities.* Production capabilities refer to the organization of production and include the skills of workers and managers, institutions, and the know-how with respect to the technical engineering of production processes. They are well reflected in the quality (value and market demand) and efficiency (cost) of production. The capabilities include firms' absorptive skills and manufacturing skills for producing modern goods.

- *Technological capabilities.* Because most countries in Sub-Saharan Africa are not at the technology frontier, industrialization largely derives not from innovations in production but from effective adoption and transfer of technologies from advanced economies. To accommodate the significant externalities in adopting these technologies, there is a large role for government

Table 1.1 Technical Capabilities: Primary Skills, Features, and Activities

	Capabilities		
	Production	Technological	R&D
Primary skills			
Absorptive	✓	✓	n.a.
Manufacturing	✓	✓	n.a.
R&D	n.a.	n.a.	✓
Features			
Learning-by-doing spillovers	✓	✓	n.a.
Imitation	n.a.	✓	n.a.
Absorption	n.a.	✓	n.a.
Innovation: Product and process improvement	n.a.	✓	n.a.
Innovation: Generation of new products and processes (technology)	n.a.	n.a.	✓
Activities			
Technology transfer activities	n.a.	✓	n.a.
R&D activities	n.a.	n.a.	✓

Source: Adapted from Yülek 2018.
Note: n.a. = not applicable. R&D = research and development.

policy to build firm and industry capabilities through learning by doing, imitation, and absorption of technologies and new products and processes.

- *Research and development (R&D) capabilities.* Government policy should be reinforced by investments in R&D capabilities so that firms can invest in developing new products and processes of production. Governments should adopt a hierarchy of policies at the national, industry, and firm level, given that these policies not only are simple aggregations at each level but also require distinct approaches to building capabilities at each stage.

Hard Industrial Policies: The Pursuit of Strategic Sectors

Countries in the region may choose from three potential models of industrialization, as alternatives or in some combination, depending on each country's initial structure and resource endowment. The models are traditional manufacturing and industry, the building of sectors with the characteristics of manufacturing, and resurgent indigenous entrepreneurship in small-scale manufacturing.

Dynamic Comparative Advantage and Traditional Manufacturing

The first variety of future industrialization in Africa is associated with the flying geese model of industrialization. That is, countries would initially target sectors and industries within the economy's existing comparative advantage, which could be dynamic and evolve as endowments change. Accordingly, targeting sectors with a current comparative advantage alters tomorrow's endowment structure, which alters tomorrow's comparative advantage and permits sustainable production diversification and upgrading relative to today (Stiglitz et al. 2013). In this case, the state facilitates private sector engagement in sectors in which the country is deemed to have a comparative advantage. The state's role can take different forms, including providing incentives, addressing coordination problems, improving the workings of market institutions, and strengthening human capital and complementary markets such as finance and other services. The details of the set of policies depend on the relative endowments of labor, skills, and natural resources. Policy makers need to identify the sectors with potential comparative advantage and the associated entry points for policies to provide incentives for growth and investment in those industries. In many African countries, this means attracting large-scale investments in labor and resource-intensive manufacturing. Continuous learning and industrial upgrading are essential so that production processes evolve along with changing comparative advantage. This does not, however, preclude African countries from joining the new industrial revolution with relatively advanced technologies.

The new industrial revolution is important, but African countries face two sets of obstacles that prevent them from fully benefiting. The first is the digital divide—that is, information and communications technology adoption is lagging in the region, with large implications for its competitiveness. The second obstacle is a skills mismatch—that is, complementary skills needed for digital transformation are lacking. Thus, the digital divide and skills mismatch make it unlikely that digitally enabled manufacturing will transform African manufacturing in the short term. African countries therefore should look to adopt a two-track approach. In track one, countries would build capacity and business ecosystems to absorb and use technology and improve skills, particularly in the science, technology, engineering, and mathematics fields and in technical and vocational education and training. In track two, countries would develop sectors that are less automated and where technology installation has been slow, but for which Africa still possesses a labor cost advantage (Banga and te Velde 2018, cited in Naudé 2019).

Sectors with the Characteristics of Manufacturing

The second variety of future industrialization involves fostering investment in services that are directly linked to manufacturing in input-output terms and in terms of factor intensity, such as providers of logistics and financial services to manufacturers. The organization of manufacturing production and coordination of the distribution of manufactured products is increasingly fragmented and complex, which has increased the content of services inputs for many manufacturers. Robust evidence suggests strong links between development in services and manufacturing performance in Africa, through the use of intermediate services inputs in manufacturing production.

In Africa today, online trading platforms are increasingly used to sell manufactured products, eliminating many of the geographical barriers that previously prevented manufacturing firms in the region from accessing larger domestic and international markets. The continuous increase in internet adoption, the increased penetration rate, and innovations such as mobile money transfers in the financial and telecommunications sectors are key drivers of these observed trends. Attracting game-changing investment that will transform the region's manufacturing sector will require efficient business services, such as consulting, accounting, legal, and business processing. These business services will not only ensure the enforcement of contracts and protection of property rights but also reduce the transaction costs associated with using the financial market. Clearly, the growing similarity and interdependence between tradable services and manufacturing are evident, and the services sector is becoming increasingly important for the growth of manufacturing in the region. Policy makers' understanding of this interdependence will play a central role in the effectiveness and success of various current industrial policies or those policies still to be rolled out in the region.

Indigenous Entrepreneurship in Small-Scale Manufacturing

The third variety of future industrialization consists of promoting high-tech start-up firms to provide platforms for small-scale manufacturers deploying the technological advances of the Fourth Industrial Revolution, such as additive manufacturing (3D printing) and robotics. Advances in these areas arguably have created new opportunities for manufacturing growth in Africa. Although 3D printing is still in its infancy in Africa, the region's adoption lag is shrinking relatively quickly. The technology could possibly make manufacturing easier and more accessible to the many artisans, small businesses, and informal entrepreneurs that form the core of most African economies.

Increasing the uptake of this technology, together with other robotics to transform the region's manufacturing sector, will require investing in producing tech entrepreneurs and in the continentwide rollout of the Internet of Things. There are encouraging signs. For example, with digital development, the region is growing more connected. The share of the region's population using the internet reached almost 30 percent in 2018, up from 13 percent in 2013. At the same time, Africa has seen a rise in the number of tech start-ups and tech hubs, and growth in the tech ecosystem. Tech hubs in the region grew by 41 percent, from 314 in 2016 to 442 in 2018. Furthermore, the volume of funding raised by tech start-ups across the continent has soared. Overall, the region's tech start-ups attracted about US$334.5 million in investment in 2018 (GSMA 2018). In addition to supporting the birth and growth of emerging entrepreneurs, promotion of innovation in small-scale manufacturing is necessary for industrial upgrading even in traditional labor-intensive sectors. Increased investment in digital and associated technologies could provide opportunities to leapfrog traditional industries.

African countries will experience a variety of industrial futures going forward, and industrialization has the potential to be the engine of growth. However, successful industrialization will require pragmatic, pluralistic, and entrepreneurial-based industrial policy approaches linked to new disruptive technologies to improve and sustain the momentum of the recent growth in the sector.

Note

1. Rijkers, Freund, and Nucifora (2014) show that Tunisia's industrial policy was used as a vehicle for rent creation for businesses owned by the then-president and his family.

References

Banga, K., and D. te Velde. 2018. "Skill Needs for the Future." Background Paper 10, Pathways for Prosperity Commission, Oxford.

Cusolito, A. P., and W. F. Maloney. 2018. *Productivity Revisited: Shifting Paradigms in Analysis and Policy*. Washington, DC: World Bank.

de Vries, G., M. Timmer, and K. de Vries. 2013. "Structural Transformation in Africa: Static Gains, Dynamic Losses." GGDC Research Memorandum 136, University of Groningen Growth and Development Center, University of Groningen.

Diao, X., K. Harttgen, and M. McMillan. 2017. *The Changing Structure of Africa's Economies*. Washington, DC: World Bank.

GSMA. 2018. *The Mobile Economy Sub-Saharan Africa 2018 Report*. London: Global System for Mobile Communications.

Hallward-Driemeier, M., and G. Nayyar. 2017. *Trouble in the Making? The Future of Manufacturing-Led Development*. Washington, DC: World Bank.

ILO (International Labour Organization). 2018. *World Employment Social Outlook: Trends 2018*. Geneva: ILO.

Johnson, C. 1982. *MITI and the Japanese Miracle: The Growth of Industrial Policy: 1925–1975*. Redwood City, CA: Stanford University Press.

Jordan, L., S. Turban, and L. Wilse-Samson. 2013. "Learning within the State: A Research Agenda." Columbia University, New York.

Kassa, W. 2020. "COVID-19 and Trade in SSA: Impacts and Policy Response." Policy Brief, June 2020, World Bank, Washington, DC.

Lind, J. T., and H. Mehlum. 2010. "With or Without U? The Appropriate Test for a U-Shaped Relationship." *Oxford Bulletin of Economics and Statistics* 72 (1): 109–18.

McMillan, M., and D. Rodrik. 2011. "Globalization, Structural Change, and Economic Growth." In *Making Globalization Socially Sustainable*, edited by M. Bachetta and M. Jansen. Geneva: International Labor Organization and World Trade Organization.

Mensah, E. B. 2020. "Is Sub-Saharan Africa Deindustrializing?" UNU-MERIT Working Paper Series 2020-045, United Nations University–Maastricht Economic and Social Research Institute on Innovation and Technology, Maastricht, Netherlands.

Naudé, W. 2019. "Three Varieties of Africa's Industrial Future." IZA Discussion Paper 12678, Institute of Labor Economics, Bonn.

Nguimkeu, P., and A. G. Zeufack. 2019. "Manufacturing in Structural Change in Africa." Policy Research Working Paper 8992, World Bank, Washington, DC.

Rijkers, B., C. Freund, and A. Nucifora. 2014. "The Perils of Industrial Policy: Evidence from Tunisia." World Bank, Washington, DC.

Rodrik, D. 2013. "Unconditional Convergence in Manufacturing." *Quarterly Journal of Economics* 128 (1): 165–204.

Rodrik, D. 2016. "Premature Deindustrialization." *Journal of Economic Growth* 21 (1): 1–33.

Stiglitz, J. E., J. Y. Lin, and C. Monga. 2013. *The Rejuvenation of Industrial Policy.* Washington, DC: World Bank.

Stiglitz, J. E., J. Y. Lin, C. Monga, and E. Patel. 2013. *Industrial Policy in the African Context.* Washington, DC: World Bank.

UNIDO (United Nations Industrial Development Organization). 2013. *Industrial Development Report 2013: Sustaining Employment Growth: The Role of Manufacturing and Structural Change.* Vienna: UNIDO.

Yülek, M. A. 2018. *How Nations Succeed: Manufacturing, Trade, Industrial Policy, and Economic Development.* Singapore: Springer Nature.

Chapter 2

Drivers of Manufacturing Job Growth

Job growth in manufacturing has been sustained and significant in several Sub-Saharan African countries over the past two decades. This process has been driven mainly by new and young firms, consistent with the experiences of countries in other regions. Job growth in the region is illustrated by the cases of Côte d'Ivoire and Ethiopia, two sharply contrasting economies that reflect some of the diversity across countries in the region.

Manufacturing job growth has occurred in both countries without pushing up wage rates until recently (near the end of the observed data). Thus, for the greater part of the past two decades, manufacturers could hire as many workers as they needed without bidding up wage rates against the competition. For most of the period, job growth was facilitated by the entry of new firms such that reducing administrative and economic barriers to entry would be all that policy makers needed to do to sustain it.

However, the evidence shows that the scope for manufacturing job growth through growth in new plant openings (at the extensive margin) is diminishing. This point is underscored by average wages in Ethiopia, which have risen with job growth in recent years, indicating that the pace of job growth over the long term would depend on the pace of growth in manufacturing productivity as well as the extent of administrative and legal barriers to entry.

Current Drivers of Growth of Manufacturing Jobs

New and Young Firms as Drivers of Job Growth

A robust research finding of the past 20 years is that new and young firms are the sole drivers of job growth across all industries in developed and developing economies alike.[1] The job-creating potential of a firm does not depend on its size but on its age, that is, on how long it has been in operation. In essence, new and young firms are the predominant source of job growth among both small and large firms.[2]

Therefore, entry and exit barriers are central to defining governments' policy agendas on job creation and growth. That the rate of job growth does not vary by firm size serves as an argument against policy interventions favoring smaller firms at the expense of larger ones for promoting job growth. Moreover, the observation that most job growth occurs in new and young firms underscores the importance of facilitating new entry and removing exit barriers.

New and young firms are the engine of job growth in any economy because they are more dynamic than older and more established firms for a variety of reasons. First, the early years of a firm's life cycle constitute a phase of passive learning through which the firm gradually discovers the nature and scale of its capabilities as an organization.[3] As a firm becomes more aware and certain of its true capabilities, it commits increasing labor and capital to specific operations, which constitutes the firm's growth process. Second, new and young firms, compared with established firms, are more likely to invest actively in learning new ways of doing things and about new technology and products.[4] Third, younger firms are more likely to increase productivity by updating their production techniques through competitive diffusion of know-how as workers and managers move between rivals and competitors over the course of their careers.[5]

Job growth is higher in new and young firms across the entire size distribution of firms. Thus, the group of firms driving job growth in an economy comprises small firms as well as large ones. Therefore, policies favoring smaller firms would likely be inferior to size-neutral interventions facilitating start-ups as instruments for promoting job growth. In effect, interventions targeting any single size group of operating firms would reduce jobs and output in the aggregate by diverting skills and know-how away from innovative firms toward operators that are less likely to develop or adopt new technologies or products.[6]

Policies favoring smaller firms at the expense of larger ones are backed by significant empirical evidence, yet such policies have led to reduced employment levels in countries such as India and Mexico. A study of manufacturing firms in India, Mexico, and the United States shows that firms of any given age on average have several times smaller employment in India and Mexico than in the United States (Hsieh and Klenow 2014).[7] This finding is a reflection of job growth being faster in start-ups and young firms in the United States than it is in similar firms in India and Mexico because of the greater barriers to investment that larger firms face in those countries relative to their counterparts in the United States.

Ethiopia

An estimated 128,000 manufacturing jobs were created in Ethiopia between 1996 and 2016, all in establishments employing 10 workers or more.[8] Figure 2.1 shows that most of these jobs were concentrated in new and young firms.[9] This pattern is especially strong after 2011. Most of the jobs are concentrated in larger establishments. However, the pace of job growth has been highly comparable over the entire size spectrum as illustrated in figure 2.2. Moreover, because job growth in new and young establishments more than offsets job losses due to contracting or exiting establishments, jobs became increasingly concentrated in larger young establishments over the two decades of observation.

About 210,000 jobs were reported in the manufacturing census in 2016, 46 percent of which were in establishments with more than 500 employees and 9 percent in establishments with fewer than 20 workers (figure 2.2). Employers of 20–100 workers accounted for about 15 percent of the jobs, with the remaining 30 percent being the share of employers of 101–500 workers. The distribution of jobs across size groups of employers has followed that pattern, with the concentration of jobs in large establishments becoming progressively higher over time since 1996.

In contrast, the relative distribution of manufacturing jobs by employer age group has shifted significantly over the past decade toward a growing concentration in younger establishments (figure 2.1). This dynamic, which began about 2009, was such that by 2016 nearly as many workers were employed

Figure 2.1 Ethiopia: Number of Workers, by Manufacturer Age Group, 1996–2016

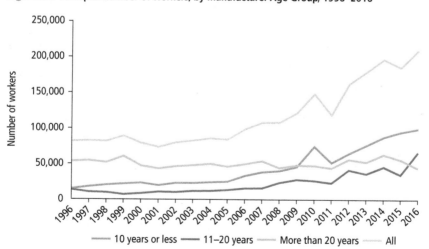

Source: Abreha et al. 2019.

Figure 2.2 Ethiopia: Number of Workers, by Manufacturer Size Group, 1996–2016

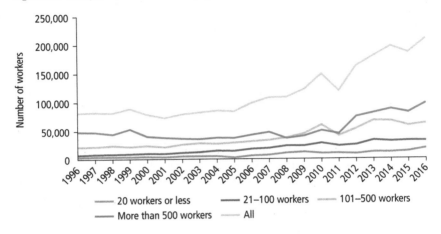

Source: Abreha et al. 2019.

in establishments that had been operating for at most 10 years as in all older establishments combined, reflecting a situation in which jobs grew fastest among establishments ages 10 years or younger, reasonably fast in establishments ages 11–20 years, and not at all in establishments older than 20 years (figure 2.1).

Thus, there has been a growing concentration of manufacturing jobs in younger establishments, and job growth in the sector is largely confined to younger establishments. These patterns hold sectorwide as well as within each size group (figures 2.3–2.6).

To further dissect the sources of job growth, it is useful to know how many of those jobs were created via entry as opposed to postentry expansion. For this purpose, the years 1996 through 2010 are considered because dissecting the sources of job growth requires tracing firms' operating status during the period under observation, and in the data it is possible to do that only until 2010.[10] Figure 2.7 portrays the breakdown of the aggregate annual flow of manufacturing jobs from 1997 to 2010 between new entrants and continuing establishments. The indication is that a large majority of jobs each year were held in continuing establishments. Thus, in 2006 more than 86 percent of manufacturing jobs were in continuing establishments; the remaining 14 percent were in start-ups.

Perhaps the most significant aspect of the observed dynamics is that the employment share of continuing establishments dropped from about 86 percent in 2006 to 61 percent over the next five years. All job growth that occurred over that period was a consequence of new jobs created by start-ups, which more than offset the job losses due to plant closures (figure 2.8). The number

Figure 2.3 **Ethiopia: Workforce Size of Manufacturers Employing 20 Workers or Less, 1996–2016**

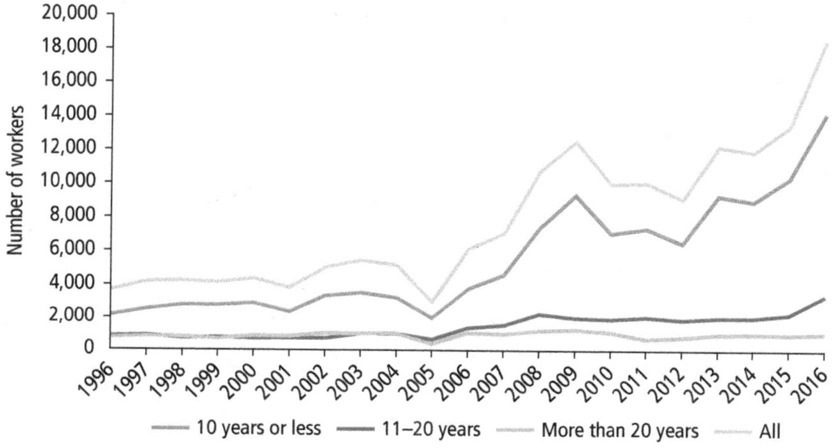

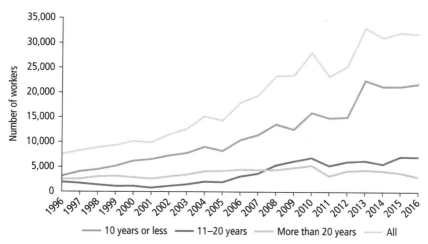

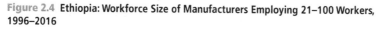

Source: Abreha et al. 2019.

Figure 2.4 **Ethiopia: Workforce Size of Manufacturers Employing 21–100 Workers, 1996–2016**

Source: Abreha et al. 2019.

Figure 2.5 Ethiopia: Workforce Size of Manufacturers Employing 101–500 Workers, 1996–2016

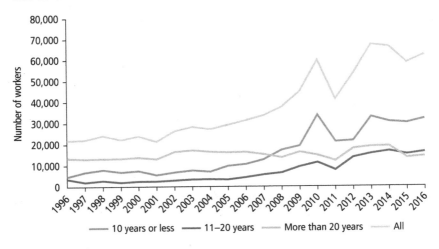

Source: Abreha et al. 2019.

Figure 2.6 Ethiopia: Workforce Size of Manufacturers Employing More Than 500 Workers, 1996–2016

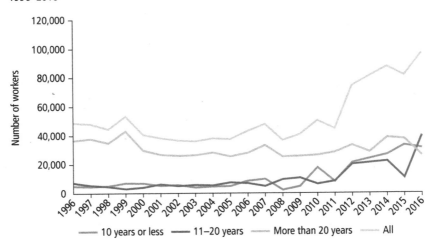

Source: Abreha et al. 2019.

Figure 2.7 Ethiopia: Workforce Size by Manufacturer Operating Status, 1997–2010

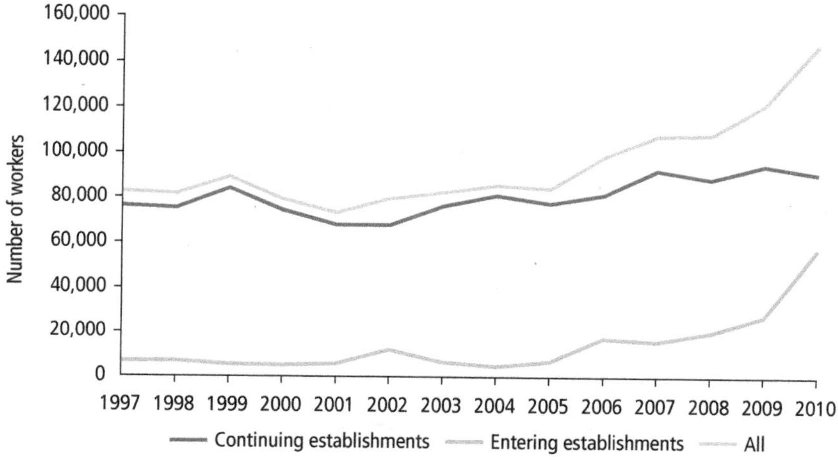

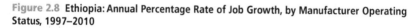

Source: Abreha et al. 2019.

Figure 2.8 Ethiopia: Annual Percentage Rate of Job Growth, by Manufacturer Operating Status, 1997–2010

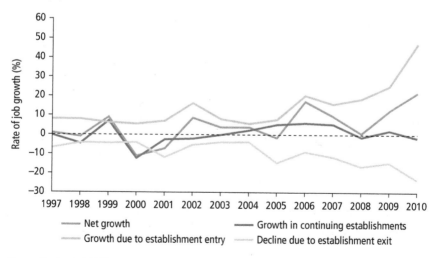

Source: Abreha et al. 2019.

of jobs created in start-ups rose by more than 40,000, which was twice the number of jobs lost because of plant closures over the period. There was some job growth in continuing establishments; however, it was intermittent and on a far smaller scale than the rate of job creation via new entries. The number of jobs in continuing establishments increased by fewer than 10,000 (or about 10 percent). See box 2.1 for a detailed discussion on job growth in Ethiopian manufacturing.

BOX 2.1

Establishment Age Effects on Job Growth across Size Groups: The Case of Ethiopia

According to the 2016 manufacturing census of Ethiopia, there were some 2,600 manufacturers in the country, with a combined regular workforce of about 210,000 employees. This represents significant job growth relative to what the census recorded 20 years earlier, during the 1996 round, which was 82,000 workers employed in about 620 establishments.

Manufacturing jobs are increasingly concentrated in younger establishments, and this pattern is evident sectorwide as well as within all but one of the size groups of establishments. Figure 2.3 shows that jobs have always been most concentrated in the youngest age group and are becoming more so. There has been significant job growth over the period 2005–16 in establishments ages 11–20 years within the smallest size group, but that is only about one-fifth of the total job growth that took place in the size group over the decade. There was no job growth among establishments in this size group that were older than 20 years.

This pattern is repeated in figure 2.4 for establishments employing 21–100 workers. Here also, little job growth is observed in establishments older than 20 years throughout the two decades of observations. Job growth accelerated substantially among establishments that were 10 years old or younger, and it was not as high but significant and steady in the 11–20 year age group.

Figure 2.5 shows a similar pattern among establishments in the 101–500 employment size group. The pattern here neatly replicates the sectorwide picture in figure 2.1, whereby the employment share of establishments that are 10 years old or younger overtakes that of the older-than-20 group following a decade of steady job growth in the younger group, which picked up momentum all the way to 2016. There has not been significant job growth at any point among establishments that have been in the market for more than 20 years. Job growth has been steady and substantial for the 11–20 year age group, although not nearly as high as that for the youngest age group.

(continued next page)

Box 2.1 Establishment Age Effects on Job Growth across Size Groups: The Case of Ethiopia (continued)

This leads to the case of the largest size group, that is, establishments employing more than 500 workers, as portrayed in figure 2.6. The main difference between the pattern here and that for the other size groups is that jobs are most concentrated in the oldest age group—those that have been in operation for more than 20 years. This is the case even though there has not been any job growth in establishments older than 20 years for this size group, as was the case for the other size groups. All the same, the job growth recorded by the largest size group is as high as that of the smaller employment groups during the 20 years of observations. As in the case of the other size groups, most of the job growth in large establishments was recorded in establishments that had been in operation for no more than 10 years. There has been steady and significant job growth in establishments ages 11–20 years but at a lower rate than that observed in younger establishments.

Côte d'Ivoire

Between 2003 and 2014, the manufacturing sector in Côte d'Ivoire generated a net total of about 24,000 jobs. During the same period, entering and surviving establishments created more than 101,000 and 19,000 jobs, respectively, whereas exiting manufacturers resulted in a loss of about 96,000 jobs (see Abreha et al. 2019). In the latter years, most of the manufacturing jobs were highly concentrated in younger establishments, especially those that had been in operation between 11 and 20 years (figure 2.9). As expected and similar to what is observed in Ethiopian manufacturing, most of the jobs were concentrated in large establishments (figure 2.10). Additionally, there are no size effects—that is, job growth was not significantly different in smaller or larger establishments (see Abreha et al. 2019).

Although most of the jobs are concentrated in continuing establishments (figure 2.11), figure 2.12 indicates substantial age effects, whereby start-ups and young establishments have been the main drivers of manufacturing job growth although their relative shares in aggregate employment have been significantly lower compared with those in Ethiopia. However, there is a significant contrast in how the age of establishments affects manufacturing job growth in the two countries, as depicted in figures 2.7 and 2.8, and figures 2.11 and 2.12, for Ethiopia and Côte d'Ivoire, respectively. New establishments have played a lesser role in job growth in Côte d'Ivoire than in Ethiopia, which seems to be related to the lower entry and exit rates in Côte d'Ivoire compared with those in Ethiopia.

Figure 2.9 Côte d'Ivoire: Number of Workers, by Manufacturer Age Group, 2003–14

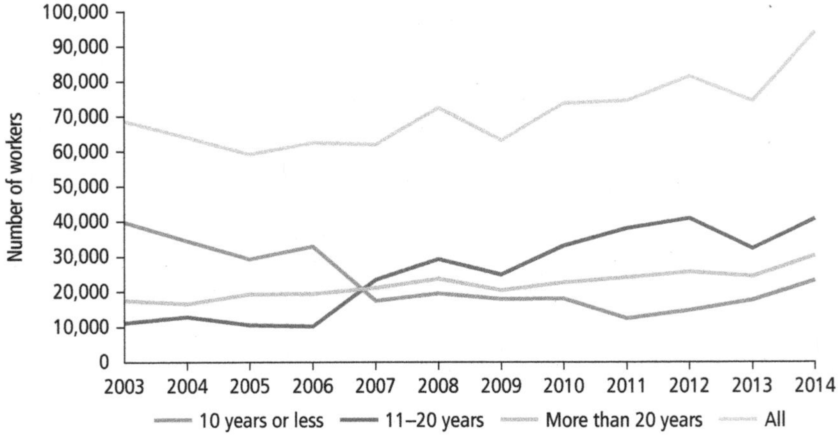

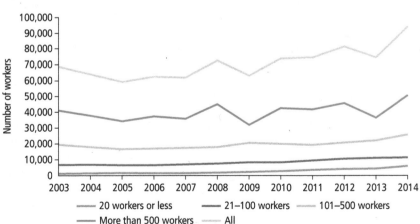

Source: Abreha et al. 2019.

Figure 2.10 Côte d'Ivoire: Number of Workers, by Manufacturer Size Group, 2003–14

Source: Abreha et al. 2019.

Figure 2.11 Côte d'Ivoire: Workforce Size, by Manufacturer Operating Status, 2003–14

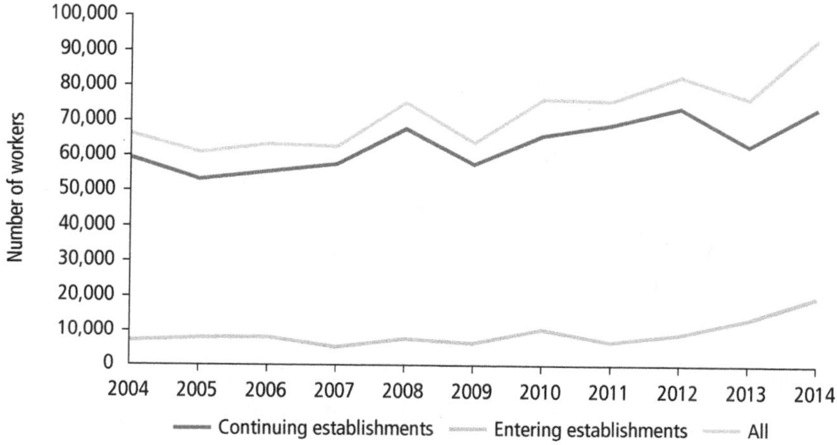

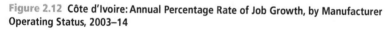

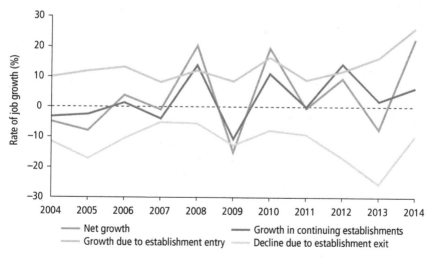

Source: Abreha et al. 2019.

Figure 2.12 Côte d'Ivoire: Annual Percentage Rate of Job Growth, by Manufacturer Operating Status, 2003–14

Source: Abreha et al. 2019.

Jobs Growth and Wage Trends

Ethiopia

An important feature of recent manufacturing job growth in Ethiopia is that it has been fueled by an environment of "unlimited labor supply"[11] at comparatively low wages. This opportunity was seized primarily by new and young establishments. However, the wage trends are only part of the story. As profit-maximizing employers, establishments equate the wage rate to the marginal productivity of labor. As a close correlate of the average returns per job to the establishments, gross profits per worker rose in new and young establishments over the period more than in other establishments, which underscores the higher jobs growth rate of the new establishments.

The average wage rate remained largely constant for new and young establishments throughout the period. Thus, the steady rise in gross profit margins per worker in those establishments mainly reflects a steady rise in average labor productivity, as measured by annual value added per employee. Nonetheless, the higher rate of job growth in new and young establishments should be attributed to the relatively low-wage environment because labor productivity rose as fast and steadily in older establishments as well, leading to comparable increases in gross profit margins per worker in both groups. By contrast, the average wage rate remained consistently and substantially higher in older establishments than in new and young establishments throughout the period.

Despite these observations, some signs suggest that the phase of job growth at low wages might be coming to an end. One of the signs is that profit margins per worker have fallen steeply across all size and age groups of establishments since 2014 (except establishments that have been in business for 20 or more years). This finding is attributable to the gradual rise in wage rates being higher than increases in labor productivity for all size groups. This situation appears to have made production in new and young establishments increasingly capital-intensive over time, reversing the trend in job growth driven by a process of increasing substitution of labor for capital among this group of establishments. Although this capital intensity will not change the fact that most job growth is concentrated in new and young establishments, it implies that fewer jobs will be created in such establishments going forward as they respond to rising wages by substituting equipment for labor in their choice of techniques of production or products.[12]

The sustained manufacturing job growth in Ethiopia between 1996 and 2016 was concentrated in increasingly labor-intensive lines until the last five years of the period. Figure 2.13 shows that the value of fixed assets per employee declined steadily throughout the first decade of the millennium in

Figure 2.13 Ethiopia: Fixed Assets per Worker, by Manufacturer Size Group, 1996–2016

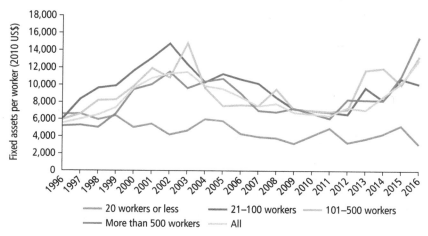

Source: Abreha et al. 2019.

aggregate and for each employment size group of establishments except those employing at most 20 workers. Most significant, the decline in fixed assets per employee was steepest in new and young establishments, where most of the job growth occurred (figure 2.14). Fixed assets per worker remained more or less the same over the years among older establishments. However, fixed assets per worker began to rise in 2012 across most of the age and size groups, but more steeply in new and young establishments, which suggests a slowing of job growth.

The decline in the labor intensity of production during the end of the period of observation was matched by a fall in gross profit margins per worker across all size and age groups of establishments except establishments older than age 20 (figure 2.15). Underlying this change was that the average wage rate, which rose quite steeply toward the end of the period across all size and age groups, had been almost constant within each group, although it was always significantly lower for new and young establishments (figure 2.16). Therefore, the concentration of job growth in new and young establishments over the two decades can be attributed to their ability to hire workers at much lower wages than those paid by older establishments.

The average labor productivity in new and young establishments was lower than that in other establishments over the same period, as shown in figure 2.17. Given their levels of labor productivity, new and young

Figure 2.14 Ethiopia: Fixed Assets per Worker, by Manufacturer Age Group, 1996–2016

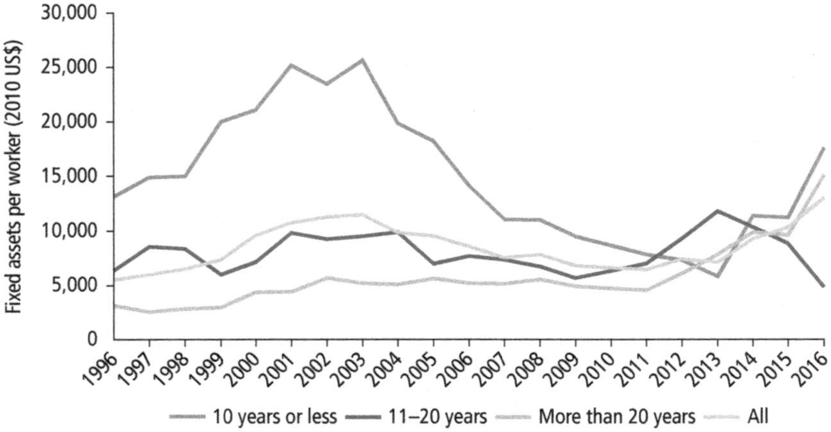

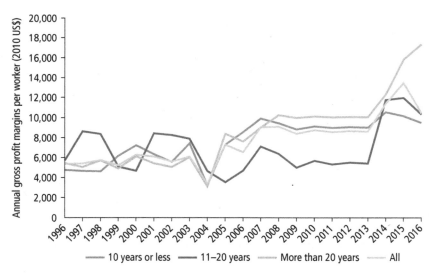

Source: Abreha et al. 2019.

Figure 2.15 Ethiopia: Annual Gross Profit Margins per Worker, by Manufacturer Age Group, 1996–2016

Source: Abreha et al. 2019.

Figure 2.16 Ethiopia: Annual Wages per Worker, by Manufacturer Age Group, 1996–2016

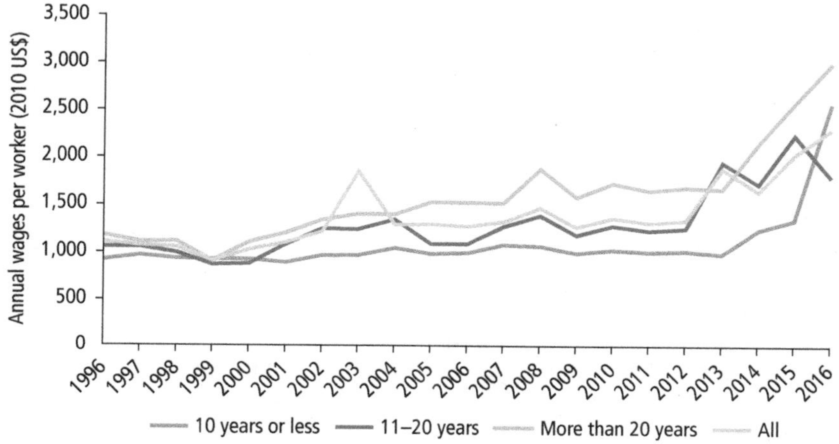

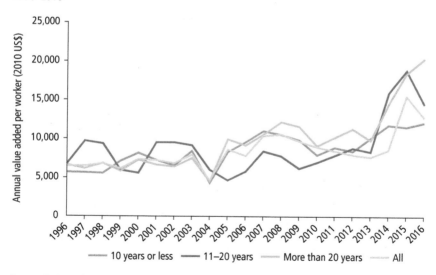

Source: Abreha et al. 2019.

Figure 2.17 Ethiopia: Annual Value Added per Worker, by Manufacturer Age Group, 1996–2016

Source: Abreha et al. 2019.

establishments were able to sustain the economywide average profit margins only because these establishments were able to hire at the economywide average wage rate. In the same vein, the steep rise in the average wage rate paid by new and young establishments explains why such establishments have invested in relatively less labor-intensive activities and processes in the latter years of the period, signaling the slowing of the growth of manufacturing jobs.

Côte d'Ivoire

Manufacturing job growth in Côte d'Ivoire has also been enabled by an environment of "unlimited labor supply" at comparatively low wages (figure 2.18). Establishments appear to have taken advantage of the low wages to invest in labor-intensive activities and techniques (figure 2.19). Manufacturers in Côte d'Ivoire continued to operate under these conditions, hiring at lower pay rates, and this is likely to persist into the near future. However, manufacturing job growth would not be sustainable in the long run without commensurate growth in productivity.

Figure 2.18 Côte d'Ivoire: Annual Wages per Worker, by Manufacturer Age Group, 2003–14

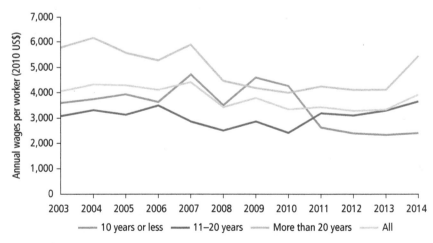

Source: Abreha et al. 2019.

Figure 2.19 Côte d'Ivoire: Fixed Assets per Worker, by Manufacturer Size Group, 2003–14

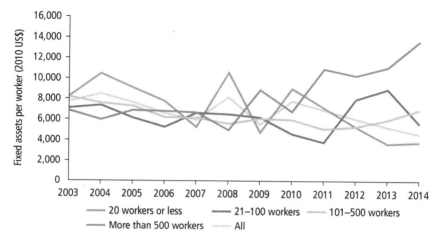

Source: Abreha et al. 2019.

Underlying Factors and Policy Interventions

The underlying factors notwithstanding, the broader policy implication of the concentration of job growth in new and young firms is that public interventions for job growth should avoid size-based support schemes. Therefore, two sets of public interventions for promoting manufacturing job growth can be implemented—those directed at lowering barriers to entry and those promoting within-firm productivity growth.

Distinguishing between the two types of interventions is important because, on the one hand, policies aimed at lowering entry barriers lead to job growth only because entry boosts aggregate productivity by inducing the reallocation of market share from less productive incumbents to more productive entrants. On the other hand, although the second set of interventions raises industrywide productivity via reallocation of market share from less productive incumbents to more productive ones, it also leads to within-firm productivity growth among incumbents and entrants.

Policy Interventions for Lowering Entry Barriers

Arguably, the most formidable bottleneck to raising rates of entry into existing and new manufacturing industries in economies like those of Côte d'Ivoire and Ethiopia is physical infrastructure for essential services, including transport and logistics, information and communication technology, and power and other utilities. Policy interventions aimed at reducing other barriers to entry by addressing infrastructure and services bottlenecks can be grouped into four broad categories, namely, business licensing and business regulation, access to external finance, trade policy, and labor market regulation.

Business Licensing and Business Regulation

Administrative and regulatory barriers to entry include all legal restrictions on the location, timing, scale, or type of production activities and related transactions, which are typically codified in explicit requirements for licenses and permits that businesses must acquire to operate. The cost of securing the licenses and permits would be negligible relative to the scale of activities of large companies in a developed economy. However, it can be quite sizable for the average small business in a developing economy.[13]

Empirical estimates suggest that license fees average 32 percent of annual output per worker in developing economies (Barseghyan and DiCecio 2011) and are reliable proxies for cross-country differences in the average cost of entry. Cross-country differences in the cost of entry are also associated with corresponding differences in the rates of entry. In turn, cross-country differences in rates of business entry lead to corresponding differences in the misallocation of factors of production and, consequently, productivity. On the basis of estimates, countries in the lowest decile of the average cost of entry per firm would have 32 to 45 percent higher total factor productivity and 52 to 75 percent higher labor productivity than countries in the top decile of the distribution of the cost of entry (Barseghyan and DiCecio 2011).

Access to External Finance

The rate of entry also depends on the ease of access to external finance. The existing evidence shows that interfirm differences in access to finance lead to distortions in the scale and interindustry patterns of entry that result in huge losses in aggregate productivity (Buera, Kaboski, and Shin 2011; Jeong and Townsend 2007). However, this finding may not hold if more productive firms tend to be less constrained financially than less productive ones (Midrigan and Xu 2010). In that case, more productive firms would tend to invest more without necessarily borrowing more given that their investments tend to be internally financed.

Moreover, the greater contribution of new and younger establishments to job growth suggests that new and younger firms tend to be more responsive to new investment opportunities compared with well-established firms (Adelino, Ma, and Robinson 2014). Supporting evidence suggests that new firms are more likely than older firms to respond to changes in local economic conditions, with the responsiveness of the new being higher where firms have easier access to external finance (Adelino, Ma, and Robinson 2014).

Trade Policy

Initial exposure to foreign trade allows domestic firms to enter industries to which they would not have access otherwise because such exposure opens export markets for products for which domestic demand may be limited or absent. Over time, continued exposure to trade boosts the aggregate productivity of domestic producers in import-competing industries because import competition forces less productive domestic firms to exit those industries, while export markets allow the more productive domestic firms to increase production and employment.[14] Therefore, the boost to job and output growth via trade occurs only among the more productive domestic firms in each industry to the extent that they export. Whether the number of jobs and domestic output will be higher than they were before exposure to trade depends on the balance between job losses due to trade-induced exit of domestic firms and job gains due to trade-induced new entry.

Labor Market Regulation

An economy's comparative advantage, which is determined by cross-country differences in production technology or relative factor endowments, is an important determinant of which industries or sectors would experience net job growth or net job losses caused by greater exposure to trade. However, cross-country patterns of comparative advantage in trade also depend on international differences in labor market regulation or flexibility (Cunat and Melitz 2011). Countries that have "more flexible" labor markets generally tend to have a comparative advantage in industries facing greater uncertainty in market demand or production outcomes. As a consequence, countries that have less flexible labor markets end up specializing in more capital-intensive industries if they are characterized by lower within-industry uncertainty.

Policy Interventions for Increasing Within-Firm Productivity Growth

Labor market policies can influence within-firm productivity to the extent that they influence human capital formation through schooling and other skills-development schemes. Other interventions for promoting within-firm productivity growth may be aimed at one or both of two areas of policy—trade policy and the provision of infrastructure and incentives for innovation and technology adoption.

Trade Policy

The boost that trade exposure gives to the aggregate productivity of domestic firms via trade-induced reallocation toward more efficient firms does not necessarily improve the productive efficiency of individual firms. Nevertheless, trade can raise productivity at the firm level through three channels: (1) through the "learning-by-exporting" mechanism, (2) through "imported inputs" that make domestic firms more productive, and (3) through "trade-induced" innovation.

The first of these channels refers to exposure to trade leading to within-firm productivity growth through a learning effect, whereby people think of new, production-related ideas by learning from those with whom they do business or compete through trade (Eaton and Kortum 2002). Indeed, if it is persistent and free enough, trade can generate growth and income convergence among economies through the flow of ideas, which, in turn, raises productivity at the firm level beyond the standard efficiency gains from reallocation effects (Alvarez, Buera, and Lucas 2013).

Infrastructure for Innovation and Technology Adoption

A case can be made for subsidizing research and development (R&D) or innovation by new entrants as another policy instrument for boosting aggregate productivity and generating welfare gains. Acemoglu et al. (2018) show that a policy of subsidizing R&D and innovation by incumbents reduces growth as well as welfare because it deters the entry of more innovative operators. By contrast, subsidizing R&D by both incumbents and new entrants increases growth and welfare if the continued operation of incumbents is taxed at the same time. These two results are complementary and explained by the strong selection effect that industrial policy seeking to promote R&D and innovation is likely to have.

Conclusion and Policy Options

Many Sub-Saharan African countries, including Côte d'Ivoire and Ethiopia, have experienced sustained and significant job growth in manufacturing over the past two decades. As in other regions and sectors, this process has been driven mainly by new and young firms. An important aspect of the process in Côte d'Ivoire, as well as in Ethiopia, is that it has been fueled mainly by an environment of "unlimited labor supply" at comparatively low wages and that, compared with established firms, new and young firms have taken advantage of this environment on a larger scale.

This is a situation in which removing or reducing administrative and economic barriers to entry is potentially the most important policy tool for promoting job growth in the sector. Addressing entry barriers should be understood in the broader sense to include an agenda for reducing entry barriers and minimizing the time and monetary costs of licensing and the postentry costs of complying with regulations. However, regulatory barriers are not the only potential deterrents to entry. Depending on the current market structure, entry into an industry can also be deterred via collusion on the part of incumbent firms unless precluded by an effective competition policy. Moreover, entry regulations and the concentration of market power as a potential entry deterrent reinforce each other as forces inhibiting job growth.[15] In addition, incumbent firms tend to have better access to infrastructure, finance, or both, compared with many potential entrants.

Furthermore, there are some indications that the observed phase of job growth might be coming to an end in Ethiopia, one such indication being that wages started rising steeply for all employers beginning in 2012. This rise probably marks a turning point at which policies aimed at promoting industrial job growth would need to include tools that help promote growth in the productivity of new and young firms in addition to tools that facilitate entry.

The situation in Côte d'Ivoire is one in which manufacturing job growth can no longer be sustained at current levels without policy interventions to boost poststart-up productivity. Unlike in Ethiopia, industrial wages in Côte d'Ivoire are not rising and do not show signs of picking up. Manufacturers in Côte d'Ivoire have been hiring at declining pay rates during the observation period, and average manufacturing labor productivity has been declining even faster, which has culminated in gross profit margins per worker being close to zero.

Reducing the cost of entry regulations, developing an effective competition policy, and improving access to infrastructure and finance for all categories of firms should be part of the policy toolkits that Côte d'Ivoire and Ethiopia adopt. However, it seems that neither country can sustain manufacturing job growth without the use of the second set of policies targeting growth in labor productivity in new and young establishments. These policies could take a variety of forms, such as in-school and postschool skills-development programs that help increase the supply of skills to those firms, enhance their capacity to adopt improved technology or develop or diversify into higher-value products, or improve their access to more reliable and cheaper transport and logistics systems and utilities. Although all manufacturing firms would benefit from such productivity-enhancing interventions, they would likely have the maximum impact on job growth only to the extent that they have a bearing on the rate of business start-ups and investment decisions that firms make after start-up to survive and establish themselves in specific industries.

Notes

1. Probably the best known and most recent international evidence for the absence of systematic size effects in job growth at the firm level is in Haltiwanger, Jarmin, and Miranda (2013). Using US census data, the paper shows that job growth was primarily driven by start-ups and young firms, with initial size playing no role in the process. In a related paper, Decker et al. (2014) report that business start-ups account for about 20 percent of gross job growth in the United States and that, all else given, younger firms have a higher share of aggregate job growth than older firms.

2. The literature on empirical evidence for the invariance of job growth with firm size extends from as far back as the 1980s to the present. It was initially focused on testing Gibrat's Law (Lucas 1978; Sutton 1997) on establishment census data in the United States and Europe. Examples are Evans (1987) and Hall (1987) on different sets of US data, Dunne and Hughes (1994) on data on the United Kingdom, and Audretsch, Santarelli, and Vivarelli (1999) on Italian data.

3. Jovanovic (1982) offers this as an explanation of why younger firms grow faster.

4. The distinction between "passive" and "active" learning is made in Pakes and Ericson (1998), who propose that firms also invest actively to enhance their capabilities, which may make older firms grow faster.

5. This relates to models of firm dynamics that do not necessarily produce faster job growth in start-ups and younger firms but are consistent with that outcome. The models include the fact that firms continually update their production techniques through competitive diffusion, as described in Jovanovic and MacDonald (1994). Hopenhayn's (1992) model of firm entry, production, and exit decisions driven by simultaneous firm- and industry-level dynamics should be added to this category.

6. See Acemoglu et al. (2018) for an economic model laying out this argument.

7. The barriers to which Hsieh and Klenow (2014) refer reduce job growth by making larger firms less productive than they would be otherwise, thereby reducing aggregate manufacturing productivity.

8. This is about a fifth of the more than 600,000 new industrial jobs that were added to the nonfarm sectors of Ethiopia's economy over 1999–2013 according to World Bank (2017). But the larger figure is based on the results of the latest labor force surveys for that period and includes cases of self-employment and own account work in microenterprises. The smaller total here relates only to job growth in the larger establishments covered by the annual manufacturing census of the Central Statistics Agency of the government of Ethiopia. The manufacturing census targets a population of manufacturers defined by a minimum employment size threshold of 10 workers.

9. In this report, the terms *enterprises, firms, establishments and manufacturers* are used interchangeably unless otherwise indicated.

10. For the period 1996–2010, there is a common establishment identification number, and the data can be treated as panel. However, the establishment identification number changed in the censuses after 2010, and the data can only be used cross-sectionally for those years. Other researchers have attempted to construct the panel for the most recent years using additional information such as establishment name, address, and so on. However, this data set is not yet available and is not used in this report.

11. This term borrows a famous phrase from a classic contribution to development economics, Lewis (1954), to characterize a state of sustained job growth under structural change at a constant wage rate.

12. This observed pattern of capital intensity is also in line with recent findings on Ethiopia by Diao et al. (2021).

13. See Barseghyan and DiCecio 2011 and World Bank 2004.

14. This is along the lines portrayed in the Melitz (2003) model.

15. See Bertrand and Kramarz (2002) for evidence on reinforcing barriers to entry based on a study of the retail industry in France.

References

Abreha, K., P. Jones, E. Lartey, T. Mengistae, and A. Zeufack. 2019. "Manufacturing Job Growth in Africa: What Is Driving It? The Cases of Côte d'Ivoire and Ethiopia." World Bank, Washington, DC.

Acemoglu, D., U. Ackicit, H. Alp, N. Bloom, and W. Kerr. 2018. "Innovation, Reallocation and Growth." *American Economic Review* 188 (11): 3450–91.

Adelino, M., S. Ma, and D. Robinson. 2014. "Firm Age, Investment Opportunities and Job Creation." NBER Working Paper 19845, National Bureau of Economic Research, Cambridge, MA.

Alvarez, F., F. Buera, and R. Lucas Jr. 2013. "Ideas, Economic Growth and Trade." NBER Working Paper 19667, National Bureau of Economic Research, Cambridge, MA.

Audretsch, D., E. Santarelli, and M. Vivarelli. 1999. "Startup Size and Industrial Dynamics: Some Evidence from Italian Manufacturing." *International Journal of Industrial Organization* 17: 965–83.

Barseghyan, J., and R. DiCecio. 2011. "Entry Costs, Industry Structure and Cross-Country Income and TFP Differences." *Journal of Economic Theory* 146 (5): 1828–51.

Bertrand, M., and F. Kramarz. 2002. "Does Entry Regulation Hinder Job Creation? Evidence from the French Retail Industry." *Quarterly Journal of Economics* 67: 1369–413.

Buera, F., J. Kaboski, and Y. Shin. 2011. "Finance and Development: A Tale of Two Sectors." *American Economic Review* 101 (5): 1964–2002.

Cunat, A., and M. Melitz. 2011. "Volatility, Labor Market Flexibility, and the Pattern of Comparative Advantage." *Journal of the European Economic Association* 10 (2): 225–54.

Decker, R., J. Haltiwanger, R. Jarmin, and J. Miranda. 2014. "The Role of Entrepreneurship in US Job Creation and Economic Dynamism." *Journal of Economic Perspectives* 28 (3): 3–24.

Diao, X., M. Ellis, M. McMillan, and D. Rodrik. 2021. "Africa's Manufacturing Puzzle: Evidence from Tanzanian and Ethiopian Firms." NBER Working Paper 28344, National Bureau of Economic Research, Cambridge, MA.

Dunne, P., and A. Hughes. 1994. "Age, Size, Growth and Survival: UK Companies in the 1980s." *Journal of Industrial Economics* 42 (2): 115–40.

Eaton, J., and S. Kortum. 2002. "Technology, Geography, and Trade." *Econometrica* 70 (5): 1741–79.

Evans, D. 1987. "Tests of Alternative Theories of Firm Growth." *Journal of Political Economy* 95: 657–74.

Hall, B. 1987. "The Relationship between Firm Size and Firm Growth in the US Manufacturing Sectors." *Journal of Industrial Economics* 35 (4): 583–606.

Haltiwanger, J., R. Jarmin, and J. Miranda. 2013. "Who Creates Jobs? Small versus Large versus Young." *Review of Economics and Statistics* 95 (2): 347–61.

Hopenhayn, H. 1992. "Entry, Exit, and Firm Dynamics in Long Run Equilibrium." *Econometrica* 60 (5): 1127–50.

Hsieh, C., and P. Klenow. 2014. "The Life Cycle of Plants in India and Mexico." *Quarterly Journal of Economics* 129 (3): 1035–84.

Jeong, H., and R. Townsend. 2007. "Sources of TFP Growth: Occupational Choice and Financial Deepening." *Economic Theory* 32 (1): 179–221.

Jovanovic, B. 1982. "Selection and the Evolution of Industry." *Econometrica* 50 (3): 649–70.

Jovanovic, B., and G. MacDonald. 1994. "Competitive Diffusion." *Journal of Political Economy* 10: 24–52.

Lewis, A. 1954. "Development with Unlimited Supplies of Labour." *The Manchester School* 22: 139–92.

Lucas Jr., R. E. 1978. "On the Size Distribution of Business Firms." *Bell Journal of Economics* 9: 508–23.

Melitz, M. 2003. "The Impact of Trade on Intra-Industry Reallocations and Aggregate Productivity." *Econometrica* 71 (6): 1695–725.

Midrigan, V., and D. Xu. 2010. "Finance and Misallocation." NBER Working Paper 15647, National Bureau of Economic Research, Cambridge, MA.

Pakes, A., and R. Ericson. 1998. "Empirical Implications of Alternative Models of Firm Dynamics." *Journal of Economic Theory* 79: 1–45.

Sutton, J. 1997. "Gibrat's Legacy." *Journal of Economic Literature* 35: 40–59.

World Bank. 2004. *Doing Business in 2004: Understanding Regulation.* Washington, DC: World Bank.

World Bank. 2017. "Ethiopia: Employment and Jobs Study." World Bank, Washington, DC.

Chapter 3

Manufacturing Productivity and the Prospects for Jobs Growth

Most Sub-Saharan African countries have experienced a significant increase in their manufacturing workforces over the past couple of decades. Cheap labor in these countries has spurred substantial job growth especially among new and young firms, irrespective of their size. For example, Côte d'Ivoire created about 24,000 manufacturing jobs between 2003 and 2014, and Ethiopia added 128,000 manufacturing jobs over the 1996–2016 period. These employment opportunities are mainly because of new establishments. In Côte d'Ivoire, survivors created 19,000 net jobs, entrants contributed 101,000 jobs, and exiters destroyed 96,000 jobs over 2004–14. Comparable figures for Ethiopia during 1997–2010 are 1,700, 195,000, and 130,000 jobs, respectively (Abreha et al. 2019).

Rapid expansion of the manufacturing workforce in Sub-Saharan African countries has occurred at about the same time as these countries have experienced productivity growth. Côte d'Ivoire and Ethiopia are again typical examples. A greater share of the observed productivity growth has been driven by the reallocation of markets and resources away from less productive establishments toward more productive ones through the expansion and contraction of incumbent producers as well as through the entrance of new establishments and closure of some incumbents. Put differently, the reallocation mechanism is strong enough to generate productivity growth even in the absence of sizable within-firm productivity gains. This feature of productivity dynamics is consistent with the observation that manufacturing job growth has occurred mainly because of new and young establishments.

Recently, however, the advantage that the manufacturing sector in these economies has had by hiring additional workers at roughly constant wage rates has been eroding, as illustrated in the pattern of job growth and dynamics of wages in Ethiopian manufacturing. When new and young establishments are less likely to be the main drivers of job creation, future job growth prospects need to come from activities that improve within-firm productivity gains, such as product and process innovations, technology adoption, and better management practices and organizational structure. Given that sustained productivity growth is needed to generate more and better jobs and achieve structural change, what drives manufacturing productivity in Sub-Saharan African countries?

This chapter addresses this question by relying on evidence mostly from Sub-Saharan African countries, but also from other developing and developed economies. The chapter establishes why any future job creation by incumbent establishments will be significantly shaped by their productivity dynamics and summarizes the features of productivity growth across industries and establishments of different sizes. Furthermore, it discusses the potential sources of and evidence for within-firm productivity gains, namely, trade participation, foreign ownership, and agglomeration economies. The chapter also briefly looks into factors affecting productivity that are industry specific, sectoral, and economywide, including market structure and competition policy, entry regulation, and infrastructure. The chapter concludes by highlighting policy options for attaining sustainable employment creation and robust productivity growth.

Jobs Growth at the Intensive Margin with Productivity as the Driver

In Sub-Saharan African manufacturing, the main driver of employment growth has been the availability of cheap labor. However, wages have increased, which implies that any future job growth will require productivity growth to compensate for the declining advantage of hiring additional workers at roughly constant wage rates. To this end, boosting productivity is the most important channel for ensuring better employment growth prospects.

Productivity growth occurs through two main channels.[1] The first channel is when individual firms become more productive. The second channel is when resources and markets reallocate toward more productive firms, away from their less productive counterparts. The most extreme reallocations take the form of entry into and exit from the market. The entry of new productive firms and exit of the least productive ones become additional avenues for productivity growth.[2] Therefore, productivity evolves through the interplay of new firms entering the market, surviving firms expanding or contracting, and inefficient firms exiting the market.

The existing evidence shows enormous cross-country differences in economic growth and income levels worldwide (for example, Hall and Jones 1999; Jones 2016).[3] Within countries, there is also considerable heterogeneity among firms in narrowly defined industries.[4] Several arguments have been put forward to explain the productivity dispersion and income differences. Among others, the obvious one is resource misallocation. Recent estimates reveal that resource misallocation can explain up to 60 percent of the aggregate total factor productivity (TFP) differences between rich and poor countries (Kalemli-Ozcan and Sorensen 2012). Widespread productivity dispersions reflect market frictions and distortions that restrict resources from being reallocated to high-productivity firms (Haltiwanger 2015). Some frictions and distortions are caused by size-based tax policies that are biased against large firms (Gunner, Ventura, and Xu 2008; Hopenhayn and Rogerson 1993), financial market frictions that distort capital allocation (Buera, Kaboski, and Shin 2011), and trade policies that prevent the equalization of marginal productivity across firms (Eaton and Kortum 2002; Eaton, Kortum, and Kramarz 2011; Melitz 2003).

Furthermore, product differentiation, transportation costs, and related market imperfections lead to situations in which the most productive firms do not take over the entire market. Such imperfections give rise to considerable markups and price dispersion across producers. They also reduce the forces of selection operating through changes in market shares as well as firms entering and exiting industries (for instance, Melitz 2003; Melitz and Ottaviano 2008; Syverson 2004a, 2004b).

Sources of Productivity Growth: Interindustry and Intraindustry Resource Reallocation

Market Distortions and Potential Growth in Jobs and Productivity

A main feature of developing countries is the sizable cross-sector productivity heterogeneities not only between the traditional and modern sectors but also among industries in the modern sectors.[5] Misallocations across as well as within sectors and industries are quite substantial in developing economies compared with those in developed economies (McMillan, Rodrik, and Verduzco-Gallo 2014).[6]

Under the condition that resources move from low- to high-productivity activities, these productivity differentials are productivity enhancing and constitute strong sources of potential job creation. Hence, the resource reallocation that comes with structural change can accelerate growth and generate gainful employment opportunities. However, this outcome is not always guaranteed. Structural change can be growth reducing, as was observed in Sub-Saharan Africa and Latin America during the 1990s. For example, it is estimated that Sub-Saharan Africa has experienced, on average, a reduction of 1.3 percentage points per year in labor productivity growth because of labor mobility from high- to low-productivity activities (McMillan, Rodrik, and Verduzco-Gallo 2014). A study on selected countries in West Africa finds that structural change patterns are mostly not accompanied by labor reallocation to high-productivity sectors (Haile 2018).

In the manufacturing sector, episodes of employment creation that have been accompanied by productivity improvement, shifts in market shares, and movement of resources away from less productive firms to more productive ones have played an important role in raising aggregate productivity. These reallocations are triggered by differences in the productivity of factors across establishments and are mainly attributed to market distortions.

A study on Ugandan firms illustrates the extent and role of the misalloca-tion that is usually observed in Sub-Saharan African manufacturing. Between 2002 and 2009, labor productivity grew, on average, by 13 percent annually (Dennis et al. 2016). Part of the productivity gains was due to improvements in the technical efficiency of operating firms, and the remainder was attribut-able to labor and capital movements across industries and across firms within industries. About 20 percent of the growth was a result of labor shifting to sectors and industries where it was more productive. Furthermore, reallo-cation of labor across firms explains 55 to 90 percent of the growth at the industry level.

Misallocation Country Cases: Côte d'Ivoire, Ethiopia, and Tanzania Compared with Bangladesh

Contribution of Market Share Reallocations to Productivity Growth

A comparison of manufacturing firms in Côte d'Ivoire, Ethiopia, and Tanzania, using Bangladesh as a benchmark, reveals clear differences in the size and sources of productivity growth between countries and across establish-ments within countries. In Ethiopian manufacturing, aggregate productivity increased by 47 percent between 1996 and 2009, whereas it increased by 6 per-cent in Côte d'Ivoire over a similar period (2004–16) (Jones et al. 2019b).[7] By contrast, Tanzania experienced a decline in productivity from 2008 to 2012. Ethiopia's productivity growth pattern resembles that of Bangladesh during its early years of industrialization, when productivity grew by 33 percent during 1995–2001.

In Côte d'Ivoire and Ethiopia, a large share of the observed productiv-ity growth was due to the reallocation of market shares from less productive establishments to more productive ones. This reallocation occurred not only through the expansion and contraction of incumbent producers but also via new plant openings (entries) and plant closures (exits). In Ethiopia, the impact of the reallocation of market share among survivors exceeded that associated with increases in productivity within plants. In addition, plant closures boosted productivity more than new plant openings did. Thus, reallocation boosted productivity by eliminating the least productive plants through exposure to greater competition from new establishments.

In Côte d'Ivoire, the reallocation effect has also been the main driver of productivity growth. However, new establishments have had a relatively larger impact in that the productivity of entering plants, on average, exceeds that of surviving plants by more than the average amount by which the productivity of closing plants falls short of that of surviving plants.

The predominance of the reallocation effect relative to the contribution of within-firm productivity changes is consistent with the implication that productivity growth and job growth have occurred in an environment of "unlimited labor supply," which implies constant wage costs. Therefore, reallocation and entry and exit were the major drivers of job creation as well as aggregate productivity growth, even in the absence of within-firm productivity gains. (See annex 3A for details on the productivity growth decomposition.)

Firm Size and Productivity Growth

A dissection of productivity growth reveals a systematic element of variation by firm size and industry. Firms in the smallest size category (with fewer than 50 employees), which encompasses most of the formal manufacturing firms, experienced the largest productivity growth in three of the four countries—Bangladesh, Ethiopia, and Tanzania. Côte d'Ivoire is the exception, with slightly larger plants (those with 50–199 workers) experiencing the fastest productivity growth. In addition, the data reveal that productivity growth is primarily driven by entrants in the size category with fewer than 200 workers, whereas exiting firms contribute negatively in the 200–499 worker size category. These findings indicate that the strength of the market selection mechanism varies for different firm size categories.

Cross-Industry Productivity Growth

Among garment and textile producers, Ethiopian plants attained the highest productivity growth compared with their counterparts in the other countries. Aggregate productivity in Ethiopia rose by 24 percent between 1996 and 2001 and by 30 percent between 2001 and 2006, but declined in Côte d'Ivoire between 2004 and 2014 and in Tanzania between 2008 and 2012. In comparison, aggregate productivity increased by 33 percent between 1995 and 2001 in Bangladesh, largely driven by more efficient survivors gaining market shares and less efficient plants exiting the market. The Ethiopian case displayed a similar pattern with a slight variation. In the first half of the period, market share reallocation was the dominant factor; in the second half, the entry of more efficient plants was the driving force.

In the food and beverages industry, aggregate productivity expanded by 11 percent in Ethiopia between 1996 and 2006, compared with 47 percent in Bangladesh between 1995 and 2001. The main drivers of growth were market share reallocations among survivors in Ethiopia and the high firm turnover rate in Bangladesh. By contrast, the industry underwent a period of productivity decline in Côte d'Ivoire and Tanzania mainly because surviving firms became less productive, relatively less efficient new producers entered in Côte d'Ivoire, and an increasing share of output was shifted to less productive plants in Tanzania.

In the furniture industry, Ethiopia experienced an increase in aggregate productivity of 36 percent between 1996 and 2006, and Côte d'Ivoire experienced an increase of 19 percent between 2004 and 2014. Productivity growth in Ethiopia was primarily driven by surviving plants becoming more productive and gaining market share. In Côte d'Ivoire, it was due to more productive survivors gaining market share and less efficient plants exiting the market.

Sources of Productivity Growth: Within-Firm Productivity Growth, Innovation, and Technology Adoption

Sources of Within-Firm Productivity Growth

Much of the growth in manufacturing productivity has resulted from plant openings and closures as well as from market share reallocation, which is consistent with the observed pattern of job creation in which new and young establishments were the prominent sources of employment, propelled by the opportunity to hire workers at roughly constant wages. In view of the recent development of rising wages, any future job growth prospects should be due to within-firm productivity gains.

When do firms experience improvement in their technical efficiency? In general, the literature identifies three drivers of firm-level productivity: participation in international trade, foreign direct investment (FDI), and agglomeration economies (see Combes and Gobillon 2015; Duranton and Puga 2004). These drivers influence productivity at the firm and aggregate levels via innovation and technology adoption. For instance, product and process innovations can be viewed within the following context: international trade exposure leads to innovation or innovation leads to international trade participation (or both); foreign capital relaxes credit constraint and provides incentives for innovation or innovation attracts foreign ownership (or both); and economic clusters improve innovation by enhancing innovation capability through the sharing of indivisible resources such as infrastructure and goods that have economies of scale, better matching between producers and inputs, and learning from enhanced exchange and transfer of knowledge and skills.

Trade Exposure

The mechanisms through which trade affects productivity and overall welfare are the consumption of a large number of varieties of final goods (in addition to local varieties), technology embodied in imported inputs, intense competition in goods markets, and reallocation of market shares and eventually resources to more productive firms (Harrison and Rodriguez-Clare 2010).

Firms that participate in international trade enjoy a productivity premium compared with their counterparts that restrict their activities entirely to domestic operations. First, under the *selection effect* participation in international trade involves nonnegligible fixed (one time and periodic) and variable trade costs. The fixed costs come from market research, advertisement expenses, investment in storage and logistics, and contract write-up and enforcement; the variable costs emanate mainly from transportation costs and tariffs. Only the most productive firms can absorb these costs to gain access to foreign markets as a destination for their products and a source of inputs for their production activities. Relatedly, firms also exert effort to improve their efficiency with the intended goal of participating in international trade.

Second, as a result of *learning-by-doing*, firms experience productivity gains from exposure to foreign demand, better technology, and a greater variety of inputs. Normally, the selection and learning effects reinforce each other. Increased trade exposure has significant learning effects and strengthens the selection mechanisms that weed out less efficient firms even further.

A large body of evidence documents the presence of significant export productivity premiums (including other firm metrics), in that manufacturing exporters outperform their domestic counterparts (for example, Bigsten et al. 2004; Mengistae and Pattillo 2004; and Van Biesebroeck 2005). There is also evidence of import premiums, and two-way traders are shown to perform better than export-only, import-only, and domestic-only firms (Abreha 2019; Foster-McGregor, Isaksson, and Kaulich 2014).

Although the results on the causal relationship between trading and productivity are mixed, most studies support the hypothesis that better-performing firms select into exporting and importing. These firms are more productive even before they become exporters and importers (Abreha 2019; Bigsten and Gebreeyesus 2009). Furthermore, several studies report a significant postentry productivity effect associated with firms becoming exporters and importers.[8] For example, based on export participation as a measure of trade exposure and TFP as an approximation for plant productivity, evidence from Côte d'Ivoire, Ethiopia, and Tanzania provides strong support for the proposition that increased trade exposure significantly raises plant-level TFP (Jones et al. 2019b).

Foreign Ownership

The productivity of foreign-owned enterprises improves because of the relaxation of credit constraints, adoption of better organizational and management practices, and diffusion of technical skills and business knowledge that come with foreign ownership. In addition, the beneficial effects of foreign investment, including technology spillovers and other pecuniary externalities and competition effects, are not limited to foreign-owned firms only but are shared by domestic firms.[9]

These effects occur through several channels (Keller 2010). First, multinational enterprises undertake part of their activities by hiring local labor in the host country. To the extent that these workers gain knowledge of the multinationals' technologies, labor turnover and mobility within and across industries constitute a mechanism of technology transfer. Second, local firms will have more opportunities to engage in business transactions with foreign-owned enterprises, and these business interactions constitute another channel of technology spillover. Transfer is further facilitated by local firms' operating in proximity to foreign-owned enterprises, thereby reducing the cost of technical and business knowledge exchange and adoption. Third, technology transfer occurs through outsourcing by foreign-owned enterprises to local producers of intermediate inputs, including but not limited to producers that are in contractual agreement with the foreign-owned enterprises. In addition, the flow of foreign capital can end up creating substantial markets for local suppliers, which, in turn, increases the number of varieties of intermediate inputs available, thereby raising the overall productivity of domestic firms. Relatedly, the supply of high-quality inputs to local producers by foreign-owned enterprises raises the overall productivity of final goods producers. Furthermore, flows of foreign capital usually trigger market and resource reallocations toward high-performing firms.

Studies that focus on horizontal FDI spillovers (that is, spillovers in the same industry) have reported an insignificant or negative effect of FDI on industry productivity in host countries (see Aitken and Harrison 1999; Blalock and Gertler 2008; Javorcik and Spatareanu 2008). A suggested explanation for the negative effect is that the adverse effect of FDI (say, through competition) outweighs the potential spillovers that come with it. However, other studies tend to find positive effects, mostly in developed economies and high-technology industries, although the size of the effect across countries and industries varies significantly.[10] Cross-country studies that find aggregate productivity growth because of FDI attribute it to selection and market reallocation effects (Alfaro and Chen 2018). On vertical FDI spillovers, it is reported for Lithuania that firms that are upstream of industries with substantial inflows of FDI turn out to be more productive compared with other domestic firms (Javorcik 2004). The results for Indonesian firms reveal a similar effect (Blalock and Gertler 2008).

In Ghana, firms that have entrepreneurs with previous experience in foreign-owned enterprises enjoy a productivity premium over other domestic firms (Gorg and Strobl 2005). Moreover, TFP is found to be 8 percent higher among domestic firms in Ethiopia that are located in districts that have attracted significant greenfield FDI. Such exposure to foreign firms enhances the efficiency of local firms through their production operations, managerial and organizational practices, infrastructure, provision of business services, and knowledge exchange and sharing about exporting (Abebe, McMillan, and Serafinelli 2018).

Clustering

Urbanization provides a platform for interactions among firms and workers in markets for final goods and services, intermediate inputs, and knowledge. These interactions constitute agglomeration economies and usually translate into innovation, productivity growth, and ultimately more and better jobs.

Three mechanisms drive the benefits of these interactions: sharing, matching, and learning (Duranton and Puga 2004). First, the *sharing channel* indicates that being in close physical proximity to other firms allows firms to use indivisible goods and infrastructure (whose production and supply are usually characterized by economies of scale) and the wide variety of intermediate inputs and specialized input services that are available. Second, the *matching channel* is where agglomeration improves firm and industry outcomes by raising the probability of better-quality matches between workers and firms in the local labor market. The matching channel also mitigates the holdup problem in certain professions, in which the presence of dense markets encourages workers to invest in their human capital. Third, the *learning channel* relates to enhanced exchange and transfer of knowledge and skills across workers and firms.

Unpacking which channels are driving agglomeration effects is difficult. There is also a distinction between urbanization and localization economies (Combes and Gobillon 2015). The former denote externalities from being in any given geographic location regardless of firms' core economic activities or any other characteristics. The latter refer to the benefits associated with the location of a specific industry to which firms belong. For example, a study shows that employment growth in US cities strongly depends on the degree of sectoral diversity in the cities, which is measured by the sectoral concentration of employment (Glaeser et al. 1992). A similar study establishes that diversified cities are more suitable for innovation; hence, urbanization economies significantly explain employment growth in cities (Duranton and Puga 2001). By contrast, another study reports that the specialization of US cities—the share of employment in each sector relative to its share at the national level—promotes economic activities. The implication is that specialization is basically localization and that, therefore, localization economies are more significant than urbanization economies (Henderson, Kuncoro, and Turner 1995).

Despite their predominantly agrarian base, Sub-Saharan African countries are undergoing rapid urbanization. In 2018, the region's rate of urbanization was 40 percent (World Development Indicators, The World Bank). With regard to agglomeration economies, city size and population density tend to have significant effects on productivity and employment (Collier, Jones, and Spijkerman 2018). However, such agglomeration effects are weaker for cities in Sub-Saharan Africa relative to cities in Asia and Latin America.

Urbanization may be driven by the formation of consumption cities that have emerged because of discovery, production, and export of resource commodities and that, in such cases, are unlikely to result in agglomeration economies. Urbanization in Côte d'Ivoire and Ghana displays these features (Gollin, Jedwab, and Vollrath 2016). Similarly, it seems that population density has not generated employment growth in Ghanaian manufacturing, which is also more likely to occur in other resource-rich countries.[11] By contrast, among Ethiopian firms, a study shows a positive and significant relationship between agglomeration and physical productivity of firms producing the same product. This finding strongly suggests that agglomeration comes with competitive pressure, forcing firms to improve their efficiency, along with positive spillover effects (Bigsten et al. 2012). More generally, however, the estimates of agglomeration effects are rather weaker than expected in Sub-Saharan African countries (Siba and Söderbom 2015), but this does not mean there is no potential for agglomeration as a key driver of productivity growth and job generation.

Market Structure, Entry Regulation, and Productivity

There are considerable cross-country productivity gaps and income differences, which partly reflect large magnitudes of resource misallocation in poor economies compared with developed economies. Recent findings show substantial misallocation in Sub-Saharan African agriculture, services, and manufacturing.[12] These results provide the context for the extent of misallocation in Sub-Saharan Africa, given that manufacturing is a rather small fraction of the economy in these countries. Key sources of resource misallocation are entry barriers and the resultant market structure. The extant evidence shows that entry costs, which are considerably higher in poor countries, lead to lower productivity and output levels because of misallocation. Entry costs also explain a great portion of the cross-country differences in productivity and income. A study shows that countries in the bottom 10 percent of the entry cost distribution have higher TFP and labor productivity compared with those at the top 10 percent of the distribution; that is, the TFP premium is 32 to 45 percent, and that of labor productivity is 52 to 75 percent (Barseghyan and DiCecio 2011).

Country case studies also confirm that entry barriers are a likely cause of misallocation. In India, entry barriers in the form of market regulation have resulted in industries characterized by the prevalence of unproductive (usually small) firms that coexist with a few productive (usually large) firms, lowering aggregate productivity (McKinsey Global Institute 2001). Similar findings hold for Brazil (McKinsey Global Institute 2006), OECD countries (Nicoletti and Scarpetta 2003), and transition economies (Bastos and Nasir 2004). In addition, product market and entry regulations tend to have a negative effect on employment growth in France (Bertrand and Kramarz 2002). In Ethiopian manufacturing, the evolution of industry productivity has been significantly shaped by the size of the local market, transportation costs, and entry barriers such as licensing fees (Jones et al. 2019a).

However, entry barriers have indirect effects on other aspects of firms' activities and hence shape productivity growth at the firm and aggregate levels. For example, the threat of entry influences the productivity growth of incumbent firms by affecting their innovation activities in manufacturing in the United Kingdom (Aghion et al. 2009). In technologically advanced industries, the threat of foreign firm entry provides incentives to incumbents to undertake innovation activities targeted toward surviving the threat of foreign entry, whereas the opposite holds in technologically laggard sectors because the threat of foreign entry lowers the expected return from innovation.

Physical Infrastructure and Productivity

Sub-Saharan Africa's economic prospects have been hampered by the extreme infrastructure gap, which is further compounded by the geographic disadvantages of remoteness from global market centers given that many countries in the region are landlocked. The gap in infrastructure has resulted in high transportation and communications costs and, consequently, limited and weak domestic and intra- and interregional connectedness.

Two key factors account for the region's underdeveloped infrastructure. The first is the lack of financial resources. Investments to develop extensive and high-quality infrastructure are constrained because of the low tax base and limited capacity to generate enough revenue to finance such projects. This shortcoming is critical, given that most infrastructure services are underpriced and often rely on public subsidies. The second factor is the lack of political commitment to encourage private sector investment, coupled with rather poor public sector management. Together, these lead to corruption, political interference, and absent or weak domestic capital markets, tax administration, and the like.

Productivity in Sub-Saharan African manufacturing firms has been constrained by the infrastructure gap, as has the overall performance of industry. In Ethiopian manufacturing, road infrastructure is strongly associated with the entry of new firms into the market. In addition, better market connectivity is an even more crucial determinant of the establishment of large firms (Shiferaw et al. 2015). Thus, the quality of road infrastructure shapes the degree of resource misallocation through the mechanism of entry of new firms and exit of incumbents.

In Ghana, substantial misallocation in the manufacturing sector is attributable to unreliable electricity supply (Ackah, Asuming, and Abudu 2018). Moreover, unreliability in electricity supply diminishes the level of investment, which hampers the prospects for economic growth (Estache and Vagliasindi 2007).

Conclusion and Policy Options

Côte d'Ivoire and Ethiopia have seen expansion of their manufacturing workforces over the observation periods. New and young establishments, irrespective of their size, have been the main drivers of manufacturing job growth. And the growth of the countries' manufacturing workforces has occurred over the same period during which they have had high productivity growth.

A large share of productivity growth is driven by reallocation of market share and resources from low-productivity firms toward more productive firms among incumbents. Plant openings and closures have also resulted in positive contributions. Furthermore, participation in international trade, foreign investment, and clustering tend to enhance productivity in Sub-Saharan African manufacturing at the firm and aggregate levels.

In Ethiopia, aggregate productivity increased by 47 percent between 1996 and 2009. The contribution of market reallocation among incumbents was larger compared with within-plant productivity growth. Furthermore, firm exit played a larger role than entry in boosting productivity. In Côte d'Ivoire, aggregate productivity grew by only 6 percent during 2004–14. Most of the growth came from market reallocation among incumbent firms. In addition, the contribution of entrants was greater than that of exiters; that is, on average, the productivity of entering plants exceeded that of incumbents by more than the productivity of closing plants fell short of that of surviving plants.

One of the key drivers of job growth in Sub-Saharan Africa, the unlimited labor supply, is unlikely to sustain job creation in the near future. Any prospect for generating enough jobs, especially in the face of the large and growing number of youth in the region, critically depends on rapid, sustained productivity growth. Therefore, efforts toward creating employment opportunities and improving manufacturing productivity should go beyond merely facilitating the entry of new establishments into operation and utilization of existing technologies.

The following policy tools are available for accelerating productivity growth through greater trade openness and integration into regional and global value chains, promotion of innovation (process, product, or both), adoption of new technologies, application of better management practices, and effective entry and competition regulation.

- Remove or reduce market entry barriers, including easing licensing requirements, developing a credible legal framework, improving access to finance, and supporting investment in infrastructure.

- Improve market conditions for entry and survival of young firms. Young firms have generated most of the observed jobs and productivity growth but are more likely to exit; and, although firm exit is not always bad, interventions to improve market contestability are needed to support the survival of younger firms.

- Promote productivity-improving interventions, especially among new and young firms. Such interventions can include skills programs and reliable and affordable transport, logistics, and utilities.

- Build and strengthen industry links in the domestic economy. The shortage of high-quality or affordable inputs is a constraining factor in firms' operations.

- Provide support that improves human resource management practices. Studies attempting to open the black box of productivity are pointing toward management practices as a crucial factor.

- Acknowledge firms' identification of the absence of market demand as the first major obstacle for their operations and full productive capacity utilization.[13] To this end, it is necessary to target entering and expanding activities in end markets as well as to improve countries' competitiveness to capture much of the value added in final consumption. Therefore, effort needs to be exerted toward gaining market access through favorable trade agreements (preferential tariffs, less restrictive nontariff trade barriers, and simplified rules of origin) as well as trade facilitation and logistics.

- Work toward more trade openness and participation in regional and global value chains, given that trade exposure is often followed by productivity growth at the firm level. Overall, better trade and investment policies need to be adopted, such as exchange rate regimes, FDI policy (identifying strategic sectors in the provision of incentive packages), and trade and investment promotion.

- Consider that policy support has usually built and strengthened agglomeration economies and oftentimes has been associated with desired productivity and employment outcomes. Hence, carefully crafted interventions need to be aimed at accelerating urbanization as well as establishing and bolstering economic clusters.
- Narrow the infrastructure gap by increasing public investment and adopting an appropriate public sector management system to facilitate job creation and productivity growth as well as accelerate much-needed structural change.

Annex 3A Productivity Growth Decomposition

Aggregate productivity (Φ_t) is defined as a weighted average of firm-level productivity (φ_{it}) in which firms' market shares (S_{it}) are used as weights. Employment shares and value-added shares can also be used as alternative weights.

$$\Phi_t = \sum_i s_{it} \varphi_{it}$$

Following Olley and Pakes (1996), aggregate productivity is further decomposed into two components:

$$\Phi_t = \overline{\varphi}_t + \sum_i \left(s_{it} - \overline{s}_t \right)\left(\varphi_{it} - \overline{\varphi}_t \right)$$

$$= \overline{\varphi}_t + cov\left(\varphi_{it}, s_{it} \right),$$

where $\overline{\varphi}_t$ is unweighted mean productivity and $\overline{s}_t$ is unweighted mean market share.

This technique does not follow firms over time, and the covariance term only captures the distribution of firm productivity and market shares in a given period t. To accommodate the contributions of incumbent, entering, and exiting firms, Melitz and Polanec (2015) extend the Olley-Pakes decomposition technique, which is dynamic OP decomposition with entry and exit.

To explain the technique, suppose S_{Kt} denotes aggregate market shares of survivors or incumbents (S), entrants (E), and exiters (X). That is,

$$S_{Kt} = \sum_{i \in K} s_{it},$$

where K represents S, E, and X. To be precise with the definitions of firm types, an incumbent is a firm that has been in operation in periods $t = 1$ and $t = 2$. An entrant is a firm that has started operations in $t = 2$ but not in $t = 1$. By contrast, an exiter is a firm that was in operation in $t = 1$ but no longer in $t = 2$.

Now, aggregate productivity levels in periods $t = 1$ and $t = 2$ and growth over time can be expressed as follows:

$$\Phi_1 = \Phi_{S1} + S_{X1}\left(\Phi_{S1} - \Phi_{X1}\right)$$

$$\Phi_2 = \Phi_{S2} + S_{E2}\left(\Phi_{E2} - \Phi_{S2}\right)$$

$$\Delta\Phi = \Phi_2 - \Phi_1 = \underbrace{\Delta\overline{\phi}_s}_{(1)} + \underbrace{\Delta\text{cov}_s}_{(2)} + \underbrace{S_{E2}\left(\Phi_{E2} - \Phi_{S2}\right)}_{(3)} + \underbrace{S_{X1}\left(\Phi_{S1} - \Phi_{X1}\right)}_{(4)},$$

where term (1) is changes in the unweighted mean productivity of incumbent firms. Term (2) is changes in the covariance term between productivity levels and market shares of incumbents. Term (3) captures the relative difference in the productivity levels of entrants and incumbents weighted by the market shares of entering firms in the second period. If entrants are relatively more productive (and have sizable market share), they positively contribute to growth in aggregate productivity. Term (4) compares the productivity levels of exiters and incumbents weighted by the market shares of exiting firms in the first period. If less productive firms leave (and previously had nonnegligible market shares), their market departure improves aggregate productivity.

The reference productivity levels vary across firm types, following from the timing assumptions on firm entry and exit. Entrants improve aggregate productivity if and only if they possess higher productivity levels than surviving firms in the period entry occurs ($t = 2$). The contribution of exiters to aggregate productivity growth is positive if and only if they have lower productivity than surviving firms in the period when exit takes place ($t = 1$).

Most techniques use the same reference productivity levels when comparing the contributions of one group of firms to contributions of another, which leads to measurement bias. The reference productivity levels in Griliches and Regev (1995) and Foster, Haltiwanger, and Krizan (2001) overestimate the contribution of entering firms to productivity growth and hence underestimate that of surviving and exiting firms. Through careful choice of appropriate references, the decomposition with entry and exit overcomes this measurement issue.

Notes

1. An economy's aggregate productivity is a weighted sum of firm-level productivity, in which the weights are firms' market, employment, or value-added shares.
2. Hopenhayn (1992) finds that about a third of the jobs and more than 40 percent of US manufacturing firms exited the market and then were replaced by new entrants during each five-year period. Haltiwanger, Jarmin, and Miranda (2013) show that, conditional on survival, young firms grow faster than older and more established firms.
3. Jones (2016) shows that the gap in income per capita across countries has been growing since the 1960s despite some stability in the first decade of the twenty-first century (see figure below). Interestingly, Jones (2016, 37–38) finds that "the poorest countries in 1960 such as Ethiopia were only about 32 times poorer than the United States. By 2011, there are many countries with relative incomes below this level, and both Niger and the Central African Republic were more than 64 times poorer than the United States."

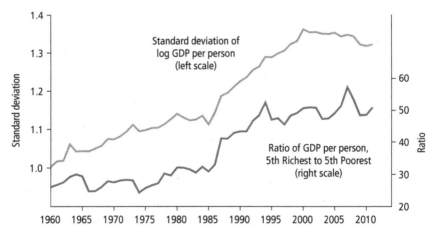

Source: Jones 2016, © Elsevier.
Note: Data from The Penn World Tables 8.0, calculated against a stable sample of 100 countries.

4. Following the availability of micro data sets, a large body of literature documents evidence of considerable and persistent productivity dispersion among producers in narrowly defined industries. In addition, low-productivity producers coexist with their high-productivity counterparts in the long run. The pioneering work in the literature is Bernard and Jensen (1995).
5. Lewis (1954) develops the first dual sector economic model.
6. In their literature survey on how distortions influence the effect of international trade in developing countries, Atkin and Khandelwal (2019) distinguish between market-level distortions and firm and sectoral distortions. The former affect all firms that are in operation and encompass factors in the labor market, including human

capital, capital markets, input markets (material, land, and other inputs), domestic market frictions, and information and knowledge asymmetries. The latter refer to factors that lead to distortions, affecting firms and sectors to varying extents, and include the high informality of firms, presence of politically connected firms as well as business groups and family firms, and imperfect competition and markups.

7. In Jones et al. (2019b), productivity is measured by labor productivity and defined as real value added per worker in 2010 US dollars.

8. Abreha (2019) and Bigsten and Gebreeyesus (2009) for Ethiopia; Bigsten et al. (2004) for selected countries in Sub-Saharan Africa; Halpern, Koren, and Szeidl (2015) for Hungary; Kasahara and Lapham (2013) and Kasahara and Rodrigue (2008) for Chile; and Van Biesebroeck (2005) for selected countries in Sub-Saharan Africa.

9. There is a distinction between inward and outward FDI spillovers. The former refer to effects in the host country, whereas the latter denote their counterparts in the source country. Because almost all Sub-Saharan African countries are net recipients of FDI and are the focus of analysis, the discussion in the report on FDI is entirely about inward FDI and Sub-Saharan African countries as hosts.

10. For example, Haskel, Pereira, and Slaughter (2007) for UK manufacturing and Keller and Yeaple (2009) for US manufacturing firms.

11. Because of the large size of the informal economy and lack of data, studies that directly address the issue of agglomeration effects in Sub-Saharan African countries are insufficient. More empirical studies are needed to arrive at some consensus on the magnitude and determinants of agglomeration economies in these countries.

12. Paganini (2016) shows that misallocation spans sectors outside manufacturing and, as illustrated in the following table, the less substitutable inputs are, the larger the degree of misallocation in a given sector.

Index / Sector	Elasticity of substitution	Mean	Standard deviation	Minimum	Maximum	Kurtosis	Number of observations
Marginal product of capital (MPK)							
Agriculture	1.31	−0.97	1.35	−3.90	3.00	3.00	179
Manufacturing	0.46	−1.15	3.10	−11.70	10.67	3.58	1981
Tertiary	0.38	0.64	4.53	−16.00	12.78	3.00	1467
Hsieh-Klenow index of distortions (HK)							
Agriculture	1.31	0.24	4.62	−7.11	5.34	5.20	179
Manufacturing	0.46	−12.00	2.91	−26.00	−1.63	3.75	1981
Tertiary	0.38	−15.00	3.77	−33.38	−1.92	3.92	1467

Source: Paganini 2016.
Note: The marginal product of capital (MPK) and the Hsieh-Klenow index of distortions (HK) are expressed in logarithms. These calculations assume a CES technology. CES = constant elasticity of substitution.

13. The Large and Medium Manufacturing Industry and Electricity Industries Survey of Ethiopian firms reveals that about 30 percent of them considered lack of market demand as a constraint for their operations and full productive capacity utilization over 1996–2011 (Abreha 2017).

References

Abebe, G., M. S. McMillan, and M. Serafinelli. 2018. "Foreign Direct Investment and Knowledge Diffusion in Poor Locations: Evidence from Ethiopia." NBER Working Paper 24461, National Bureau of Economic Research, Cambridge, MA.

Abreha, K. 2017. "Corporate Taxation, Import Competition and Productivity: Evidence from Ethiopian Manufacturing." HESPI Working Paper 05/17, The Horn Economic and Social Policy Institute, Addis Ababa, Ethiopia.

Abreha, K. 2019. "Importing and Firm Productivity in Ethiopian Manufacturing." World Bank Economic Review 33 (3): 772–92.

Abreha, K. G., P. Jones, E. Lartey, T. Mengistae, and A. Zeufack. 2019. "Manufacturing Job Growth in Africa: What Is Driving It? The Cases of Côte d'Ivoire and Ethiopia." World Bank, Washington, DC.

Ackah, C. G., P. O. Asuming, and D. Abudu. 2018 "Misallocation of Resources and Productivity: The Case of Ghana." Institute of Statistical, Social and Economic Research, University of Ghana, Accra.

Aghion, P., R. Blundell, R. Griffith, P. Howitt, and S. Prantl. 2009. "The Effects of Entry on Incumbent Innovation and Productivity." Review of Economics and Statistics 91 (1): 20–32.

Aitken, B., and A. Harrison. 1999. "Do Domestic Firms Benefit from Direct Foreign Investment? Evidence from Venezuela." American Economic Review 89 (3): 605–18.

Alfaro, L., and M. X. Chen. 2018. "Selection and Market Reallocation: Productivity Gains from Multinational Production." American Economic Journal: Economic Policy 10 (2): 1–38.

Atkin, D., and A. Khandelwal. 2019. "How Distortions Alter the Impacts of International Trade in Developing Countries." NBER Working Paper 26230, National Bureau of Economic Research, Cambridge, MA.

Barseghyan, L., and R. DiCecio. 2011. "Entry Costs, Industry Structure, and Cross-Country Income and TFP Differences." Journal of Economic Theory 146 (5): 1828–51.

Bastos, F., and J. Nasir. 2004. "Productivity and Investment Climate: What Matters Most?" Policy Research Working Paper 3335, World Bank, Washington, DC.

Bernard, A. B., and J. B. Jensen. 1995. "Exporters, Jobs, and Wages in US Manufacturing: 1976–1987." Brookings Papers on Economic Activity: Microeconomics 1995 (1): 67–119.

Bertrand, M., and F. Kramarz. 2002. "Does Entry Regulation Hinder Job Creation? Evidence from the French Retail Industry." Quarterly Journal of Economics 117 (4): 1369–413.

Bigsten, A., P. Collier, S. Dercon, M. Fafchamps, B. Gauthier, J. W. Gunning, A. Oduro, et al. 2004. "Do African Manufacturing Firms Learn from Exporting?" Journal of Development Studies 40 (3): 115–41.

Bigsten, A., and M. Gebreeyesus. 2009. "Firm Productivity and Exports: Evidence from Ethiopian Manufacturing." Journal of Development Studies 45 (10): 1594–614.

Bigsten, A., M. Gebreeyesus, E. Siba, and M. Söderbom. 2012. "Enterprise Agglomeration, Output Prices, and Physical Productivity: Firm-Level Evidence from Ethiopia."

UNU-WIDER Working Paper 2012/85, United Nations University–World Institute for Development Economics Research, Helsinki, Finland.

Blalock, G., and P. Gertler. 2008. "Welfare Gains from Foreign Direct Investment through Technology Transfer to Local Suppliers." *Journal of International Economics* 74 (2): 402–21.

Buera, F. J., J. P. Kaboski, and Y. Shin. 2011. "Finance and Development: A Tale of Two Sectors." *American Economic Review* 101 (5): 1964–2002.

Collier, P., P. Jones, and D. Spijkerman. 2018. "Cities as Engines of Growth: Evidence from a New Global Sample of Cities." University of Oxford, Oxford, U.K.

Combes, P. P., and L. Gobillon. 2015. "The Empirics of Agglomeration Economies." In *Handbook of Regional and Urban Economics*, volume 5, edited by J. V. Henderson and J.-F. Thisse, 247–348. Amsterdam: Elsevier.

Dennis, A., T. Mengistae, Y. Yoshino, and A. Zeufack. 2016. "Sources of Productivity Growth in Uganda: The Role of Interindustry and Intra-Industry Misallocation in the 2000s." Policy Research Working Paper 7909, World Bank, Washington, DC.

Duranton, G., and D. Puga. 2001. "Nursery Cities: Urban Diversity, Process Innovation, and the Life Cycle of Products." *American Economic Review* 91 (5): 1454–77.

Duranton, G., and D. Puga. 2004. "Micro-foundations of Urban Agglomeration Economies." In *Handbook of Regional and Urban Economics*, volume 4, edited by J. V. Henderson and J.-F. Thisse, 2063–117. Amsterdam: Elsevier.

Eaton, J., and S. Kortum. 2002. "Technology, Geography, and Trade." *Econometrica* 70 (5): 1741–79.

Eaton, J., S. Kortum, and F. Kramarz. 2011. "An Anatomy of International Trade: Evidence from French Firms." *Econometrica* 79 (5): 1453–98.

Estache, A., and M. Vagliasindi. 2007. "Infrastructure for Accelerated Growth for Ghana: Needs and Challenges." In *Ghana Country Economic Memorandum: Meeting the Challenge of Accelerated and Shared Growth*, Report No. 40934-GH. Washington, DC: World Bank.

Foster, L., J. C. Haltiwanger, and C. J Krizan. 2001. "Aggregate Productivity Growth: Lessons from Microeconomic Evidence." In *New Directions in Productivity Analysis*, edited by E. Dean, M. Harper, and C. Hulten, 303–72. Cheltenham, U.K.: Edward Elgar.

Foster-McGregor, N., A. Isaksson, and F. Kaulich. 2014. "Importing, Exporting and Performance in Sub-Saharan African Manufacturing Firms." *Review of World Economics* 150 (2): 309–36.

Glaeser, E. L., H. D. Kallal, J. A. Scheinkman, and A. Shleifer. 1992. "Growth in Cities." *Journal of Political Economy* 100 (2): 1126–52.

Gollin, D., R. Jedwab, and D. Vollrath. 2016. "Urbanization with and without Industrialization." *Journal of Economic Growth* 21 (1): 35–70.

Gorg, H., and E. Strobl. 2005. "Spillovers from Foreign Firms through Worker Mobility: An Empirical Investigation." *Scandinavian Journal of Economics* 107 (4): 693–709.

Griliches, Z., and H. Regev. 1995. "Firm Productivity in Israeli Industry: 1979–1988." *Journal of Econometrics* 65 (1): 175–203.

Gunner, N., G. Ventura, and Y. Xu. 2008. "Macroeconomic Implications of Size-Dependent Policies." *Review of Economic Dynamics* 11 (4): 721–44.

Haile, F. 2018. "Structural Change in West Africa: A Tale of Gain and Loss." Policy Research Working Paper 8336, World Bank, Washington, DC.

Hall, R. E., and C. Jones. 1999. "Why Do Some Countries Produce So Much More Output per Worker Than Others?" *Quarterly Journal of Economics* 114 (1): 83–116.

Halpern, L., M. Koren, and A. Szeidl. 2015. "Imported Inputs and Productivity." *American Economic Review* 105 (12): 3660–703.

Haltiwanger, J. 2015. "Job Creation, Job Destruction, and Productivity Growth: The Role of Young Businesses." *Annual Review of Economics* 7 (1): 341–58.

Haltiwanger, J., R. Jarmin, and J. Miranda. 2013. "Who Creates Jobs? Small versus Large versus Young." *Review of Economics and Statistics* 95 (2): 347–61.

Harrison, A., and A. Rodríguez-Clare. 2010. "Trade, Foreign Investment, and Industrial Policy for Developing Countries." In *Handbook of Development Economics,* volume 5, edited by D. Rodrik and M. Rosenzweig, 4039–214. Amsterdam: Elsevier.

Haskel, J., S. Pereira, and M. Slaughter. 2007. "Does Inward Foreign Direct Investment Boost the Productivity of Domestic Firms?" *Review of Economics and Statistics* 89 (3): 482–96.

Henderson, V., A. Kuncoro, and M. Turner. 1995. "Industrial Development in Cities." *Journal of Political Economy* 103 (5): 1067–90.

Hopenhayn, H. 1992. "Entry, Exit, and Firm Dynamics in Long Run Equilibrium." *Econometrica* 60 (5): 1127–50.

Hopenhayn, H., and R. Rogerson. 1993. "Job Turnover and Policy Evaluation: A General Equilibrium Analysis." *Journal of Political Economy* 101 (5): 915–38.

Javorcik, B. 2004. "Does Foreign Direct Investment Increase the Productivity of Domestic Firms? In Search of Spillovers through Backward Linkages." *American Economic Review* 94 (3): 605–27.

Javorcik, B., and M. Spatareanu. 2008. "To Share or Not to Share: Does Local Participation Matter for Spillovers from Foreign Direct Investment?" *Journal of Development Economics* 85 (1–2): 194–217.

Jones, C. I. 2016. "The Facts of Economic Growth." In *Handbook of Macroeconomics,* volume 2, edited by J. B. Taylor and H. Uhlig, 3–69. Amsterdam: Elsevier.

Jones, P., E. Lartey, T. Mengistae, and A. Zeufack. 2019a. "Market Size, Sunk Costs of Entry, and Transport Costs." Policy Research Working Paper 8875, World Bank, Washington, DC.

Jones, P., E. Lartey, T. Mengistae, and A. Zeufack. 2019b. "Sources of Manufacturing Productivity Growth in Africa." Policy Research Working Paper 8980, World Bank, Washington, DC.

Kalemli-Ozcan, S., and B. E. Sorenson. 2012. "Misallocation, Property Rights, and Access to Finance: Evidence from within and across Africa." NBER Working Paper 18030, National Bureau of Economic Research, Cambridge, MA.

Kasahara, H., and B. Lapham. 2013. "Productivity and the Decision to Import and Export: Theory and Evidence." *Journal of International Economics* 89 (2): 297–316.

Kasahara, H., and J. Rodrigue. 2008. "Does the Use of Imported Intermediates Increase Productivity? Plant-Level Evidence." *Journal of Development Economics* 87 (1): 106–18.

Keller, W. 2010. "International Trade, Foreign Direct Investment, and Technology Spillovers." In *Handbook of the Economics of Innovation*, volume 2, edited by B. Hall and N. Rosenberg, 793–829. Amsterdam: Elsevier.

Keller, W., and S. Yeaple. 2009. "Multinational Enterprises, International Trade, and Productivity Growth: Firm-Level Evidence from the United States." *Review of Economics and Statistics* 91 (4): 821–31.

Lewis, A. 1954. "Development with Unlimited Supplies of Labour." *The Manchester School* 22 (2): 139–91.

McKinsey Global Institute. 2001. "India: The Growth Imperative." September. https://www.mckinsey.com/~/media/mckinsey/featured%20insights/india/growth%20imperative%20for%20india/mgi_the_growth_imperative_for_india.ashx.

McKinsey Global Institute. 2006. "How Brazil Can Grow." McKinsey Global Institute Perspective, December 1, 2006. https://www.mckinsey.com/~/media/mckinsey/featured%20insights/americas/how%20brazil%20can%20grow/mgi_how_brazil_can_grow_full_perspective.pdf.

McMillan, M., D. Rodrik, and I. Verduzco-Gallo. 2014. "Globalization, Structural Change, and Productivity Growth, with an Update on Africa." *World Development* 63: 11–32.

Melitz, M. J. 2003. "The Impact of Trade on Intra-Industry Reallocations and Aggregate Industry Productivity." *Econometrica* 70 (6): 1695–725.

Melitz, M. J., and G. I. Ottaviano. 2008. "Market Size, Trade and Productivity." *Review of Economic Studies* 75 (1): 295–316.

Melitz, M. J., and S. Polanec. 2015. "Dynamic Olley-Pakes Productivity Decomposition with Entry and Exit." *Rand Journal of Economics* 46 (2): 362–75.

Mengistae, T., and C. Pattillo. 2004. "Export Orientation and Productivity in Sub-Saharan Africa." *IMF Staff Papers* 51 (2): 327–53.

Nicoletti, G., and S. Scarpetta. 2003. "Regulation, Productivity and Growth: OECD Evidence." *Economic Policy* 18 (36): 9–72.

Olley, G. S., and A. Pakes. 1996. "The Dynamics of Productivity in the Telecommunications Equipment Industry." *Econometrica* 64 (6): 1263–97.

Paganini, M. 2016. "An Efficiency Analysis of Firms: Evidence from Sub-Saharan Africa." PhD dissertation, University of Kent.

Shiferaw, A., M. Söderbom, E. Siba, and G. Alemu. 2015. "Road Infrastructure and Enterprise Dynamics in Ethiopia." *Journal of Development Studies* 51 (11): 1541–58.

Siba, E., and M. Söderbom. 2015. "Enterprise Agglomeration and Firm Performance in Sub-Saharan Africa." In *Handbook on Trade and Development*, edited by O. Morrissey, R. Lopez, and K. Sharma, 169–78. Cheltenham, U.K.: Edward Elgar.

Syverson, C. 2004a. "Market Structure and Productivity: A Concrete Example." *Journal of Political Economy* 112 (6): 1181–222.

Syverson, C. 2004b. "Product Substitutability and Productivity Dispersion." *Review of Economics and Statistics* 86 (2): 534–50.

Van Biesebroeck, J. 2005. "Exporting Raises Productivity in Sub-Saharan African Manufacturing Firms." *Journal of International Economics* 67 (2): 373–91.

World Bank. Forthcoming. "Boosting Productivity in Sub-Saharan Africa." World Bank, Washington, DC.

Chapter 4

Industrializing across Global Value Chains

Manufacturing activities, for the most part, occur within global value chains (GVCs), such that many firms in different countries are involved in tasks ranging from the design of products, to the procurement of parts and components, to the final delivery of products to end users in the global market. This breakdown of the manufacturing process across GVCs straddling international borders has made it easier for developing countries to industrialize, by delinking the process of innovation and product development from the production process and employment (Baldwin 2011; Taglioni and Winkler 2016). Moreover, it has created opportunities for countries to kick-start the industrialization of their economies by initially specializing in lower-value-added tasks in which they have a comparative advantage along a given GVC, while at the same time actively investing in activities that culminate in developing a comparative advantage in higher-value-added tasks at later stages.

This model largely fits the path to industrialization that China adopted and pursued for the past three decades. China combined an export-oriented growth strategy with a system of incentives for attracting inward foreign direct investment, placing Chinese firms at the center of triangular trade within which they imported parts and components from East Asian economies (the Republic of Korea; Japan; Taiwan, China; and others), assembled them into finished products, and exported them to US and European markets. The apparent success of the model in China and its ongoing emulation in South Asia and other countries in East Asia, including Cambodia and Vietnam, arguably makes it an attractive option for countries in Sub-Saharan Africa to adopt as a path to industrialization, and as a key component of governments' strategies for promoting badly needed job growth.

The policy challenges of promoting industrial job growth should therefore be framed as devising instruments for facilitating entry of domestic firms into manufacturing GVCs at links deemed to maximize the expected gains in jobs and productivity. However, the nature of the instruments and the chances of their success are likely to depend on the structure and dynamics of existing linkages between the region's economies and manufacturing GVCs.

This chapter presents an account of the levels and dynamics of participation in manufacturing GVCs in Sub-Saharan Africa, with an assessment of the role of differences in natural resource endowment and economic geography in explaining variations in linkages to manufacturing GVCs. Moreover, it analyzes the impact of trade policy on participation in manufacturing GVCs.

In broad terms, the findings reveal that GVC participation rates vary by resource endowments, such that resource-rich countries exhibit high forward links driven by commodity exports, whereas non-resource-rich countries demonstrate higher backward links. In addition, participation rates have been rising in minerals- and metals-rich countries but declining significantly in non-resource-rich countries. However, the prospects for industrialization are good for some countries within each group, as reflected in the variation in GVC participation rates within the groups.

In particular, within different industries in countries in each country group, the evidence shows that there are establishments that export manufactured goods with import content that reflects backward and forward links, with linkage rates comparable to those of manufacturers in the benchmark countries. Thus, although to some extent natural resources define the general trends in GVC participation in Sub-Saharan Africa and carry implications for policy formulation, barriers to export markets, import tariffs, and skills shortages, among other factors, have been found to affect entry into GVCs. These factors should guide the formulation of industrial policies that exploit comparative advantages in specific industries to enhance the prospects for industrialization in the region via GVC participation, including among the non-resource-rich country group for which participation rates have declined.

Global Value Chains: Definition and Measures

The term *value chain* refers to the sequence of stages of productive or value-creating activities or tasks, starting from conception and design to the intermediate phases of a production plan and its execution, leading to the delivery of a product as a final good or service. The concept relates to the technique of value chain analysis, which is a method of identifying cost-saving or product-differentiation opportunities across the various stages of production or delivery of a good or service. A value chain is referred to as a GVC if it involves processes and tasks in the framework of contractual relations between firms across international borders that are not necessarily in the same region.

In a GVC, firms from different countries are tied together in a vertically integrated system of production (or supply chain) of goods and services at each link at which a participating firm is importing inputs for producing items to export to another link participant in another region or country. This system of "importing to export" involves more than trade transactions among participating firms. It includes sharing blueprints and management practices, through which new ideas and know-how are continuously transferred across national and international borders and regions.

Links to a manufacturing GVC occur along two dimensions: backward linkages and forward linkages. The indicator of backward linkages to a GVC is the relative share of import content, that is, the foreign value added (FVA) in the country's gross exports. Deducting the FVA component from gross exports yields the country's domestic value-added (DVA) in exports. The indicator of forward linkages to a GVC is the relative share in the total value-added exports of that country that is used as intermediate inputs to other countries' exports to third countries (DVX). A country's GVC participation rate, that is, the overall rate of linkage to GVCs, is the sum of the relative share of FVA in gross exports and the relative share of DVX in gross exports.

Levels and Patterns of Participation in Manufacturing GVCs

Integration of Sub-Saharan African Countries into Manufacturing GVCs and the Overall Participation Rate

The participation rate in manufacturing GVCs in Sub-Saharan Africa is greater than 40 percent (figure 4.1), which indicates that a significant share of the region's trade occurs along value chains, a trend that has been observed in other studies (Allard et al. 2016; Balié et al. 2017; Foster-McGregor, Kaulich, and Stehrer 2015; Foster-McGregor and Stehrer 2013; UNCTAD 2013). Furthermore, the two indicators—backward and forward linkages—reveal that Sub-Saharan Africa's participation in GVCs is more pronounced in forward integration (DVX) compared with backward integration (FVA). By implication, most of Sub-Saharan Africa's integration into GVCs is dominated by exports of primary products rather than imports of foreign value added or intermediates for further upgrading for export.

Nearly a third of the countries have backward linkages constituting at least 40 percent of their overall GVC participation rates (figure 4.2). This signifies that most of the countries are integrated into GVCs via forward linkages. A large share of the exports for this set of countries, especially Eswatini, São Tomé and Príncipe, and Lesotho, is composed of imported intermediates. In contrast, resource-rich economies, including Angola, the Democratic

Figure 4.1 Trends in Sub-Saharan Africa's Participation in GVCs, 1990–2015

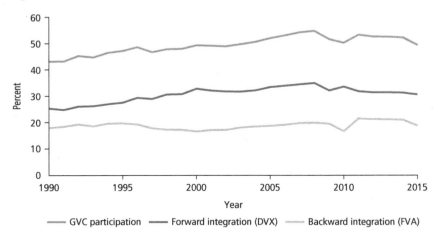

Source: Abudu and Nguimkeu 2019.
Note: DVX = indirect value added; FVA = foreign value added; GVC = global value chain.

Republic of Congo, Côte d'Ivoire, Ghana, and Nigeria, with predominantly commodity exports, are countries whose GVC participations have the weakest backward linkages. Evidence suggests that there is a negative correlation between backward integration and forward integration such that, in the context of Sub-Saharan African countries participating in GVCs, dependence on commodity exports is likely to act as a disincentive to the development of manufacturing activities that create and enhance backward links.

To the extent that imported intermediates are essential for quality upgrading and productivity enhancement (Amiti and Khandelwal 2013; Amiti and Konings 2007; Halpern, Koren, and Szeidl 1993), Sub-Saharan African countries should pursue policies that create the environment for manufacturing activities that facilitate backward links so as to foster transfer of knowledge and technology through imported intermediate inputs. Nevertheless, the stark heterogeneity in the observed backward and forward linkage rates suggests that there should be some variation in the set of economic policies aimed at promoting integration into GVCs at the national and subregional levels.

Similarity between Links to Manufacturing GVCs in Sub-Saharan Africa and Those in South Asia and Southeast Asia

Linkage rates of manufacturers in Sub-Saharan Africa to GVCs are reasonably high compared with those of a benchmark group of countries that includes Bangladesh, Cambodia, Indonesia, and Vietnam (box 4.1). Linkage rates are

Figure 4.2 Backward and Forward Integration across Countries

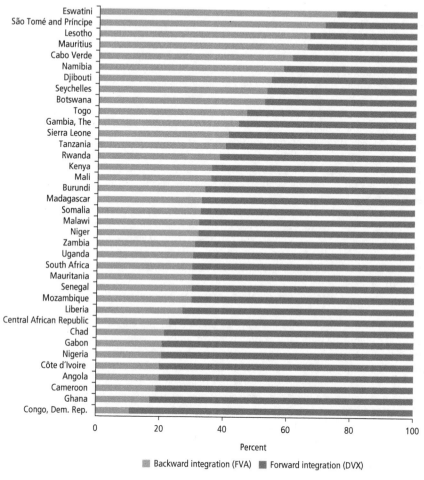

Source: Abudu and Nguimkeu 2019.
Note: DVX = indirect value added; FVA = foreign value added.

higher for oil exporters (oil-resource-rich countries) and minerals and metals exporters (non-oil-resource-rich countries). The links to manufacturing GVCs range from 59 percent for oil exporters, to 45 percent for the group of minerals and metals exporters, to 37 percent for the non-resource-rich group. These rates are high even when compared with the average for the benchmark group of countries, which is about 55 percent (figure 4.3).

BOX 4.1

Country Groups and Comparators

The country groupings used in the global value chain analysis are based on classification by natural resource endowment, population size, and per capita income. In each group, a comparison is drawn between trends in the larger economies with a population-weighted average of other economies within the group while benchmarking against a similarly weighted average for a group of international comparators drawn from outside the region.

The oil-exporting economies include Angola, Cameroon, Chad, the Republic of Congo, Equatorial Guinea, Gabon, and Nigeria. The minerals- and metals-rich economies are Botswana, Burkina Faso, the Central African Republic, the Democratic Republic of Congo, Ghana, Guinea, Mali, Namibia, Niger, Sierra Leone, South Africa, and Zambia.

The middle-income countries in the non-resource-rich group are Cabo Verde, Côte d'Ivoire, Eswatini, Kenya, Lesotho, Mauritius, São Tomé and Príncipe, and Seychelles; and the low-income economies are (1) Benin, The Gambia, Liberia, Madagascar, Malawi, Mozambique, Senegal, and Zimbabwe in Southern Africa and West Africa, and (2) Burundi, Eritrea, Ethiopia, Rwanda, Somalia, Sudan, Tanzania, and Uganda in East Africa.

The group of external comparators comprises Bangladesh, Cambodia, Indonesia, and Vietnam. These countries were selected because they are comparable to the larger countries in the region in population size and income per capita, and they are in the process of industrializing. The population sizes in 2017 were 16 million in Cambodia, 96 million in Vietnam, 158 million in Bangladesh, and 261 million in Indonesia. These numbers are comparable to 16 million in Zambia, 83 million in the Democratic Republic of Congo, 105 million in Ethiopia, and 191 million in Nigeria. All four countries in the benchmark group are middle-income economies with per capita incomes for 2017 of about US$4,000 in Bangladesh and Cambodia, US$6,900 in Vietnam, and US$12,400 in Indonesia. These per capita incomes compare with US$1,180 in Malawi, US$3,500 in Kenya, US$5,900 in Nigeria, and US$13,500 in South Africa. Thus, for example, Indonesia is reasonably comparable to Nigeria in natural resource endowment and population size.

Note: The population estimates are from the CEPII Gravity database, except for the Democratic Republic of Congo, for which estimates were obtained from the World Bank's World Development Indicators database, which is also the source of the estimates of income per capita.

The dynamics of GVC participation between 1995 and 2015 reveal striking differences across the country groups, with linkage rates having declined steeply in recent years in non-resource-rich countries while rising sharply in the group of minerals and metals exporters (the non-oil-resource-rich group), as is evident in figure 4.3. Between 1995 and 2015, GVC participation fell in the non-resource-rich group and oil exporters, by 7 and 11 percent, respectively,

Figure 4.3 Links to All Manufacturing GVCs, by Country Group

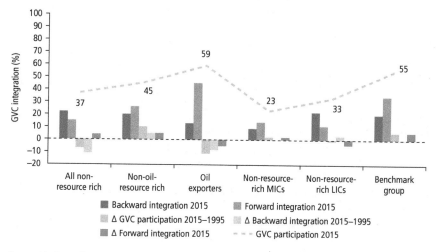

Source: Abreha et al. 2019.
Note: GVC = global value chain; LICs = low-income countries; MICs = middle-income countries.

while rising by 10 percent in minerals and metals exporters (non-oil-resource rich) and 6 percent in the external comparators. Therefore, minerals and metals exporters were integrating into manufacturing GVCs more than the external comparators during that period.

Oil exporters and minerals and metals exporters show higher forward links compared with non-resource-rich countries, whereas non-resource-rich countries have higher backward links relative to the other two groups. This evidence suggests that the higher forward links are potentially associated with exports of natural resources, which in turn explains a significant part of the higher GVC participation rates of oil exporters and minerals and metals exporters. Thus, the FVA content of exports of countries endowed with natural resources tends to be low, whereas the DVX tends to be high, predominantly constituting exports of low-value-added oil, minerals, and metals.

Resource Endowment and Participation in Manufacturing GVCs

Variation between Oil Exporters, Minerals and Metals Exporters, and Non-Resource-Rich Countries

In the non-resource-rich group, Rwandan manufacturers have greater linkage rates to GVCs in aggregate compared with their counterparts in Malawi, Senegal, and Uganda. However, backward links are stronger in Uganda and

Malawi, and backward links grew the most in Uganda between 1995 and 2015, as shown in figure 4.4. In addition, links to GVCs increased in some countries (for example, Malawi and Uganda) but declined in others (for example, Rwanda and Senegal).

Among minerals and metals exporters, the Democratic Republic of Congo has the highest GVC participation rate because of strong forward links, and South Africa has the highest backward linkage rate (figure 4.5). GVC participation rates are higher for Zambia than for Ghana, but forward links are slightly higher in Ghana. Moreover, forward and backward linkage rates increased in Ghana, the Democratic Republic of Congo, and South Africa, but they remained the same (forward linkage) or declined (backward linkage) in Zambia. Among oil exporters, participation rates are higher in Nigeria than in Cameroon but have declined in Nigeria (figure 4.6). Thus, not all resource-rich countries have experienced an increase in participation rates.

Characteristics That Facilitate Links to Manufacturing GVCs

Links to manufacturing GVCs are facilitated by an economy's size and structure, closeness to larger economies, common language and borders, regional trade agreements, and colonial ties.

The cross-country differences in participation rates within each group of countries are attributable to some of the factors highlighted in annex 4A.

Figure 4.4 Links to Manufacturing GVCs: Non-Resource-Rich Countries

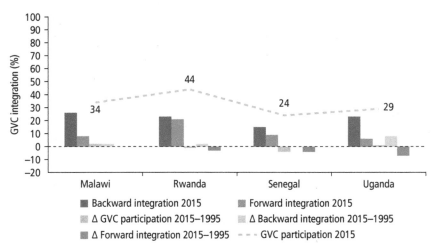

Source: Abreha et al. 2019.
Note: GVC = global value chain.

Figure 4.5 Links to Manufacturing GVCs: Minerals and Metals Exporters

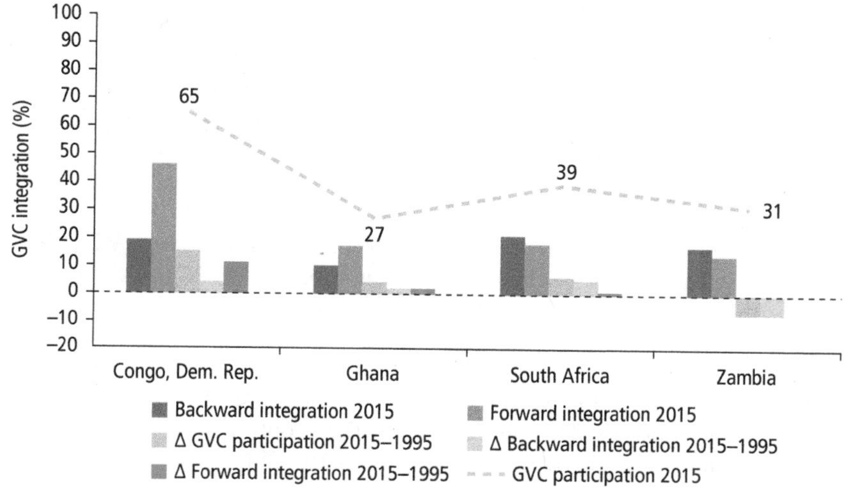

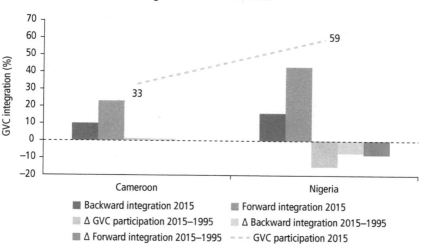

Source: Abreha et al. 2019.
Note: GVC = global value chain.

Figure 4.6 Links to Manufacturing GVCs: Oil-Rich Countries

Source: Abreha et al. 2019.
Note: GVC = global value chain.

Participation rates in GVCs for local firms are likely to be greater with counterparts in larger economies, neighboring countries, and countries with common colonial ties. Participation in common regional trade agreements is also likely to promote entry into manufacturing GVCs. Physical distance to major international markets is another important determinant of links to manufacturing GVCs, but this is the case only for non-resource-rich countries.[1] These factors, identified as potential influencers of participation in manufacturing GVCs, are pertinent to backward and forward links.

Variation in the Level, Growth, and Direction of Links to GVCs

Variation in the level, growth, and direction of links to GVCs across industries within countries and country groups provides a basis for industrial policies to exploit comparative advantages to facilitate links to manufacturing GVCs.

Links to GVCs were substantially higher in some industries, such as food and beverages and textiles and apparel, in the group of non-resource-rich countries than in the benchmark group in 2015. The higher links in food and beverages reflect higher import content of exports of that industry in the non-resource-rich group, as measured by the indicator for backward links

Figure 4.7 Links to Manufacturing GVCs, by Industry: Benchmark Countries

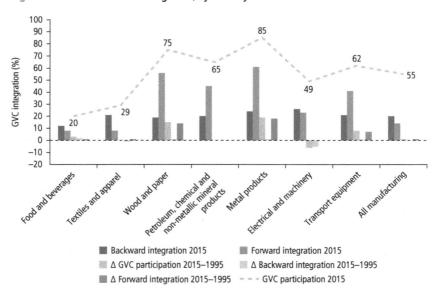

Source: Abreha et al. 2019.
Note: GVC = global value chain.

(figures 4.7 and 4.8). The share of exports of food and beverages that ended up as inputs in the exports of destination countries to third parties was slightly higher for the benchmark group, reflecting lower exports of intermediates in the non-resource-rich countries in comparison. Links to manufacturing GVCs declined by large margins across all seven industries in the non-resource-rich country group over the period.

In countries exporting minerals and metals, links in textiles and apparel and electrical and machinery were higher than in the benchmark group, with stronger forward links in electrical and machinery, which reflects higher exports of intermediates in the industry in 2015. The import content of electrical and machinery exports, as captured by backward linkage rates, was identical in the two country groups. However, there was a decline in GVC links in electrical and machinery in the benchmark group because of backward links, whereas backward links increased in that industry among minerals and metals exporters in Sub-Saharan Africa during the period (figures 4.7 and 4.9).

Characteristics of Establishments Linked to GVCs
Establishments that are linked to GVCs through the export of products with imported intermediate input content tend to be relatively large enterprises of

Figure 4.8 Links to Manufacturing GVCs, by Industry: Non-Resource-Rich Countries

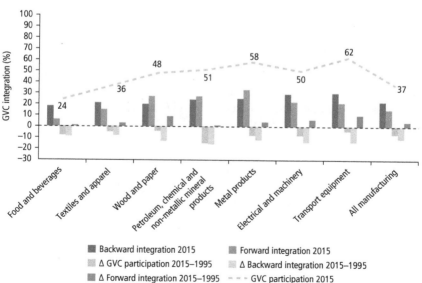

Source: Abreha et al. 2019.
Note: GVC = global value chain.

Figure 4.9 Links to Manufacturing GVCs, by Industry: Minerals and Metals Exporters

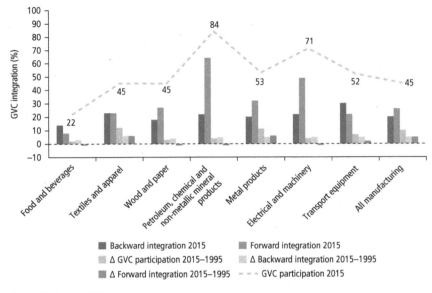

Source: Abreha et al. 2019.
Note: GVC = global value chain.

100 or more employees, have been in business for five years or longer, and are more likely to have foreign equity or possess a foreign technology license.

Participants in GVCs that are importers of intermediate inputs and exporters are more likely to be owned by foreign investors (or more likely to receive foreign direct investment) than other manufacturers, particularly in countries such as Kenya, Senegal, and Uganda among the non-resource-rich group; Ghana and Zambia among the minerals- and metals-rich group; and Cameroon and Nigeria among oil exporters. This is also the case in the key comparator countries, including Indonesia and Vietnam. Such establishments are more likely than other establishments to operate under a foreign technology license in countries such as Uganda in the non-resource-rich group, South Africa in the minerals- and metals-rich group, and Cameroon and Nigeria in the oil exporters, as is the case in Vietnam.

Comparison of Establishments in Sub-Saharan Africa and Benchmark Countries

Establishments with backward and forward links are present in different industries across the different country groups in Sub-Saharan Africa and are comparable to their counterparts in the benchmark countries.

Within the textiles and apparel industry, establishments tend to export outputs that have imported input content, similar to textiles and apparel manufacturers in the four external comparators. This is particularly the case in Kenya and Senegal (non-resource-rich group). In the metal products industry, establishments are linked to manufacturing GVCs via backward and forward links, and thus they export goods with imported input content. This is the case for countries such as Kenya (non-resource rich); Cameroon (oil exporter); and Ghana, South Africa, and Zambia (minerals and metals exporters). Along manufacturing GVCs in chemicals and non-metallic minerals industries, establishments in Côte d'Ivoire and Kenya (non-resource rich); Ghana, South Africa, and Zambia (minerals and metals exporters); and Cameroon (oil exporter) manufacture goods for export using imported intermediate goods. There are no establishments with this profile in metal products and chemicals and non-metallic minerals industries among the comparators. By contrast, establishments in the transport equipment industry in Vietnam have backward and forward links to manufacturing GVCs, as do establishments in the electrical goods and machinery industry in Indonesia. There are no establishments in Sub-Saharan Africa that export goods with input content in these two industries.

Three broad characteristics emerge pertaining to Sub-Saharan Africa's links to manufacturing GVCs. First, resource-rich economies exhibit higher forward links fueled by commodity exports. Second, non-resource-rich countries have higher backward links. Third, participation rates have been rising in minerals- and metals-rich countries but declining significantly in non-resource-rich countries and oil exporters. However, there is variation in GVC participation rates within each group, such that the prospects for industrialization are bright for some countries in every group.

Characteristics of Establishments That Only Import or Only Export

Firms participating in GVCs that only import or only export tend to be midsize enterprises with at least 20 workers, are younger, and are more likely to have foreign equity and hold a foreign technology license.

Operating under a foreign technology license and foreign equity are important factors affecting participation in manufacturing GVCs. Moreover, younger, midsize enterprises that are connected to GVCs are likely to exhibit backward or forward links but not necessarily both. Therefore, policies that are favorable to the operations of multinationals in the region should serve to facilitate the integration of firms into manufacturing GVCs.

Establishments in Sub-Saharan Africa with forward or backward links in manufacturing GVCs and that are likely to have foreign equity (as in Indonesia and Vietnam) are mainly located in Malawi and Uganda (non-resource rich), the Democratic Republic of Congo and Zambia (minerals and metals exporters), and Cameroon and Nigeria (oil exporters). Countries in which such enterprises are likely to operate under a foreign technology license include Nigeria, Uganda, and Zambia.

Industries with enterprises in this category include transport equipment and electrical and machinery. Those enterprises with backward or forward links to manufacturing GVCs in transport equipment are in Côte d'Ivoire and Malawi; the Democratic Republic of Congo, Ghana, and Zambia; and Indonesia and Vietnam among the comparators. Those with forward or backward links to GVCs in electrical and machinery are in Côte d'Ivoire, South Africa and Zambia, and the comparator country, Bangladesh.

In addition, when considering enterprises with forward or backward links to manufacturing GVCs, Kenya, South Africa, and Zambia have links in metals products, as do Bangladesh, Cambodia, and Vietnam. Participants in GVCs in manufacturing chemicals and non–minerals and metals products include Malawi and Kenya; the Democratic Republic of Congo, South Africa, and Zambia; and Cameroon.

Evolution of Sourcing Patterns for Intermediate Inputs among Manufacturing Firms

Domestic Markets as Sources of Intermediate Inputs

Manufacturers in Sub-Saharan Africa have relied more on domestic intermediates in the organization of manufacturing production, with significant variation across countries, accounting for 77 percent in Djibouti, 66 percent in Rwanda, and more than 50 percent in Cameroon, Guinea, Madagascar, Mali, and Mauritania (figure 4.10). Overall, the share of domestically sourced inputs, on average, is 48 percent; the share of imported intermediate inputs is 14 percent; and the share of value added created domestically is 38 percent.

Overall, countries in the region differ in the sources of inputs for producing manufactures, but the share of imported inputs varies less across countries, except in Zambia. Botswana, Mauritius, and Namibia seem to have a more balanced structure in the sources of inputs for manufacturing.

Multinational Firms Source Intermediate Inputs from Domestic Firms

Small manufacturing firms import about 22 percent of their inputs, a share that has increased steadily over time. Multinational firms in the region are more active in international engagement than domestic firms. Still, a sizable share of intermediate inputs (44 percent) used by multinational firms is sourced from domestic firms in the region. However, domestic sourcing by multinationals in the region has weakened in recent years (figure 4.11).

Figure 4.10 Sources of Intermediate Inputs in Manufacturing, 2015

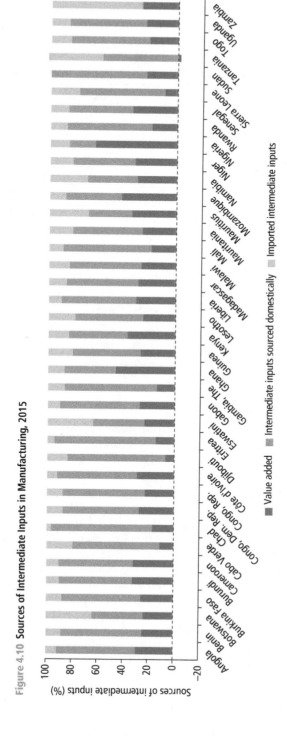

■ Value added   ■ Intermediate inputs sourced domestically   ■ Imported intermediate inputs

Source: World Bank illustration based on data from Van Biesebroeck and Mensah 2019.

Figure 4.11 Sourcing of Intermediate Inputs, Multinationals versus Domestic Manufacturers

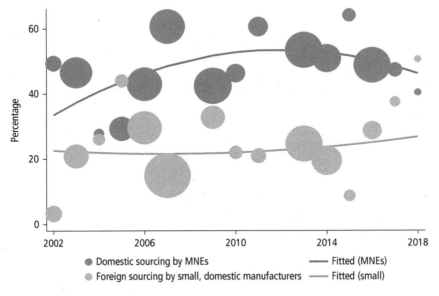

Source: Van Biesebroeck and Mensah 2019.
Note: The circles show the average values for the two GVC measures averaged over the firms in all countries that were surveyed in a given year. The size of the circles reflects the number of firms surveyed. The fitted line is obtained from a firm-level regression of each GVC measure on year and year squared, controlling for country fixed effects. GVC = global value chain; MNEs = multinational enterprises.

The share of imported inputs of multinationals in the region is highly dependent on the share of the inputs domestic firms in the region can supply. Thus, policy reforms could enhance increased integration of domestic manufacturing with multinationals and raise the domestic contribution to production for export.

Sub-Saharan Africa as a Source of Intermediate Inputs
In 2015, the 28 member countries of the European Union (EU) contributed, on average, about 5.4 percent of inputs to Sub-Saharan Africa, compared with 0.4 percent from the United States.[2] However, this represents a declining share of imported inputs from the EU. The United States also declined in significance between 1995 and 2015 for many countries in Sub-Saharan Africa with regard to sourcing intermediate inputs for manufactures production. Imports of intermediates from China are low, at about 1 percent, but they are growing rapidly (figure 4.12). There is also limited intraregional value-added trade activity within Sub-Saharan Africa, with intermediate inputs from countries

Figure 4.12 Imported Intermediate Inputs to the Manufacturing Sector, 2015

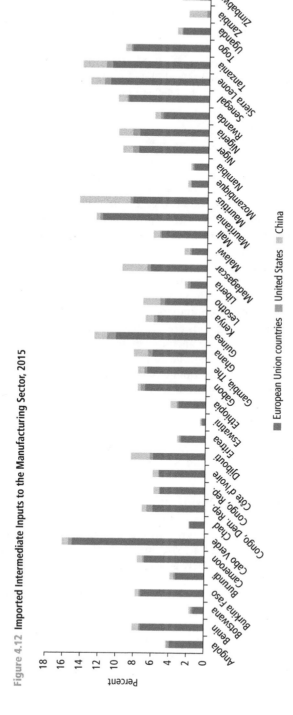

Source: World Bank illustration based on data from Van Biesebroeck and Mensah 2019.

within the region cumulatively accounting for an average of 1.52 percent of total manufacturing output value. Furthermore, the shares of China and East Asia are rising whereas the shares of the EU and the United States in the FVA component of Sub-Saharan African exports are declining (Van Biesebroeck and Mensah 2019), suggesting an important shift in global trade and the need to reorient Sub-Saharan Africa's trade and industrialization strategies toward East Asia.

Patterns of Destinations and End Uses of Manufactured Goods

The fast pace of globalization over the past 20 years increased export exposure for many countries, yet the average export share of manufactures in Sub-Saharan Africa is quite low, with approximately 48 percent of the countries exporting less than 5 percent of their manufacturing output as of 2015 (figure 4.13). However, there has been a slight increase in the average export share, by 0.9 percentage point, one-third of which is due to exports for final demand, whereas the remainder represents exports of intermediate inputs used in further production in destination countries (Van Biesebroeck and Mensah 2019). Annex 4C presents a case study of manufacturing firms in Rwanda.

Although manufactured goods are exported from Sub-Saharan Africa to different parts of the world, several countries, including Côte d'Ivoire, Ghana, Liberia, and Senegal, export a significant proportion of their manufactures to EU countries (figure 4.14). The United States is an important destination for manufactures from Côte d'Ivoire and Ghana, and China is an important destination for Mauritania and Zambia.

Patterns of Intraregional Trade and Prospects of Regional Value Chains

Regional Integration and Production Networks

Regional integration of trade and production is quite weak in Sub-Saharan Africa—the main partners of the region are the EU and China and to some extent India (figures 4.15 and 4.16). China's rising role is in raw materials (forward integration) and also increasingly as a source for import of intermediate goods into African countries (backward integration). Imported inputs from within the region account, on average, for 1 percent of total output value in both resource-rich and non-resource-rich country groups. This amount is not negligible but is notably lower than the shares imported from other regions except for Latin America.

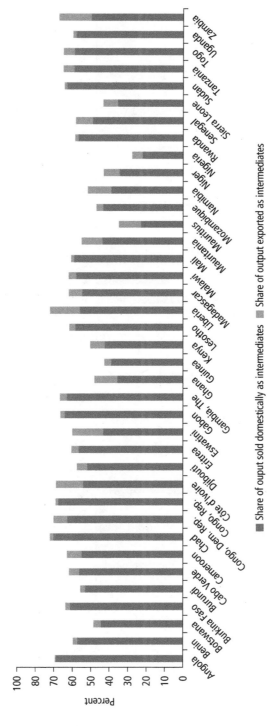

Figure 4.13 Destination Shares of Manufactured Output from Sub-Saharan Africa Sold as Intermediate Inputs, 2015

■ Share of ouput sold domestically as intermediates   ■ Share of output exported as intermediates

Source: World Bank illustration based on data from Van Biesebroeck and Mensah 2019.
Note: The figure reflects only the shares sold as intermediates.

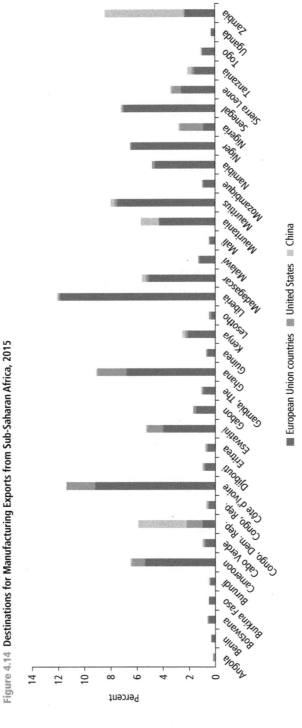

Figure 4.14 Destinations for Manufacturing Exports from Sub-Saharan Africa, 2015

■ European Union countries   ■ United States   ■ China

Source: World Bank illustration based on data from Van Biesebroeck and Mensah 2019.
Note: The figure reflects only the shares sold in the European Union, the United States, and China.

Figure 4.15 Links to Manufacturing GVCs in Non-Resource-Rich Countries, by Source and Destination, 2015

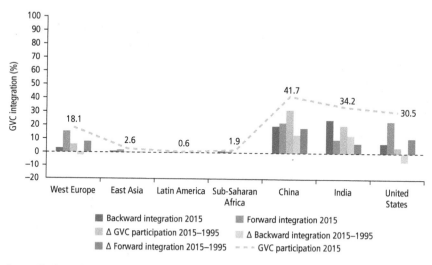

Source: Abreha et al. 2019.
Note: GVC = global value chain.

Figure 4.16 Links to Manufacturing GVCs in Resource-Rich Countries, by Source and Destination, 2015

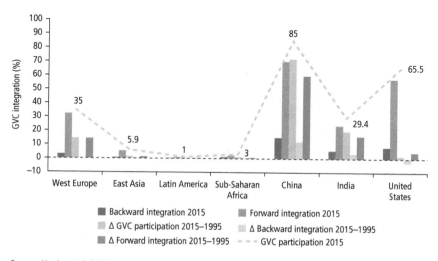

Source: Abreha et al. 2019.
Note: GVC = global value chain.

However, some strong regional value chains are in place across economies that neighbor South Africa. Countries located within Southern Africa, for example, Botswana, Eswatini, Namibia, Zambia, and Zimbabwe, are strongly connected to South Africa in the regional production system, sourcing substantial amounts of foreign value added from South Africa (figure 4.17). More distant Sub-Saharan African countries systematically show remarkably low integration in the regional production system. Proximity to countries with important manufacturing industries is critical to the development of such production networks.

Figure 4.17 Strong Regional Value Chains for Countries That Neighbor South Africa

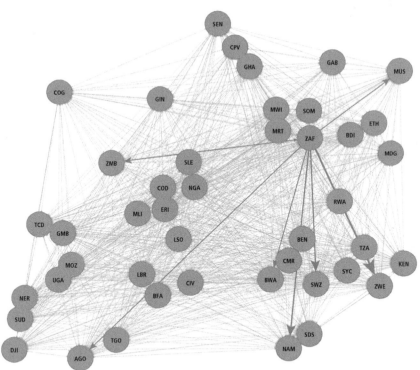

Source: World Bank illustration using indicators of global value chain participation (share of foreign value added) calculated from the United Nations Conference on Trade and Development Eora database.
Note: Line thickness indicates strength of relationship between the two countries. Figure is based on weights of foreign value-added trade between countries in the region.

Prospects for Developing Regional Value Chains

The low levels of regional integration and high levels of resource endowments of countries in Sub-Saharan Africa offer enormous opportunities for building regional production networks and developing regional value chains in manufacturing, which would facilitate the processing of raw materials and value addition to exports, enhance the production of manufactures for regional markets, and propel integration into manufacturing GVCs while strengthening existing links.

For example, the continent is endowed with sufficient resources to become both self-sufficient and a net exporting region for fertilizer. However, despite its substantial reserves, primary fertilizer production is confined to 10 countries, of which 6 are in North Africa. In addition, more than half of African ammonia imports are sourced from the Russian Federation, with the remainder coming from the Caribbean, the Middle East, and the United States. There is enormous potential for future fertilizer demand growth as a result of projected population growth and the need for food security, and increasing fertilizer self-sufficiency is likely to boost future fertilizer demand potential.

Thus, there is an opportunity to develop regional value chains by leveraging regional trade agreements, bilateral agreements, or public-private partnerships. As a case in point, under the partnership between Togo and the Dangote Group, Togo processes phosphate before export to Nigeria (value addition) instead of exporting in raw form. The output then becomes an input to the production of fertilizer in Nigeria, which would be both supplied to the domestic market and exported to the region.

Conclusion and Policy Options

Sub-Saharan Africa accounts for a tiny fraction of the volume of trade in manufactures as compared to China, Western Europe, and the United States, with linkage rates to manufacturing GVCs consequently being extremely low. However, linkage rates across manufacturing GVCs vary significantly between countries in Sub-Saharan Africa, driven by various factors including resource endowments and other country-specific characteristics that matter for participation and upgrading in GVCs (Kummritz, Taglioni, and Winkler 2017).

Trade policy, investments in infrastructure and connectivity, and education and skills strategies, among others, are associated with strengthening competitiveness in manufacturing.

Trade policy could play an essential role in driving participation in manufacturing GVCs by enhancing preferential access to the export markets of developed economies, mainly Asia, the EU, and the United States. Access to these markets would have implications for manufacturing GVC participation, particularly in textiles and apparel exports, in addition to the potential in agro-processing and processing of natural resources before export. Among the types of policy support that developed countries can provide, facilitating access to exports from developing countries is a straightforward proposition (Van Biesebroeck and Zaurino 2019). Light manufacturing, especially labor-intensive production of textiles and apparel products, is a prime example of the types of industries in which developing countries have a natural comparative advantage and are likely to enjoy great gains.

Higher tariff rates are negatively associated with GVC participation, and higher tariffs on imports of capital goods are even more restrictive for value chain participation (Abudu and Nguimkeu 2019; Slany 2019). For instance, upgrading and adding value to the natural resource exports of resource-rich economies requires that production equipment and intermediate inputs be imported at lower costs.

The labor force in most Sub-Saharan African countries is predominantly low skilled or unskilled, which partly explains why most of the countries in the region are not linked to high-value-added activities in manufacturing GVCs. Cognitive skills, such as literacy, numeracy, and problem-solving, and noncognitive skills, including management and communication skills, information and communications technology skills, and readiness to learn and think creatively, have been identified as critical factors in a country's capacity to thrive in GVCs (Grundke et al. 2017). Therefore, effective engagement in GVCs and upgrading within GVCs would require policy makers in Sub-Saharan Africa to align their industrial and trade policies with formal education policies and programs, as well as with training and reskilling programs to reinforce and build their workers' skills, not just in one area but in improving the overall set of skills of workers.

GVCs have become increasingly important for manufacturing activities. Thus, policy makers' efforts aimed at promoting job growth through industrialization would succeed only to the extent that they facilitate entry of domestic firms into manufacturing GVCs at links deemed to maximize the expected gains in jobs and productivity.

See box 4.2 for a discussion of the effects of COVID-19 (coronavirus) on GVCs.

BOX 4.2

COVID-19 (Coronavirus) and Potential Disruptions to Global Value Chains

The impact of COVID-19 (coronavirus) on the manufacturing sector is expected to be significant in the short run, given that the share of trade in the national income of most economies in the region is relatively large. The impact of disruptions in global value chains (GVCs) driven by the global demand slump would predominantly occur in countries with strong forward GVC links—mainly exporting raw materials used in other countries for production for export. Raw material exports account for the largest share of the region's trade and GVC integration. In addition, supply shocks introduce direct supply disruptions in African countries that are increasingly becoming more integrated into GVCs. Non-resource-rich Sub-Saharan African countries that have been centers of robust growth in the region over the past two decades will be the most affected by these supply shocks. The largest declines in trade are likely to be in sectors with highly integrated GVCs. African economies that have recently been integrating or are well integrated into manufacturing GVCs, including Eswatini, Ethiopia, Kenya, Lesotho, and South Africa, will be affected the most in the immediate short run. For example, the garment industry, a budding manufacturing subsector in the region accounting for a large share of the sector's employment and exports, is hard hit by worldwide retail closures and furloughs coupled with the collapse in consumer confidence.

In the long run, the combination of trade-policy shocks[a] and the enduring public health concerns from COVID-19 have created uncertainty about the future of international trade, resulting in a rethinking of GVCs in manufacturing. Because of COVID-19 and emerging geopolitical trends in advanced economies, there is a growing preference for resilience or a "de-risking" strategy. COVID-19 is expected to reinforce an already ongoing change in GVCs with respect to geographic rebalancing (Kassa 2020). It has been estimated that between 16 and 26 percent of global exports would move to different countries between 2020 and 2025 (McKinsey Global Institute 2020). The change in heavily traded labor-intensive manufacturing GVCs, where many African countries' comparative advantages lie, is expected to be significant. Textiles and apparel GVCs are expected to feature the highest share of trade that shifts to other countries.[b] This shift in GVCs is expected to create opportunities for developing economies. For example, Bangladesh and Vietnam have been, and are expected to continue to be, the main beneficiaries of the most recent shift. With the right policy mix and active industrial policies, African countries could present a viable alternative for some of these investments, based on their comparative advantages. African countries with relatively higher backward links in manufacturing GVCs may need to reposition themselves to reap any gains that may arise from fundamental changes in GVCs caused by global shocks, including the COVID-19 pandemic.

a. These shocks include rising protectionism in advanced economies, China-US trade tensions, and Brexit.
b. McKinsey Global Institute (2020) estimates that, relative to all other value chains, textiles and apparel features the highest share of trade that could most likely shift (36 to 57 percent in apparel and 23 to 45 percent in textiles), representing a range of $67 billion to $393 billion in value.

Annex 4A Gravity Model of Global Value Chain Participation

The most recent analyses of GVC links in Sub-Saharan Africa include Allard et al. (2016) and AfDB, OECD, and UNDP (2014). Allard et al. (2016) make use of the Eora database to estimate indicators of GVC participation for Sub-Saharan African countries. AfDB, OECD, and UNDP (2014) look specifically at the role of GVC participation using estimates of backward linkages (FVA) and forward linkages (DVX) for a wider range of two- or three-digit International Standard Industrial Classification industries than those reported in Allard et al. (2016).

Allard et al. (2016) conclude that many countries in the region have a comparative advantage in tasks that might have high shares in the value added of final goods in manufacturing industries, which is consistent with the conclusion of AfDB, OECD, and UNDP (2014), based on the Eora database, that in Africa as a whole—including North Africa—local manufacturers are more integrated into GVCs compared with domestic firms in agriculture, mining, or services.

The main hypothesis of this gravity model analysis is that natural resource endowments and economic geography are important determinants of countries' links to manufacturing GVCs (as illustrated in figure 4.3 and discussed in the section "Resource Endowment and Participation in Manufacturing GVCs"). The effects of these determinants can be estimated and identified in the framework of an econometric factor proportions–based gravity model of "supply-side differences" between countries as partners in trade in goods and services or tasks. Antras and de Gortari (2020) provide a theoretical structure for such a model, with implications for the likelihood of countries participating in specific GVCs.

The implication of the main prediction of the model in Antras and de Gortari (2020) is that coastal, larger, or wealthier countries are more likely to attract downstream production stages in manufacturing GVCs, compared with landlocked or poorer countries. The estimated model is extended by adding equations that can capture empirical regularities that are not necessarily included in Antras and de Gortari's (2020) model and yet are consistent with it. One such regularity is that countries that are rich in natural resources tend to be less integrated into GVCs.

This annex describes a model of backward and forward linkages of economies across manufacturing GVCs by categories of natural resource endowment. In the model, equation (4A.1) specifies influences on backward linkages on aggregate at the country level. Equation (4A.2) does the same for forward linkages.

$$FVA_{i,j,t} = \alpha_0 + \alpha_1 \ln (DISTANCE_{i,j}) + \alpha_2 CONTIGUITY_{i,j} + \alpha_3 LANGUAGE_{i,j}$$
$$+ \alpha_4 COLONY_{i,j} + \alpha_5 RTA_{i,j,t} + \alpha_6 \ln(1+TARIFF_{i,j,t}) + \alpha_7 GDP_{i,t}$$
$$+ \alpha_8 GDP_{j,t} + MRT_{i,t} + MRT_{j,t} + \varepsilon_{i,j,t}) \qquad (4A.1)$$

$$DVX_{i,j,t} = \alpha_0 + \alpha_1 \ln (DISTANCE_{i,j}) + \alpha_2 CONTIGUITY_{i,j} + \alpha_3 LANGUAGE_{i,j}$$
$$+ \alpha_4 COLONY_{i,j} + \alpha_5 RTA_{i,j,t} + \alpha_6 \ln(1+TARIFF_{i,j,t}) + \alpha_7 GDP_{i,t}$$
$$+ \alpha_8 GDP_{j,t} + MRT_{i,t} + MRT_{j,t} + \varepsilon_{i,j,t} \qquad (4A.2)$$

where i is the exporting country, j is the importing country (or country group), and t is the year.

$FVA_{i,j,t}$ denotes the value of foreign value added in gross exports of country i to country j in year t, measuring the degree of backward integration in the bilateral trade relationship between the countries.

$DVX_{i,j,t}$ denotes the value of indirect value added in gross exports of country i to country j in year t, measuring the extent of forward integration in the bilateral trade between countries i and j.

$DISTANCE_{i,j}$ stands for population-weighted bilateral geographic distance between i and j in kilometers.

$CONTIGUITY_{i,j}$ is a dummy variable that equals 1 if countries i and j are contiguous.

$LANGUAGE_{i,j}$ is a dummy variable for common official or primary language in countries i and j.

$COLONY_{i,j}$ is a dummy variable that equals 1 if country i was ever a colony of country j.

$RTA_{i,j,t}$ is a dummy variable that equals 1 if country i and country j belong to a common regional trade agreement area or monetary union.

$TARIFF_{i,j,t}$ is a trade-weighted applied tariff rate that exports from country i face when shipped to country j.

$GDP_{i,t}$ is the gross domestic product (GDP) of exporting country i in year t.

$GDP_{j,t}$ is the GDP of importing country j in year t.

$MRT_{i,t}$ is an outward multilateral resistance term.

$MRT_{j,t}$ is an inward multilateral resistance term.

Data on gravity variables such as bilateral distance, GDP, population, and regional trade agreements were obtained from the CEPII database, and the tariff data came from the United Nations Conference on Trade and Development–Trade Analysis Information System (UNCTAD-TRAINS) via the World Integrated Trade Solution (WITS) database.

Annex 4B Analysis of Enterprise-Level Data

In the main text of this chapter, the section "Comparison of Establishments in Sub-Saharan Africa and Benchmark Countries" reports findings based on an analysis of data from the World Bank Enterprise Surveys to identify instances of participation in GVCs. Typically, a business establishment is considered to be part of a GVC if it is exporting downstream goods that it has produced using imported inputs. To distinguish instances of participation in GVCs from cases of nonparticipation in the production activities of the population of establishments in an economy, the factors that affect participation at the firm level are analyzed. For this purpose, data from the World Bank Enterprise Surveys are used to estimate a linear probability model of firms' GVC participation:

$$P(y = 1 \mid X) = X\beta, \tag{4B.1}$$

where y equals 1 if a firm operates along a GVC and 0 otherwise. The analysis adopts two definitions of GVC participation. The first is a standard definition in which a given firm is considered active in GVCs if it is exporting and importing. Alternatively, the analysis follows a less exclusive definition, which deems a manufacturer to be operating along a GVC if it exports any part of its output without necessarily using imported inputs, or if it does not necessarily export any part of its output that is produced using imported inputs.

The covariates X include age group, employment size categories, foreign ownership (equals 1 if there is any foreign ownership in the establishment and 0 otherwise), technology license (equals 1 if the firm uses technology licensed from a foreign company and 0 otherwise), and indicators of industry classification.

Annex 4C Rwandan Firms in Manufacturing Global Value Chains

Only a few firms in Rwanda are globally engaged, despite the increase in the number of exporting firms in the country between 2008 and 2015. Goods-producing firms in Rwanda are very inward-looking and active domestically, but they have remarkably limited engagement in GVCs. Although strong growth in the number of exporting firms in the country began in 2009, it stalled and even declined in 2015.

A greater percentage of the larger exporting firms in Rwanda are in the mining sector, but the manufacturing sector has become increasingly important, registering an increase in the number of exporters, particularly among medium-size firms (figure 4C.1). The productivity of exporting firms in the manufacturing sector is also high; the sector's largest exporters have sales of US$158,000 per worker, and the marginal exporting firm's average sales per worker is US$45,000. Moreover, the share of manufactures in total exports rose from 6 percent to 21 percent between 2008 and 2016, an indicator of employment creation potential for the economy.

Figure 4C.1 **Rwanda: Distribution of Exporters across Sectors**

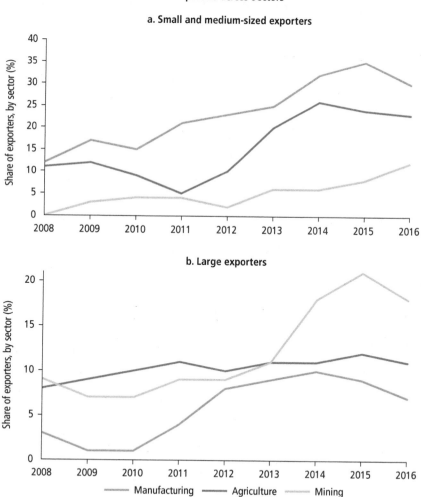

a. Small and medium-sized exporters

b. Large exporters

Manufacturing ——— Agriculture ·········· Mining

Source: Frazer and Van Biesebroeck 2019.

Share of Intermediate Inputs Sourced Domestically

In general, the Rwandan economy is less integrated into international markets, having a combined share of about 88 percent of manufacturing value added generated and inputs sourced domestically, which declined by only a percentage point between 1995 and 2015 (figure 4C.2, panel a). Invariably, imports of intermediates are low, coming mostly from the EU (39 percent), with much smaller shares from China (4.5 percent) and the United States (2.3 percent) in 2015 (figure 4C.2, panel b). However, intraregional intermediate inputs and value-added trade activity between Rwanda and other Sub-Saharan African countries have increased.

Destination for Manufacturing Products

In 2015, 57 percent of manufactured goods was sold domestically as intermediate inputs and 41 percent as final demand (figure 4C.3, panel a), whereas only 2 percent was exported, mainly as intermediate inputs (figure 4C.3, panel b). Although it increased from 1.8 percent in 1995, the share of manufactures exported remains much lower than the regional average.

The concentration of manufacturing exports by destination is remarkably high. The bulk of the small share of manufactures that is exported goes to at most five destinations, with the closest neighbors, the Democratic Republic of Congo and Burundi, being the top two.

Between 2008 and 2016, the Democratic Republic of Congo was the most important destination for manufacturing exports from Rwanda, accounting for 44 percent in 2008 and 82 percent in 2013 but falling to 60 percent in 2016. In comparison with agriculture and mining exports, the importance of export destinations outside Sub-Saharan Africa is relatively lower for manufacturing exports. Between 2008 and 2016, only China, India, Italy, the Netherlands, Singapore, Spain, Switzerland, the United Kingdom, and the United States appeared among the top five destinations for the country's manufacturing exports outside Sub-Saharan Africa. The majority of the manufacturing exports end up in neighboring countries because of proximity and lower transport costs. Nevertheless, exporting to more-distant destinations will require efforts to overcome barriers in logistical requirements and product standards.

Product Concentration of Manufacturing Exports

In 2008, the top 10 (of 90) product categories accounted for 98 percent of total exports for large firms and almost 100 percent for smaller firms. In 2016, the share for large exporting firms had declined to 89 percent and that of small exporting firms was 90 percent. Similar patterns emerge for the top 3 (of 90) product categories for large and small firms. Small exporting firms export relatively different product categories with a high churn, mostly trading in plastic and rubber, furniture and wood products, and chemicals. The exports of large exporting firms, in contrast, are concentrated in vegetable products, foodstuffs, mineral products, and footwear and leather.

Figure 4C.2 Rwanda: Share of Value Added and Domestic Inputs versus Imported Inputs

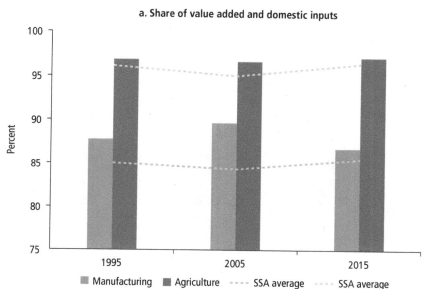

a. Share of value added and domestic inputs

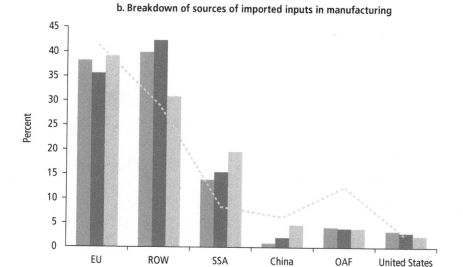

b. Breakdown of sources of imported inputs in manufacturing

Source: Frazer and Van Biesebroeck 2019.
Note: EU = European Union; OAF = other African countries (South Africa and North African countries, that is, Morocco including Western Sahara, Algeria, Arab Republic of Egypt, Libya, and Tunisia); ROW = rest of world; SSA = Sub-Saharan Africa.

Figure 4C.3 Rwanda: Share of Manufactures Sold Domestically versus Exported

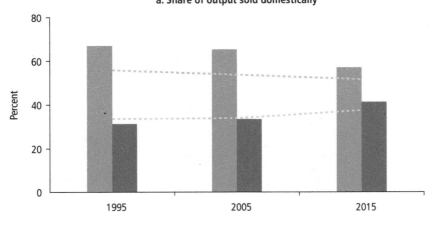

a. Share of output sold domestically

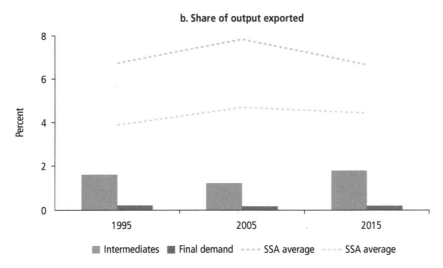

b. Share of output exported

▨ Intermediates ■ Final demand ---- SSA average ---- SSA average

Source: Frazer and Van Biesebroeck 2019.
Note: SSA = Sub-Saharan Africa.

Notes

1. Refer to annex 4B for details on the analysis of the enterprise-level data.
2. In 2015, total output value comprised own value-added (40.6%), domestically sourced intermediates (44.5%), imported intermediates from the European Union (5.4%), the United States (0.4%), and China (1.0%). Averages are calculated using the data for the countries as reflected in figure 4.12.

References

Abreha, K., E. K. K. Lartey, T. A. Mengistae, S. Owusu, and A. G. Zeufack. 2019. "Africa in Manufacturing Global Value Chains: Cross-Country Patterns in the Dynamics of Linkages." World Bank, Washington, DC.

Abudu, D., and P. Nguimkeu. 2019. "Public Policy and Country Integration to Manufacturing Global Value Chains: The Roles of Trade, Labor Market Regulation and Tax Incentives." World Bank, Washington, DC.

AfDB, OECD, and UNDP (African Development Bank, Organisation for Economic Co-operation and Development, and United Nations Development Programme). 2014. *African Economic Outlook 2014: Global Value Chains and Africa's Industrialization.* Paris: OECD Publishing.

Allard, C., J. I. Canales Kriljenko, W. Chen, J. Gonzalez-Garcia, E. Kitsios, and J. Treviño. 2016. "Trade Integration and Global Value Chains in Sub-Saharan Africa: In Pursuit of the Missing Link." African Department, International Monetary Fund, Washington, DC.

Amiti, M., and A. K. Khandelwal. 2013. "Import Competition and Quality Upgrading." *Review of Economics and Statistics* 95 (2): 476–90.

Amiti, M., and J. Konings. 2007. "Trade Liberalization, Intermediate Inputs, and Productivity: Evidence from Indonesia." *American Economic Review* 97 (5): 1611–38.

Antras, P., and A. de Gortari. 2020. "On the Geography of Global Value Chains." *Econometrica*, 84 (4):1553–1589.

Baldwin, R. 2011. "Trade and Industrialization after Globalization's 2nd Unbundling: How Building and Joining a Supply Chain Are Different and Why It Matters." NBER Working Paper 17716, National Bureau of Economic Research, Cambridge, MA.

Balié, J., D. Del Prete, E. Magrini, P. Montalbano, and S. Nenci. 2017. "Agriculture and Food Value Chains in Sub-Saharan Africa: Does Bilateral Trade Policy Impact on Backward and Forward Participation?" Working Paper 4/17, Sapienza University of Rome.

Foster-McGregor, N., F. Kaulich, and R. Stehrer. 2015. "Global Value Chains in Africa." UNU-MERIT Working Paper Series 2015-024, United Nations University–World Institute for Development Economics Research, Helsinki, Finland.

Foster-McGregor, N., and R. Stehrer. 2013. "Value Added Content of Trade: A Comprehensive Approach." *Economic Letters* 120 (2): 354–57.

Frazer, G., and J. Van Biesebroeck. 2019. "The Extent of Engagement in Global Value Chains by Firms in Rwanda." Policy Research Working Paper 8979, World Bank, Washington, DC.

Grundke, R., S. Jamet, M. Kalamova, and M. Squicciarini. 2017. "Having the Right Mix: The Role of Skill Bundles for Comparative Advantage and Industry Performance in GVCs." OECD Science, Technology and Industry Working Paper 2017/03, Organisation for Economic Co-operation and Development, Paris.

Halpern, L., M. Koren, and A. Szeidl. 1993. "Imported Inputs and Productivity." *American Economic Review* 105 (12): 3660–703.

Kassa, W. 2020. "COVID-19 and Trade in SSA: Impacts and Policy Response." World Bank Policy Brief, World Bank, Washington, DC.

Kummritz, V., D. Taglioni, and D. Winkler. 2017. "Economic Upgrading through Global Value Chain Participation: Which Policies Increase the Value-Added Gains?" Policy Research Working Paper 8007, World Bank, Washington, DC.

McKinsey Global Institute. 2020. "Risk, Resilience, and Rebalancing in Global Value Chains." McKinsey Global Institute.

Slany, A. 2019. "The Role of Trade Policies in Building Regional Value Chains: Some Preliminary Evidence from Africa." *South African Journal of Economics* 87 (3): 326–53.

Taglioni, D., and D. Winkler. 2016. *Making Global Value Chains Work for Development.* Washington, DC: World Bank Group.

UNCTAD (United Nations Conference on Trade and Development). 2013. *World Investment Report 2013: Global Value Chains: Investment and Trade for Development.* Geneva: UNCTAD.

Van Biesebroeck, J., and E. B. Mensah. 2019. "The Extent of GVC Engagement in Sub-Saharan Africa." Policy Research Working Paper 8937, World Bank, Washington, DC.

Van Biesebroeck, J., and E. Zaurino. 2019. "Effects of Trade Liberalization on Textile and Apparel Exports from Sub-Sahara Africa." Policy Research Working Paper 8936, World Bank, Washington, DC.

Chapter 5

Job Gains, Productivity Growth, and the Role of Upgrading in Manufacturing Global Value Chains

Participation in manufacturing global value chains (GVCs) can stimulate productivity growth through various channels, including specialization in core tasks, access to imported inputs, knowledge spillovers from multinationals, and the effects of global competition (Criscuolo and Timmis 2017). Moreover, upgrading through GVCs or moving to higher-value activities has become important for job creation and economic development.

Participation in manufacturing GVCs is likely to raise productivity growth but not necessarily employment growth (Pahl and Timmer 2020). This result is based on the premise that, with the emergence of GVCs, the employment effects of exporting have become less visible. Employment in exports is now a composite of domestic activities by several firms in different industries; it includes direct jobs in the exporting industry and indirect jobs through the production of intermediate inputs in other domestic firms. Those indirect contributions can be sizable and depend on the strength of backward links to domestic firms, which is where low-income countries, including those in Africa, are weak.

In addition, firms that participate in GVCs might be successful at absorbing advanced technologies and raising productivity, but they may be less successful at employing labor because the technologies associated with production along manufacturing GVCs reduce the possibilities for substitution of unskilled labor for other factors of production (Reijnders and de Vries 2018; Reijnders, Timmer, and Ye 2016; Rodrik 2018). Thus, although current trends in manufacturers in the region linking to GVCs are favorable for industrialization in their respective countries, the question that arises is whether participation in manufacturing GVCs has contributed to job growth and productivity gains.

This chapter sets out to answer this question. First, the chapter analyzes the extent to which countries in Sub-Saharan Africa have benefited from GVC participation to grow jobs in the manufacturing sector. Although the emphasis is on job growth in manufacturing, the chapter also examines the contribution of GVC participation to job growth in the agriculture and services sectors. Second, the chapter documents and discusses the productivity growth effect of GVC participation in the region. The third section discusses the role of upgrading in manufacturing GVCs in Sub-Saharan Africa, examining the link between GVC integration and industrial upgrading, and the drivers of industrial upgrading through participation in GVCs. Each section highlights policy options for achieving sustainable job gains, productivity growth, and industrial upgrading in the region through integration into GVCs.

Current Trends in Job Growth in Sub-Saharan Africa across GVCs

GVC Participation and Job Growth in Manufacturing

The manufacturing sector in Sub-Saharan Africa has generated jobs through GVC participation. In South Africa, the most industrialized country in the region, a total of 629,000 manufacturing GVC jobs accounted for slightly more than 20 percent of all GVC jobs in 2014. In Senegal and Ethiopia, there were 24,000 and 215,000 manufacturing GVC jobs, respectively, accounting for less than 10 percent of GVC jobs in each country in 2014 (figure 5.1). When compared with other developing countries, the region has, on average, the lowest share of formal manufacturing jobs in overall GVC jobs, at about 15 percent. For example, the share of formal manufacturing jobs in overall GVC jobs in comparator countries, such as Bangladesh, Brazil, China, India, and Malaysia, is above 35 percent (Pahl et al. 2019).

Despite having a lower share of manufacturing workers, Ethiopia, Kenya, and Senegal recorded increases in the number of jobs in manufacturing GVCs between 2000 and 2014: 150,000, 64,000, and 3,000, respectively. The number of jobs in manufacturing GVCs declined by 184,000 in South Africa during that period. The recorded gains in manufacturing GVC jobs can be attributed to the implementation of significant GVC-oriented industrial policies in these countries, particularly in Ethiopia.

The contribution of GVC participation to jobs is even higher for the agriculture and services sectors in the region. In Ethiopia, Kenya, and Senegal, the number of GVC jobs was highest in agriculture, followed by services. In 2014, the agriculture sector was responsible for about 2.5 million jobs in Ethiopia, accounting for 75 percent of the overall GVC jobs; comparable figures were 1.3 million (65 percent) in Kenya, 171,000 (64 percent) in Senegal, and 781,000

Figure 5.1 Number of Workers in GVCs, by Sector of Employment, in Sub-Saharan Africa and Benchmark Countries, 2014

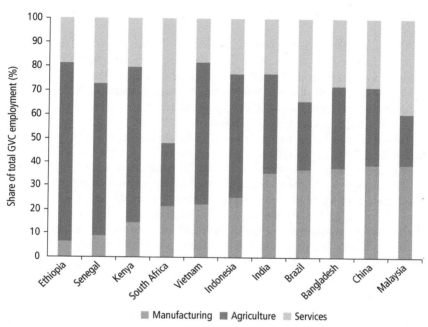

Source: Pahl et al. 2019.
Note: Countries are ranked by manufacturing share of global value chain employment. Agriculture includes fishing and forestry. Services are all other sectors of the economy. The coverage of manufacturing differs by country. For Bangladesh and Ethiopia, it covers all establishments with 10 or more employees; for Kenya, data pertain to establishments with 5 or more persons engaged; for Malaysia, Senegal, South Africa, and Vietnam, the scope of the data is all registered establishments. Data for Brazil, China, India, and Indonesia include all manufacturing firms (formal and informal).

(27 percent) in South Africa. The total number of jobs in GVCs in the services sector was about 586,000 (18 percent) in Ethiopia, 395,000 (20 percent) in Kenya, 55,000 (21 percent) in Senegal, and 1.3 million (45.6 percent) in South Africa. Between 2000 and 2014, more GVC jobs were generated in the agricultural sector in Ethiopia and Kenya, adding 691,000 and 471,000, respectively. In contrast, the number of jobs in the sector declined by 78,000 and 318,000 in Senegal and South Africa, respectively. In comparison, during the same period, jobs created in agriculture through GVCs declined by 673,000 whereas the number of jobs in manufacturing increased by 28 million in China. In Bangladesh and India, job creation in GVCs increased in all sectors but was highest in the manufacturing sector (Pahl et al. 2019).

Although the emphasis here is on job growth in manufacturing, it is noteworthy that the distinction between services and manufacturing activities has become increasingly blurry, given that GVC jobs in services may include workers involved in activities auxiliary to manufacturing, such as business processing services, communications, transport, finance, and after-sales services.[1]

Through participation in GVCs, job growth in the manufacturing sector in Sub-Saharan African countries has benefited from the expanding global demand for manufactured goods in the world economy. Between 2000 and 2014, global demand added 1.69 log points to manufacturing GVC job growth in Ethiopia.[2] In Kenya, Senegal, and South Africa, respectively, it added 0.89, 0.63, and 0.46 log points to GVC job growth.

However, the boost to job growth through participation in GVCs in Sub-Saharan Africa as well as in comparator countries has been weakened by two proximate cause factors: (1) the decline in competitiveness and (2) the decline in the labor requirement needed per unit of output arising from the adoption of labor-saving technologies to replace routine production jobs along GVCs (Pahl et al. 2019). The decline in labor demand in the execution of activities along GVCs reduced job growth by 0.25 log points in Senegal, 0.35 log points in South Africa, and 0.44 log points in Kenya (figure 5.2). In contrast, labor requirements in manufacturing went up by 0.34 log points in Ethiopia. The decline in labor requirements experienced in some of the countries was plausibly due to the quite advanced level of the manufacturing sector in these countries around 2000, such that further increases in productivity were minimal relative to improvements made in the nonagricultural sectors to which the manufacturing sector had backward links (Pahl et al. 2019).

In addition, Ethiopia, Kenya, Senegal, and South Africa lost market share in global competitiveness, which further depressed the creation of jobs within GVCs. Similarly, countries such as Brazil and Malaysia were barely able to increase job growth through improvement in competitiveness with respect to participation in GVCs.[3] In contrast, other developing countries, such as Bangladesh, China, Indonesia, and Vietnam were able to improve GVC competitiveness to boost job growth (figure 5.2).

Increasing the Share of Manufacturing Value Added in GVCs

The share of value added in GVCs has increased in a host of countries in Sub-Saharan Africa as a result of specialized and more diversified baskets of manufacturing industries. For example, between 2000 and 2014, the global share of manufacturing value added in GVCs in Ethiopia increased by 2.5 percent (the most in Sub-Saharan Africa) and in Kenya by 1.7 percent. Other countries have had different experiences, as value-added shares in GVCs have not been growing fast in Senegal and declined in South Africa. Among the comparator countries, the global share of GVC income in China and Vietnam quadrupled during the same period. Countries such as Bangladesh, Brazil, Indonesia, India,

Figure 5.2 GVC Participation and Manufacturing Job Growth: The Roles of Technology, Competitiveness, and Demand in Sub-Saharan Africa and Benchmark Countries, 2000–14

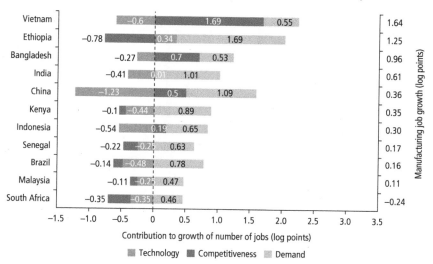

Source: Pahl et al. 2019.
Note: Countries are ordered by growth in number of manufacturing jobs (workers), indicated on the right-hand side (ignoring approximation error). "Technology" measures the effect of the change in labor requirement per value added; "competitiveness" captures the effect attributed to the change in a country's income share in the GVCs; "demand" refers to the effect of growth in world expenditure on final goods completed in the GVCs. GVC = global value chain.

and Malaysia recorded increases in the global share of GVC income but at levels lower than the increase recorded in Ethiopia (figure 5.3).

The increase in the global share of manufacturing value added in GVCs is generated from specialization of countries in particular product GVCs (Pahl et al. 2019).[4] Whereas countries in East Asia, such as China and Malaysia, derive most of the value added in GVCs in electronics and machinery, Ethiopia, Kenya, and Senegal stand out as generating major shares of value added in GVCs from specialized activities related to food manufacturing and activities higher in the chain, in particular, the cultivation of food crops in agriculture. In addition, Ethiopia is specialized in contributing to textiles GVCs, which includes the value added generated in the domestic agricultural production of cotton that is used in textile production. Senegal is specialized in GVCs of chemical products; Kenya in fabricated metals, basic metals, and paper products; and South Africa in a more diversified basket of furniture and paper products, refined petroleum, chemicals, machinery, motor vehicles, basic metals, and food. It is notable that South Africa's profile most closely resembles that of Brazil in GVC activity specialization.

Figure 5.3 Manufacturing GVC Income Shares in Sub-Saharan Africa and Benchmark Countries, 2000 and 2014

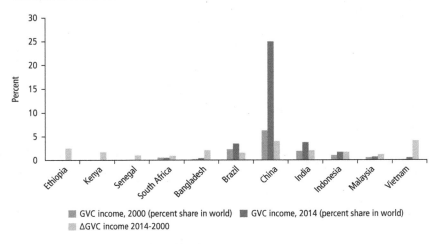

■ GVC income, 2000 (percent share in world)   ■ GVC income, 2014 (percent share in world)
▨ ΔGVC income 2014–2000

Source: World Bank calculations based on Pahl et al. 2019.
Note: GVC = global value chain.

Therefore, Sub-Saharan African countries still have viable options for growing jobs through integration into GVCs to offset the decline in labor requirements in GVC production. One strategy would be for countries to facilitate an increase in the global share of value added in GVCs in specialized and more diversified baskets of manufacturing industries.

Entering and Expanding Activities in High-Growth End Markets

The end markets for manufacturing value added in GVCs vary widely across Sub-Saharan African countries. However, a feature common to all countries in the region is the growing importance of the European Union and home markets as end markets for manufacturing value added in GVCs. In 2014, 12.9 percent of Ethiopia's manufacturing value added in GVCs ended up in the European Union market, 4.2 percent in the US market, 4.7 percent in the Chinese market, and 59.3 percent in domestic demand. Kenya and Senegal depend significantly on domestic final demand, which accounted for 78.2 and 66.7 percent of their value added in GVCs, respectively.

Although the domestic market share is relatively small compared with other Sub-Saharan African countries, it is very important for manufacturing value added in GVCs in South Africa. Of the country's value added in GVCs, 47.2 percent ends up in domestic demand and 13 percent goes to the European Union (figure 5.4). Unlike for some countries in Asia, for countries

Figure 5.4 **End Markets for Manufacturing GVC Value Added in Sub-Saharan Africa and Benchmark Countries, 2014**

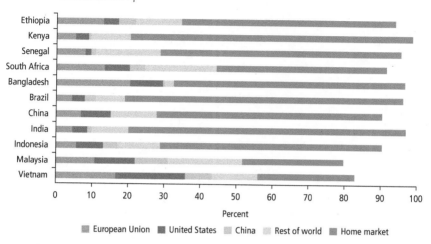

Source: World Bank, based on Pahl et al. 2019.
Note. "European Union" is the 28 member countries of the European Union as of 2014, plus Switzerland; United States includes the United States and Canada. The shares to East Asia (the Republic of Korea, Japan, and Taiwan, China) and Other emerging (Brazil, India, Indonesia, Mexico, the Russian Federation, and Turkey) are not included in the figure although they are included in the original estimation so that bars add up to 100, except for rounding.

in Sub-Saharan Africa, the United States is relatively less important as an end market for manufacturing value added in GVCs.

Thus, another potential approach to enhancing job creation via participation in GVCs would be to aim to enter and expand activities in high-growth end markets and improve the region's shares in serving those markets. In this strategy, fast-growing end markets such as the European Union are as important as domestic demand.

Manufacturing GVCs and Productivity Growth

GVC Participation and Productivity Growth in Sub-Saharan Africa

There is robust evidence of the positive productivity growth effects from GVC integration in Sub-Saharan Africa, with some variation across the region—countries that have high GVC participation rates exhibit relatively higher labor productivity levels and growth. Figure 5.5 compares productivity across two groups based on classification of countries into low and high GVC participation rates. In panel a, high GVC participation comprises linkage rates above the 25th percentile, and low GVC participation comprises linkage rates equal to and below that

Figure 5.5 GVC Participation and Manufacturing Productivity Growth in Sub-Saharan Africa

a. GVC linkage rates above and below the 25th percentile

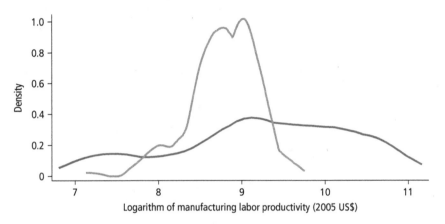

b. GVC linkage rates at the 75th percentile

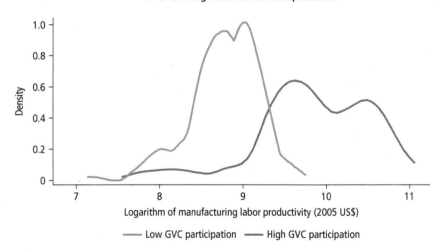

Low GVC participation   High GVC participation

Source: World Bank calculations using data from the United Nations Conference on Trade and Development's Eora database and the Expanded Africa Sector Database.
Note: GVC = global value chain.

threshold. Panel b compares productivity at linkage rates at the 75th percentile and above (high GVC participation) with those at the 25th percentile and below (low GVC participation). In both cases, higher productivity is linked to higher GVC participation rates, with the mean productivity level for low GVC participation at $7,040 (in 2005 US$) and that for high GVC participation at $15,960 (in 2005 US$).[5] The average productivity growth at low GVC participation rates is 0.067 and that at high GVC participation rates is 0.075. A 1 percent increase in GVC participation is associated with a 0.016-percentage-point increase in the growth of labor productivity. Thus, an increase in the GVC participation rate from the 25th to the 75th percentile is associated with a 1.3-percentage-point increase in labor productivity growth (Pahl and Timmer 2020).

Stronger Productivity Gains for Countries with Relatively Low Levels of Labor Productivity

GVC integration overall is associated with higher productivity growth in the long run for all countries, but the effect is stronger through backward participation and for countries that are more integrated into GVCs and those that

Figure 5.6 GVC Participation and Manufacturing Labor Productivity Growth

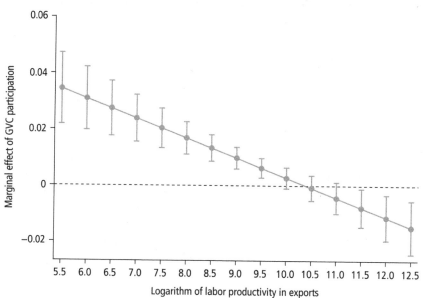

Source: Pahl and Timmer 2020.
Note: The figure shows the marginal effect of global value chain participation on manufacturing labor productivity growth, by levels of labor productivity in exports based on estimates for 56 countries (18 developed and 38 developing). Industry-time dummies are included in the estimation to account for the effect of price changes across industries and over time on labor productivity in exports.

are further from the productivity frontier. Figure 5.6 shows that the marginal effect of changes in the GVC participation index varies by the level of labor productivity in manufacturing exports, being significantly positive for values of labor productivity that are less than or equal to 10. Thus, being further from the productivity frontier, Sub-Saharan African countries will potentially make significant gains in productivity growth by integrating into GVCs. For the least productive countries, the estimated impact of increasing the GVC participation rate from the 25th to the 75th percentile is an increase in labor productivity growth of 2.8 percentage points.

Role of Industrial Upgrading in Jobs Growth in Manufacturing in Sub-Saharan Africa

Industrial Upgrading

In the context of this report and specifically for this chapter, industrial upgrading is defined as rapid growth (in relative terms) and redistribution of employment and value added toward knowledge-intensive industries. In other words, it is the movement of workers from labor-intensive industries to more sophisticated knowledge-intensive industries, captured by the rise and fall in the shares of employment and value added in these industries over time. This parsimonious definition was adopted because of the limited data on Sub-Saharan Africa with which to capture industrial upgrading in the context of GVCs. Nevertheless, this working definition of industrial upgrading is somewhat similar to the standard definition of the term in the context of GVCs. For instance, in a typical GVC context, upgrading could be defined as the integration or movement of workers into more sophisticated business functions in GVCs or from doing mainly assembly activities (more labor intensive and less knowledge intensive) in the value chain to own-equipment manufacturing, to ultimately branding own manufactures over time.

Other industrial upgrading trajectories could take the form in which firms in industry move from performing assembly activities to product design and redesign, logistics, after-sales services, and repairs. All these processes involve industrial shifts in employment share distribution and value-added creation (see de Vries et al. 2019; Gereffi 1999; Humphrey and Schmitz 2002; Sturgeon and Lee 2005). In this definition, industrial upgrading would be expected to result in increased shares of employment and value added in more knowledge- and capital-intensive industries at the expense of labor-intensive industries.

Using the working definition, the industries are grouped into three non-overlapping categories—agriculture-based and labor-intensive industries comprising food and beverages, textiles and apparel, and wood and paper;

mining-based and capital-intensive industries comprising chemical and non-metal products and metal products; and knowledge-intensive industries comprising electrical and machinery and transport equipment.

The level of development and initial level of a country's capabilities matter for the contribution of upgrading within GVCs to employment growth. For instance, in high-income Asian economies such as the Republic of Korea, GVC jobs are unevenly distributed across industries. Between 2000 and 2011, the number of fabrication manufacturing GVC workers[6] in Korea declined by 538,000. In Japan, the number of fabrication workers declined by almost 2.5 million, and in Taiwan, China, it declined by 166,000 over the same period. At the same time, GVC jobs in other related business functions, such as logistics, sales and marketing, administration and back office, research and development, and other support services, increased in Korea and Taiwan, China. These economies have relied on functional upgrading to generate manufacturing GVC jobs that are unevenly spread across the various business functions (de Vries et al. 2019). This change has occurred through shifting workers employed in fabrication toward business-related functions while creating new industries to grow jobs.

In Africa, however, the extent of upgrading within GVCs is lower than in other developing regions. Industrial upgrading in the region has occurred mostly in relatively less knowledge-intensive manufacturing industries. For instance, in Ethiopia, between 1998 and 2015, a total of 44,000 jobs were created in the food and beverages industry, 28,000 in the textiles and apparel industry, 23,000 in the wood and paper industry, and 20,000 in the metal products industry. These four industries combined contributed more than half of total employment growth in the manufacturing sector (table 5.1). Interestingly, the relatively capital-intensive chemical and non-metal products industry created the most jobs (141,000) over the same period, whereas the more knowledge-intensive electrical and machinery industry created the least jobs in the sector.[7] Similar trends in employment levels are observed in the other countries in Africa. The growth in manufacturing employment in Africa has generally been highest in less knowledge-intensive industries (table 5.1).

Despite these general trends, there is some heterogeneity across countries given that industrial upgrading has occurred in high knowledge-intensive and low knowledge-intensive industries. There is also evidence that some of these successful cases have been able to export their products at higher prices while maintaining market share, suggesting gains from economic upgrading (Foster-McGregor, Kaulich, and Stehrer 2015). For instance, in Cameroon and Senegal, in addition to the food and beverages, textiles and apparel, wood and paper, and metal products industries, which recorded increases in industry employment growth, electrical and machinery, as well as the transport equipment industry, also recorded increases in employment growth. The transport equipment industry in Ethiopia, Malawi, and South Africa and the electrical and machinery industry in Kenya have also seen increases in employment growth (table 5.1). Increasing the value-added growth in these industries is associated with positive employment growth effects. Whereas the positive employment growth effect is stronger among low-knowledge-intensive industries, it is strong among high-knowledge-intensive industries in countries such as Ethiopia, Kenya, Malawi, and Senegal (table 5.2).

Similarly, in other comparator Asian economies, the number of jobs in less knowledge-intensive industries has increased, although it has decreased as a share of total employment. India and China added 12 million and 24 million jobs, respectively, in manufacturing fabrication between 2000 and 2011. There was also a substantial increase in GVC fabrication jobs in Bangladesh (about 11 million), Vietnam (about 5 million), the Philippines (2.3 million), and Indonesia (1.1 million) during that period. At the same time, the share of GVC jobs in related capital-intensive and knowledge-intensive industries and business functions, such as logistics, sales and marketing, administration and back office, research and development, and other support services, increased in these economies (de Vries et al. 2019).

Upgrading along GVCs generates manufacturing jobs, but these jobs could be unevenly spread across industries, being favorable toward more skilled manufacturing and functional business-related jobs, as is evident in high-income countries with high initial capabilities. Thus, although it is important to upgrade in GVCs to create more jobs, it is equally essential to ensure that there are job opportunities for the region's large unskilled workforce, which would mean specializing more in low-skill activities in the value chain. In addition, GVCs lead to more inclusive growth, especially when beneficiary sectors or industries are involved in activities that are labor intensive and employ relatively lower-skilled labor (Allard et al. 2016). The volume of the activity performed in the GVC matters as much as or even more than specializing in sophisticated activities in the value chain because important benefits accrue from specializing in less sophisticated assembly activities and performing them on a large scale (Kowalski et al. 2015).

An overwhelming majority of the share of the labor force in the manufacturing sector in Sub-Saharan African countries is employed in less knowledge-intensive industries. In Côte d'Ivoire, the four less knowledge-intensive industries (food and beverages, textiles and apparel, wood and paper, and metal products) together absorbed 83.8 percent of the manufacturing labor force. In Cameroon, these four industries absorbed 81.1 percent of manufacturing workers; in Ethiopia, 49.9 percent; in Ghana, 78.6 percent; in Kenya, 80.6 percent; in Malawi, 88.0 percent; in Senegal, 65.9 percent; and in South Africa, 56.5 percent (table 5.3).

Table 5.1 Employment Growth in Manufacturing Industries in Sub-Saharan Africa and Benchmark Countries (%)

	Period	Food and beverages	Textiles and apparel	Leather products	Wood and paper	Chemical and non-metal products	Metal products	Electrical and machinery	Transport equipment	Total manufacturing
Sub-Saharan Africa										
Côte d'Ivoire	1994–97	11.5	9.1	—	4.3	4.8	5.0	2.8	–2.0	35.6
Cameroon	1998–2008	1.7	4.8	8.0	1.8	–3.0	4.3	5.1	4.0	26.7
Ethiopia	1998–2015	12.6	8.9	14.6	14.2	22.8	21.1	4.9	21.2	120.2
Ghana	1995–2003	10.0	–1.0	10.0	0.9	3.3	0.1	–1.7	–5.0	16.6
Kenya	1998–2015	8.9	10.0	25.6	4.2	6.5	8.2	6.8	–10.8	59.5
Malawi	1998–2012	3.0	–4.3	13.1	–3.5	0.8	–1.2	–13.1	13.1	7.9
Senegal	1998–2014	4.2	1.5	10.9	4.6	4.5	–3.9	5.7	5.9	33.2
South Africa	1998–2015	0.9	–6.8	–5.8	–1.8	–1.2	–0.8	–1.0	1.5	–14.9
Asian benchmarks										
Bangladesh	1998–2011	9.9	10.1	5.8	6.6	18.7	17.5	7.9	4.5	81.0
Indonesia	1998–2015	4.3	2.5	0.9	–1.3	2.7	3.3	3.6	8.3	24.4
Vietnam	1998–2015	16.5	17.6	17.9	19.1	16.5	19.1	20.4	18.6	145.8

Source: World Bank calculations using data from the United Nations Industrial Development Organization's Industrial Statistics Database at the 2-digit level of ISIC (INDSTAT2).
Note: The reported figures are midpoint growth rates in percentages. Employment growth for each industry is calculated by dividing employment growth of individual industries by the sum of employment growth of all industries multiplied by employment growth in the total manufacturing sector of respective countries. Manufacturing industries are classified according to the International Standard Industrial Classification Rev. 3 at the 2-digit level: Food and beverages: food and beverages (15) and tobacco (16); Textiles and apparel: textiles (17) and garments (18); Wood and paper: wood (20), paper (21), recorded media (22), and furniture (36); Chemical and non-metal products: refined petroleum products (23), chemicals (24), plastics and rubber (25), and non-metallic mineral products (26); Metal products: basic metals (27) and fabricated metals (28); Electrical and machinery: machinery and equipment (29), electronics (31 and 32), and precision instruments (33); Transport equipment: transport machines (34 and 35). — = not available.

Table 5.2 Employment Growth Response to a Change in Value Added: Manufacturing Industries in Sub-Saharan Africa and Benchmark Countries (%)

Country	Food and Beverages	Textiles and apparel	Leather products	Wood and paper	Chemical and non-metal products	Metal products	Electrical and machinery	Transport equipment	Total manufacturing
Sub-Saharan Africa									
Côte d'Ivoire	1.04	0.94	—	1.69	1.52	0.80	0.16	-0.30	1.07
Cameroon	-0.22	-0.60	—	-0.23	0.37	-0.53	-0.63	-0.50	-0.13
Ethiopia	1.18	-1.68	0.78	1.16	1.20	0.98	0.26	0.87	1.11
Ghana	1.00	-0.56	1.00	0.65	0.52	-0.15	0.50	-0.50	1.09
Kenya	0.63	0.53	1.00	0.23	0.47	0.47	1.64	-0.65	0.49
Malawi	0.42	0.68	1.00	-0.76	0.26	0.48	n.a.	n.a.	0.10
Senegal	1.43	-0.15	-3.26	0.71	0.60	4.57	0.54	0.27	0.70
South Africa	0.35	0.71	2.13	-1.45	-0.37	0.54	-0.95	1.27	-0.99
Asian benchmarks									
Bangladesh	0.99	0.52	-1.18	0.58	1.31	0.80	0.97	0.40	0.69
Indonesia	0.26	0.20	0.06	-0.12	0.17	0.22	0.22	0.49	0.16
Vietnam	0.85	0.89	0.85	0.86	0.78	0.84	0.86	0.80	0.82

Source: World Bank calculations, using data from the United Nations Industrial Development Organization's Industrial Statistics Database at the 2-digit level of ISIC (INDSTAT2) and the United Nations Conference on Trade and Development's Eora database.

Note: Data periods used: Côte d'Ivoire (1994–97), Cameroon (1998–2008), Ethiopia (1998–2015), Ghana (1995–2015), Kenya (1998–2015), Malawi (1998–2012), Senegal (1998–2014), South Africa (1998–2015), Bangladesh (1998–2011), Indonesia (1998–2015), Vietnam (1998–2015). Manufacturing industries are classified according to the International Standard Industrial Classification Rev. 3 at the 2-digit level: Food and beverages: food and beverages (15) and tobacco (16); Textiles and apparel: textiles (17) and garments (18); Wood and paper: wood (20), paper (21), recorded media (22), and furniture (36); Chemical and non-metal products: refined petroleum products (23), chemicals (24), plastics and rubber (25), and non-metallic mineral products (26); Metal products: basic metals (27) and fabricated metals (28); Electrical and machinery: machinery and equipment (29), electronics (31 and 32), and precision instruments (33); Transport equipment: transport machines (34 and 35). Value added at producers' prices, converted into 2010 US$ values using gross domestic product deflator as price index. — = not available.

Table 5.3 Employment Shares in Manufacturing Industries in Sub-Saharan Africa and Benchmark Countries

Country	Industry employment share (%)							
	Food and beverages	Textiles and apparel	Leather products	Wood and paper	Chemical and non-metal products	Metal products	Electrical and machinery	Transport equipment
Sub-Saharan Africa								
Côte d'Ivoire	38.0	17.7	0	24.3	14.0	3.8	0.9	1.3
Cameroon	28.1	20.0	0.4	25.8	15.8	7.2	1.7	0.9
Ethiopia	19.1	15.4	6.6	9.2	41.5	6.2	0.1	1.9
Ghana	19.9	9.4	0.5	41.3	19.3	8.0	1.4	0.2
Kenya	39.7	22.0	1.9	11.9	13.7	7.0	2.3	1.5
Malawi	66.4	9.1	0.5	10.4	10.7	2.1	—	0.9
Senegal	44.6	7.7	2.8	8.7	27.7	4.9	2.1	1.5
South Africa	19.1	6.7	1.2	16.5	18.6	14.2	14.6	9.1
Asian benchmarks								
Bangladesh	6.9	71.4	1.5	2.3	12.7	3.3	1.4	0.4
Indonesia	24.1	22.8	6.0	14.6	16.9	4.3	6.5	4.8
Vietnam	10.3	24.4	18.8	13.3	11.4	6.3	11.9	3.7

Source: World Bank calculations, using data from the United Nations Industrial Development Organization's Industrial Statistics Database at the 2-digit level of ISIC (INDSTAT2).
Note: Data periods used: Côte d'Ivoire (1997), Cameroon (2008), Ethiopia (2015), Ghana (2003), Kenya (2015), Malawi (2012), Senegal (2014), South Africa (2015), Bangladesh (2011), Indonesia (2015), Vietnam (2015). Manufacturing industries are classified according to the International Standard Industrial Classification Rev. 3 at the 2-digit level: Food and beverages: food and beverages (15) and tobacco (16); Textiles and apparel: textiles (17) and garments (18); Wood and paper: wood (20), paper (21), recorded media (22), and furniture (36); Chemical and non-metal products: refined petroleum products (23), chemicals (24), plastics and rubber (25), and non-metallic mineral products (26); Metal products: basic metals (27) and fabricated metals (28); Electrical and machinery: machinery and equipment (29), electronics (31 and 32), and precision instruments (33); Transport equipment: transport machines (34 and 35). — = not available.

The growth in employment shares in these industries is notable, the highest being recorded in the food and beverages industry, at 21.6 percent and 46.6 percent in Côte d'Ivoire and Malawi, respectively.[8] The textiles and apparel industry recorded growth in employment shares of 24.2 percent in Kenya. In Senegal, the growth in employment shares in these industries has been moderate, at 4.4 percent in the food and beverages industry and 8.7 percent in the wood and paper industry. In Ethiopia, only the metal products industry recorded growth in employment share among the four less knowledge-intensive upgrading sectors.[9]

Furthermore, wage growth in these industries has been impressive. In Malawi, where the food and beverages industry employs about 66 percent of manufacturing workers, for instance, the industry's wage rate grew by 50.1 percent between 1998 and 2012. In Ethiopia, the wage rate in the food and beverages industry grew by 60.2 percent between 1998 and 2015. The wage rate in the metal products industry grew by as much as 80.5 percent in Senegal between 1998 and 2014, and it grew by 81.8 percent in the wood and paper industry in Malawi. These wage rises suggest an improvement in the welfare of the labor force in these industries.[10]

GVCs as a Driver of Job Growth and Industrial Upgrading in Sub-Saharan Africa

The heterogeneity across countries in Sub-Saharan Africa notwithstanding, GVC participation is found to be positively associated with industrial employment growth,[11] ranging from a low association of 0.23 in the textile and apparel industry and 0.27 in the electrical and machinery industry to as high as 0.59 in the transport equipment and wood and paper industries (figure 5.7).

Decomposing GVC participation into backward and forward links and the resultant association with employment growth suggests that the positive association between GVC integration and employment growth occurs mostly through backward links (figure 5.7). Backward integration allows firms to access higher-quality and more sophisticated intermediate inputs as well as benefits from technology transfer to stimulate productivity growth and facilitate upgrading to expand the scale of production and subsequent creation of skilled and decent jobs. Presently, in the context of Africa, forward integration creates jobs but these jobs are likely to be at the bottom of the value chain, that is, lower paid and with limited opportunity for upgrading.

In addition, there is evidence of a positive association between GVC participation and industry upgrading (figures 5.8 and 5.9). Figure 5.8 shows evidence of a positive association between GVC participation and employment elasticity with respect to value added across all the manufacturing industries

Figure 5.7 Correlation between GVC Participation and Manufacturing Job Growth

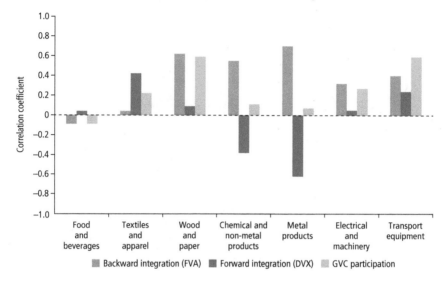

Source: World Bank calculations using data from the United Nations Conference on Trade and Development's Eora database and the United Nations Industrial Development Organization's Industrial Statistics Database at the 2-digit level of ISIC (INDSTAT2).
Note: The data are for Côte d'Ivoire, Cameroon, Ethiopia, Ghana, Kenya, Malawi, Senegal, and South Africa. Backward integration is foreign value-added shares in exports (FVA); forward integration is indirect value-added shares in exports (DVX); GVC participation rate = FVA + DVX. For the leather industry, the GVC participation rate cannot be computed because of data unavailability. Correlation coefficients are significant except for backward integration in textiles and apparel and food and beverages; forward integration in food and beverages, wood and paper, and electrical and machinery; and GVC participation in food and beverages, chemical and non-metal products, and metal products. GVC = global value chain.

in Sub-Saharan Africa. In other words, participation in GVCs increases the industry's value addition, which triggers positive responsiveness in employment growth across those industries.

Figure 5.9 focuses on the association between GVC participation and changes in industry employment shares; this association is also positive. Based on a different measure of upgrading (export upgrading), using highly disaggregated product-level export data for 122 countries and indicators of GVC integration and export quality over 1996–2015, Ndubuisi and Owusu (2021) find robust evidence of a positive association between GVC participation and export upgrading. The positive export upgrading effect of GVC participation occurs only through backward links in GVCs in developing countries, but it occurs through both forward and backward links in developed countries. GVC participation, particularly through backward links, not only raises the export quality upgrading level but also brings the level of

Figure 5.8 Correlation between GVC Participation, Value Added, and Employment Elasticity

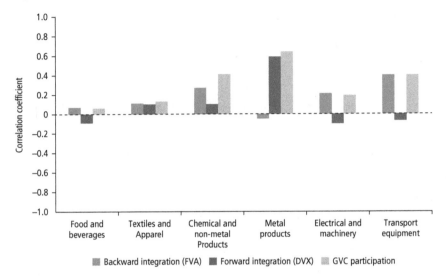

Backward integration (FVA) ■ Forward integration (DVX) GVC participation

Source: World Bank calculations using data from the United Nations Conference on Trade and Development's Eora database and the United Nations Industrial Development Organization's Industrial Statistics Database at the 2-digit level of ISIC (INDSTAT2).
Note: The data are for Côte d'Ivoire, Cameroon, Ethiopia, Ghana, Kenya, Malawi, Senegal, and South Africa. Backward integration is foreign value-added shares in exports (FVA); forward integration is indirect value-added shares in exports (DVX); GVC participation rate = FVA + DVX. For the leather industry, the GVC participation rate cannot be computed because of data unavailability. Correlation coefficients are significant except for forward integration in textiles and apparel, food and beverages, chemical and non-metal products, electrical and machinery, and transport equipment; backward integration in metal products and food and beverages; and GVC participation in food and beverages. GVC = global value chain.

export quality upgrading closer to the frontier (Criscuolo and Timmis 2017; Faruq 2010; Xu and Mao 2018).

Conclusion and Policy Options

The manufacturing sector has historically been the growth engine, accounting for a substantial share of economywide productivity growth and decent job creation. However, the shares of manufacturing in gross domestic product and employment have been declining in developed economies, emerging market economies, and low-income developing countries. In Sub-Saharan Africa, it has been six decades since the implementation of various industrial policies, but industrialization remains elusive (see Owusu, Szirmai, and Foster-McGregor 2020).

Figure 5.9 Correlation between GVC Participation and Changes in Industry Employment Shares

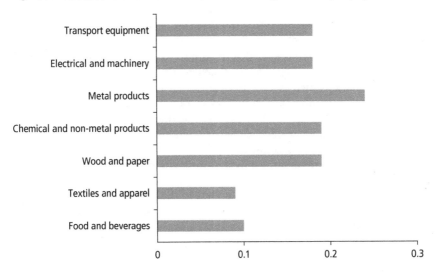

Source: World Bank calculations using data from the United Nations Conference on Trade and Development's Eora database and the United Nations Industrial Development Organization's Industrial Statistics Database at the 2-digit level of ISIC (INDSTAT2).
Note: The data are for Côte d'Ivoire, Cameroon, Ethiopia, Ghana, Kenya, Malawi, Senegal, and South Africa. Global value chain participation rate = foreign value-added shares in exports + indirect value-added shares in exports. For the leather industry, the GVC participation rate cannot be computed because of data unavailability. Correlation is significant except for food and beverages, textiles and apparel, chemical and non-metal products, and metal products. GVC = global value chain.

The manufacturing employment share remains relatively small in the region although it is increasing, and it is fair to say that many countries in the region are yet to have trends of successful industrialization. Nevertheless, industrialization will still be a key engine of growth in Sub-Saharan Africa, creating decent jobs, boosting productivity growth, and making a significant contribution to inclusive growth. The potential is huge, and there are reasons to be optimistic about the region's industrial future. Sub-Saharan African manufacturing shares of employment and value added, although lower than the region's comparators, are more stable than the shares in other regions and are increasing steadily, albeit from a low base (Naude 2019).

Integration into GVCs is providing new windows of opportunity to grow jobs and increase productivity in the manufacturing sector. Countries in the region have benefited from insertion into GVCs to grow jobs. Not only has the region expanded jobs in manufacturing through GVCs, but the contributions of GVC participation to job growth in the other key sectors—agriculture and services—are even higher. And, although the use of labor-saving technologies has depressed GVC job growth, the region still has viable options for increasing jobs through integration into GVCs to offset this decline.

The available viable policy options are to aim to enter and expand activities in high-growth end markets as well as to improve countries' competitiveness in capturing much of the value added in final consumption. In this strategy, fast-growing end markets such as the European Union are as important as domestic demand. Achieving entry into these end markets will require exerting effort toward gaining market access through favorable trade agreements (preferential tariffs, less restrictive nontariff trade barriers, and simplified rules of origin) as well as trade facilitation and logistics.

Sustaining and increasing the jobs and productivity gains from manufacturing GVCs in the region will also require the implementation of policies that would attract lead firms and global suppliers in the value chain. Strengthening cooperation between public and private global and local actors will be needed to remove impediments and allow countries in the region to leverage international supply chain links or dynamics, to improve their role in global and regional chains (cf. Gereffi 2014). Such efforts would include adopting better trade and investment promotion policies, such as competitive exchange rate regimes, favorable and attractive but strategic foreign direct investment policies that target priority industries and sectors, an improved business environment (such as property rights protection), labor market regulation, and good transport infrastructure.

Inadequate supply of high-quality or affordable foreign inputs is a constraining factor in productivity and job growth. Policies and bottlenecks that inhibit access to these crucial foreign intermediates should be removed or strategically reformed to allow domestic firms to access these inputs. While sourcing intermediate inputs from abroad, a complete national export success strategy for countries in the region will require additional policies that focus on efforts to create regional integration agreements that would promote the sourcing of a sizable share of production inputs from countries in the region, which would strengthen Sub-Saharan African countries' export positions in the global economy.

Industrial upgrading in Sub-Saharan Africa has occurred mostly in relatively labor-intensive and less knowledge-intensive manufacturing industries. These industries also absorb the greater share of the labor force in the sector, and they are predominantly low skilled and unskilled. Although the region needs to upgrade into higher-value-added manufacturing GVCs, it is equally essential to specialize in the short term in more low-skilled activities in GVCs. Important benefits accrue from specializing in less sophisticated assembly activities and performing them on a large scale. While pursuing this strategy, countries in the region should actively and effectively invest in activities that would later position them in higher-value-added tasks along the GVCs. Investing in building absorptive capacity through the introduction of carefully designed educational policies and skills-training programs that align well with countries' industrial strategies should be a major priority. For countries with high initial industrial capacity, upgrading to sophisticated activities and functions in GVCs is recommended.

Notes

1. Unlike the agriculture and services sectors, GVC jobs in manufacturing cover only formal jobs.
2. Multiplying log point growth by 100 yields growth rate in percentage terms.
3. GVC income or competitiveness in GVCs is measured as the share of value added that is added in the last stage of production (that takes place in a manufacturing industry).
4. A variant of the well-known Balassa index is used to construct the GVC specialization index.
5. The data comprise 18 Sub-Saharan African countries that together make up about 80 percent of the region's gross domestic product.
6. This is classified as a less knowledge-intensive industry within the manufacturing sector.
7. The analysis here relies on data from the United Nations Industrial Development Organization's (UNIDO) Industrial Statistics Database at the 2-digit level of ISIC (INDSTAT2); although the numbers are substantially higher, the increasing trend—particularly strong after 2010—that is observed using the UNIDO INDSTAT2 data is similar to the observed patterns using the Ethiopian manufacturing census data.
8. The periods are defined in the note to table 5.1.
9. World Bank calculations using data from UNIDO's INDSTAT2 for the periods defined in table 5.1.
10. World Bank calculations, using data from UNIDO's INDSTAT2 database. Wage: Wages and salaries paid to employees, converted into 2010 US$ values using the gross domestic product deflator as the price index.
11. Except in the food and beverages industry, although the correlation is weak and not significantly different from zero.

References

Allard, C., J. I. Canales Kriljenko, W. Chen, J. Gonzalez-Garcia, E. Kitsios, and J. Treviño. 2016. *Trade Integration and Global Value Chains in Sub-Saharan Africa: In Pursuit of the Missing Link*. Washington, DC: Africa Department, International Monetary Fund.

Criscuolo, C., and J. Timmis. 2017. "The Relationship between Global Value Chains and Productivity." *International Productivity Monitor, Centre for the Study of Living Standards* (32): 61–83.

de Vries, G., Q. Chen, R. Hasan, and Z. Li. 2019. "Do Asian Countries Upgrade in Global Value Chains? A Novel Approach and Empirical Evidence." *Asian Economic Journal* 33 (1): 13–37.

Faruq, H. 2010. "Impact of Technology on Export Quality." *Journal of Developing Areas* 44 (1): 167–87.

Foster-McGregor, N., F. Kaulich, and R. Stehrer. 2015. "Global Value Chains in Africa." UNU-MERIT Working Paper Series 2015-024, The United Nations University–Maastricht Economic and Social Research Institute on Innovation and Technology, Maastricht, Netherlands.

Gereffi, G. 1999. "International Trade and Industrial Upgrading in the Apparel Commodity Chain." *Journal of International Economics* 48: 37–70.

Gereffi, G. 2014. "A Global Value Chain Perspective on Industrial Policy and Development in Emerging Markets." *Duke Journal of Comparative and International Law* 24: 433–58.

Humphrey, J., and H. Schmitz. 2002. "How Does Insertion in Global Value Chains Affect Upgrading in Industrial Clusters?" *Regional Studies* 36 (9): 1017–27.

Kowalski, P., J. L. Gonzalez, A. Ragoussis, and C. Ugarte. 2015. "Participation of Developing Countries in Global Value Chains: Implications for Trade and Trade-Related Policies." OECD Trade Policy Paper 179, Organisation for Economic Co-operation and Development, Paris.

Naude, W. 2019. "Three Varieties of Africa's Industrial Future." IZA Discussion Paper 12678, Institute of Labor Economics, Bonn.

Ndubuisi, G., and S. Owusu. 2021. "How Important Is GVC Participation to Export Upgrading?" *The World Economy*. https://onlinelibrary.wiley.com/doi/10.1111/twec.13102.

Owusu, S., A. Szirmai, and N. Foster-McGregor. 2020. "The Rise of the Service Sector in the Global Economy." UNU-MERIT Working Paper 056, The United Nations University–Maastricht Economic and Social Research Institute on Innovation and Technology, Maastricht, Netherlands.

Pahl, S., M.P. Timmer, R. Gouma, and P. J. Woltjer. 2019. "Jobs in Global Value Chains: New Evidence for Four African Countries in International Perspective." Policy Research Working Paper 8953, World Bank, Washington, DC.

Pahl, S., and M. P. Timmer. 2020. "Do Global Value Chains Enhance Economic Upgrading? A Long View." *Journal of Development Studies*, 56 (9): 1683–1705.

Reijnders, L. S. M., and G. J. de Vries. 2018. "Technology, Offshoring and the Rise of Non-Routine Jobs." *Journal of Development Economics* 135: 412–32.

Reijnders, L. S. M., M. P. Timmer, and X. Ye. 2016. "Offshoring, Biased Technical Change and Labour Demand: New Evidence from Global Value Chains." GGDC Research Memorandum 164, Groningen Growth and Development Centre, University of Groningen, Netherlands.

Rodrik, D. 2018. "New Technologies, Global Value Chains, and Developing Economies." NBER Working Paper 25164, National Bureau of Economic Research, Cambridge, MA.

Sturgeon, T., and J.-R. Lee. 2005. "Industry Co-Evolution: A Comparison of Taiwan and North-American Electronics Contract Manufacturers." In *Global Taiwan: Building Competitive Strengths in a New International Economy*, edited by S. Berger and R. Lester, 33–75. Armonk, NY: M. E. Sharpe.

Xu, J., and Q. Mao. 2018. "On the Relationship between Intermediate Input Imports and Export Quality in China." *Economics of Transition and Institutional Change* 26 (3): 429–67.

Chapter 6

Industrialization in Sub-Saharan Africa: A Policy Framework

The expansion of global value chains (GVCs) implies that industrial policy must change in several ways. Among other things, industrial policy must shift from the traditional stance aimed at developing entire industries domestically to one that focuses on moving into higher-value-added tasks associated with manufacturing industries. In addition, success in the advent of GVCs requires easy and cheap access to imports of essential intermediate inputs. Therefore, industrial policy should address the challenges associated with the cost of importing intermediate goods, such as nontariff barriers (NTBs), which could impede competitiveness.

Moreover, a broader industrial policy should focus on strategically negotiating and linking with multinational companies rather than attempting to build domestic capacity to compete with leading transnational companies as in traditional industrial policy. This broader perspective has become necessary because the challenges facing firms and governments require moving up through the chain of production of a particular commodity or set of commodities.

Sub-Saharan African manufacturing firms' links to GVCs are generally as strong as those of their counterparts in South Asia and East Asia, albeit with some variation across countries based on geography, natural resource endowments, and other factors. However, links to manufacturing GVCs have declined steeply over the past two decades in non-resource-rich countries in the region, while they have increased sharply in non-oil-resource-rich countries. These developments are attributable to high import tariffs in some of the countries, rising barriers to export markets, and skills shortages that hinder inward foreign direct investment (FDI) along GVCs. Therefore, participation in GVCs is associated with a set of national-level policies that are pertinent to strengthening manufacturing competitiveness, including policies associated with enhancing productive capacity, improving infrastructure and services, and promoting trade and investment.

This chapter addresses policy issues in the context of facilitating entry into GVCs to enhance industrialization prospects for Sub-Saharan African countries. It considers the role of policy in promoting structural transformation and addresses policy priorities for maximizing job creation and facilitating industrialization and productivity growth in the region.

Trade Policy

Expanding Market Access to Advanced and Emerging Market Economies through Preferential Trade Agreements

Changes in external trade policies, including preferential access to the export markets of developed economies, mainly East Asia, the European Union, and the United States, have implications for participation in manufacturing GVCs. Access to export markets is particularly crucial for textile and apparel exports, agro-processing, and processing of natural resources before export. Light manufacturing industries, especially labor-intensive production of textile and apparel products, are prime examples of the types of industries in which developing countries have a natural comparative advantage and from which they could benefit the most (box 6.1). Among the types of policy support that developed countries can provide, facilitating access for goods exported from developing countries to their markets is one of the most straightforward propositions (Van Biesebroeck and Zaurino 2019).

Despite having preferential market access, Sub-Saharan African countries are not exhaustively using their market access opportunities in the European Union (EU) and North America. One reason is very restrictive NTBs. For instance, when the EU embarked on its policy to foster biofuels in its transport sector, most developing countries expected to benefit, and there was a prediction that there would be a rise in Sub-Saharan African biofuel exports to the EU (Charles et al. 2009; Jank et al. 2007). However, this rise has not materialized. The EU biofuel policy is argued to have been structured in ways that act as an NTB under the EU Renewable Energy Directive, which has limited Sub-Saharan Africa's access to the EU biofuel market (Schuenemann and Kerr 2019). In this context, policies pertaining to rules of origin, most favored nation agreements, and NTB agreements with the international market must be framed to ensure that countries in the region exhaustively use market access opportunities, while ensuring that a significant share of gross exports from the region consists of domestic content.

BOX 6.1

Trade Liberalization Schemes and Light Manufacturing in Sub-Saharan Africa: The Role of the African Growth and Opportunity Act, Everything But Arms, and the Generalized System of Preferences

The African Growth and Opportunity Act (AGOA) was passed by the United States in 2000. It unilaterally granted duty- and quota-free access to the US market to the majority of Sub-Saharan African countries. The US trade concessions are uniform across all countries eligible for AGOA, but they differ for apparel and nonapparel items. For nonapparel products, AGOA is based on the Generalized System of Preferences (GSP). Approximately 1,800 items were added to the list of products with zero import duty under the GSP. As a result, the number of goods on the US GSP list for AGOA countries expanded from 4,600 to more than 6,400 items, defined using the eight-digit Harmonized System product classification. Once a country is declared AGOA eligible, it can export any of these items duty-free to the United States.

Duty-free access to the US market for apparel exports from a Sub-Saharan African country is not automatic when AGOA eligibility is granted. Countries need to be specifically declared eligible for the apparel provision, which allows duty-free and, more important, quota-free access to the US market for most apparel products, provided that the fabric (or yarn or thread) comes from the United States or an AGOA country. Although the country-level quotas have been removed, a regional AGOA quota remains for apparel. The quota was initially set at 1.5 percent of US imports, but was increased to 3.5 percent over eight years. These caps were doubled under a set of amendments called AGOA II, and the new set of caps has not proved binding. Under the additional administrative requirements, exporting countries must adopt effective enforcement and verification procedures to validate the sources of the various components of their exports to the United States.

Everything But Arms (EBA) is a special GSP arrangement for low-income countries that was introduced in 2001. The program allows duty-free access to the European Union (EU) market for all products except arms and ammunition.

AGOA and the extension of the EU trade preferences through the EBA program and the GSP have boosted the growth of exports of textiles and apparel from Sub-Saharan Africa. During the period 1995–2016, exports to the EU rose by an average of 12.9 percent for the entire Sub-Saharan African region because of EBA, which is more than twice as much as under the baseline GSP. Sub-Saharan African countries that benefit from the Special Rule for Apparel under AGOA, with more liberal rules of origin, have registered significant increases in textile exports. In addition, the foreign value-added content of their exports has increased significantly (Kassa and Owusu, forthcoming).

There remains significant potential for export-driven growth in the textiles sector given the high demand and low initial share of textile exports from the region.

However, these trade liberalization schemes could also become a double-edged sword; although they may encourage exports when the schemes are more liberal, they may also restrict domestic value addition and the strengthening of links to domestic industries by encouraging imports of low-cost intermediate inputs.

(continued next page)

Box 6.1 Trade Liberalization Schemes and Light Manufacturing in Sub-Saharan Africa: The Role of the African Growth and Opportunity Act, Everything But Arms, and the Generalized System of Preferences (continued)

The main beneficiaries of the schemes are countries that qualify for the EU's EBA arrangement, which eliminates tariffs (figure B6.1.1). Still, there is an important additional role for developed economies to play by liberalizing tariffs on imports of light manufacturing and agricultural products to support industrialization and economic transformation in the region (Kassa and Coulibaly 2019). The AGOA apparel provision is almost as generous as the EBA with regard to tariff preferences. If countries do not benefit from any preference scheme, their average tariffs for textile products are significantly higher, which could impede industrialization efforts.

Figure B6.1.1 Ad Valorem Tariffs, by Preference Scheme for Sub-Saharan African Countries, 2016

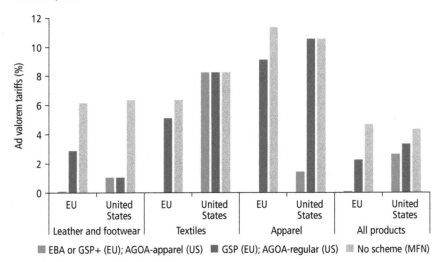

Source: Van Biesebroeck and Zaurino 2019.
Note: AGOA = African Growth and Opportunity Act; EBA = Everything But Arms; EU = European Union; GSP = Generalized System of Preferences; MFN = most favored nation.
EU-GSP: Cameroon, Republic of Congo, Côte d'Ivoire, Ghana, Kenya, Nigeria, Swaziland; EU-GSP+: Cabo Verde; EU-EBA: Angola, Benin, Burkina Faso, Burundi, Central African Republic, Chad, Democratic Republic of Congo, Djibouti, Eritrea, Ethiopia, The Gambia, Guinea, Guinea-Bissau, Lesotho, Liberia, Madagascar, Malawi, Mali, Mauritania, Mozambique, Niger, Rwanda, Senegal, Sierra Leone, Sudan, Tanzania, Togo, Uganda, Zambia; EU-No scheme (MFN): Botswana, Gabon, Mauritius, Namibia, South Africa, Zimbabwe; US-AGOA (regular): Angola, Burundi, Republic of Congo, Djibouti, Gabon, Guinea-Bissau, Mali, Mauritania, Togo; US-AGOA (apparel): Burkina Faso, Benin, Botswana, Cabo Verde, Chad, Côte d'Ivoire, Cameroon, Ethiopia, Ghana, Guinea, Kenya, Liberia, Lesotho, Madagascar, Mauritius, Malawi, Mozambique, Namibia, Niger, Nigeria, Rwanda, Sierra Leone, Senegal, Tanzania, Uganda, South Africa, Zambia; US-No scheme (MFN): Central African Republic, Democratic Republic of Congo, Eritrea, Gambia, Sudan, Swaziland, Zimbabwe.

Note: This box draws heavily on Van Biesebroeck and Zaurino (2019).

Entering and Expanding Activities in High-Growth Markets

The impact of GVC participation on job growth in Sub-Saharan Africa has been due, primarily, to growing global demand in specific product categories in which the region's firms have participated. There are sectoral variations in job gains such that agricultural GVCs have succeeded in generating a large number of jobs.

Viable options for generating employment opportunities should include entering and expanding activities in high-growth end markets as well as improving countries' competitiveness in capturing much of the value added in final consumption. These options would involve building trade negotiation capabilities to ensure lower preferential tariffs, less restrictive NTBs, and simplified rules of origin in end markets and input markets (Coulibaly, Kassa, and Zeufack, forthcoming). These actions need to be accompanied by effective trade facilitation and logistics efforts (including transportation, roads, storage facilities, distribution networks, and administrative requirements) that reduce the fixed and variable costs of production and trade operations.

Although optimistic that a substantial share of the organization of manufacturing production will continue to occur through GVCs and that high-growth markets will remain crucial for developing countries such as those in Africa, the challenge that remains to be tackled is how to turn GVC participation into favorable socially and environmentally sustainable outcomes. In this regard industry position in the value chain; the type of activities performed in the value chain; power relations in a GVC between global lead firms and suppliers; and international labor, health and safety, and environmental standards that guide this relation will go a long way toward determining how policies should be framed to maximize the sustainability impact of the activities of manufacturing industries in GVCs. Adopting international standards in environmental, health and safety, and labor practices is becoming increasingly important to successfully breaking into the markets of advanced economies because of the rising awareness of and social concerns associated with production processes in developing economies, which may pose risks to attracting FDI.

Reducing Intermediate Input Import Tariffs That Limit Active GVC Participation

The trade policies of Sub-Saharan African countries affect trading costs associated with stringent rules and regulations as well as tariffs on importing and exporting. These policies play a significant role in countries' efforts to integrate into regional and global value chains. Reducing trade barriers and lowering the costs of international trade are necessary conditions for the emergence of GVCs and the strengthening of links. For example, high import tariffs directly influence firms' costs of importing or exporting and, hence, their participation in GVCs. Higher tariff rates exert a negative impact on GVC participation (Balie et al. 2018; Nguimkeu and Abudu 2019). Higher tariffs on imports of capital goods are even more restrictive to value chain participation. For resource-rich economies, upgrading and adding value to their natural resource exports requires that they are able to import production equipment and intermediate inputs at lower cost.

Declining tariff rates are associated with increased forward and backward participation in manufacturing GVCs in Sub-Saharan Africa (figure 6.1). Despite this downward trend, however, trade protection levels in the region are among the highest in the world. Exports from Sub-Saharan African economies face high tariffs in developing countries in Asia and Latin America but less so in the European Union and the United States.

The high intraregional tariffs faced by countries in the region are more concerning (figure 6.2). Countries in Sub-Saharan Africa impose high barriers on trade with each other, which raises the cost of production, diminishes potential comparative advantages, and hinders integration into GVCs. Although they are declining, tariffs on inputs imported into the region are also high, especially for transport equipment and parts and accessories (table 6.1 and figure 6.3). The growing fragmentation of production across borders highlights the need for the region to negotiate and implement policies on tariffs, NTBs, and competitive exchange rate regimes. Such policies would facilitate more open, predictable, and transparent trade relations; increase market access with trading partners; and build and strengthen existing GVC links. Policies should also aim to reduce tariffs on imports and exports (on capital, intermediate, and consumer goods) to enable integration into GVCs.

Deepening Regional Trade and Integration to Support the Emergence of Regional Value Chains

A regional industrial policy in the context of the African Continental Free Trade Area (AfCFTA) could bolster scale economies and complementarities to drive more production, processing, and higher-value exports from the region, and facilitate industrialization through GVCs.

High trade barriers affect the investment and production decisions of firms in GVCs. Export tariffs between countries in the region averaged 18.1 percent in 1990. By 2000, this figure had dropped by only 3 percentage points, and, by 2015, it had dropped by an additional 5 percentage points. Despite a declining trend, it was still higher than the average export tariff to Western Europe (6.3 percentage points higher), the United States (8.0 percentage points higher), and China (6.2 percentage points higher) in 2015 (figure 6.2).

Intraregional trade within Sub-Saharan Africa in 2017 was 16.6 percent of total trade; by comparison, intraregional trade was 68.1 percent in Europe, 59.4 percent in Asia, and 55.0 percent in North America (Odijie 2019). Reducing these tariff barriers and other cumulative border protections would further boost Sub-Saharan Africa's trade and participation in GVCs, allowing firms access to quality foreign intermediate inputs for production and increased exports. The AfCFTA will be critical to facilitating such policy changes.

Figure 6.1 Tariffs and GVC Participation in Sub-Saharan Africa, 1990–2015

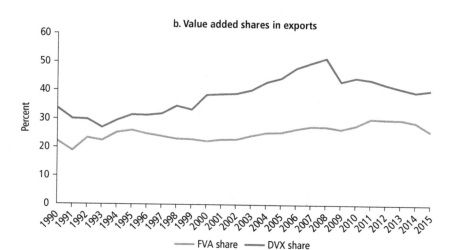

Source: World Bank calculations based on the World Bank World Integrated Trade Solution and the United Nations Conference on Trade and Development's Eora database.
Note: DVX = share in total value added in exports used as intermediate inputs to other countries' exports to third countries; FVA = share of foreign value added in exports.

Figure 6.2 Tariffs Faced by Sub-Saharan African Exports, by Region of Destination, 1995–2015

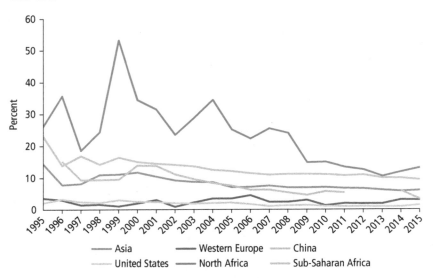

Source: World Bank calculations, based on World Integrated Trade Solution data.
Note: Asia includes China.

Table 6.1 Tariffs on Imported Goods to Sub-Saharan Africa, by Product Group (%), 1990–2015

Product group	1990	1995	2000	2005	2010	2015
Capital goods	6.4	13.0	4.3	3.1	3.7	3.2
Transport equipment and parts and accessories	24.8	22.1	14.9	11.4	11.6	9.9
Consumer goods	19.4	27.2	14.0	11.7	12.3	10.9
Intermediate goods (industrial supplies, primary)	5.8	9.5	8.1	4.8	5.9	2.0
Intermediate goods (industrial supplies, processed)	13.3	11.6	8.9	7.1	8.0	6.7

Source: World Bank calculations, based on World Integrated Trade Solution data.
Note: Capital goods are all capital goods except transport equipment. Tariffs are the weighted average of the effective tariffs applied and defined in the World Integrated Trade Solution as the lowest available tariff. If a preferential tariff exists, it is used as the effective applied tariff. Otherwise, the most favored nation applied tariff is used.

The AfCFTA agreement covers trade in goods and services, investment, intellectual property rights, and competition policy. By requiring member countries to eliminate up to 90 percent of the tariffs on goods and reducing NTBs to trade, the AfCFTA is expected to create a larger tariff-free market for countries in the region so they can trade effectively and competitively

Figure 6.3 Tariffs on Imported Goods to Sub-Saharan Africa, by Product Group, 1990–2015

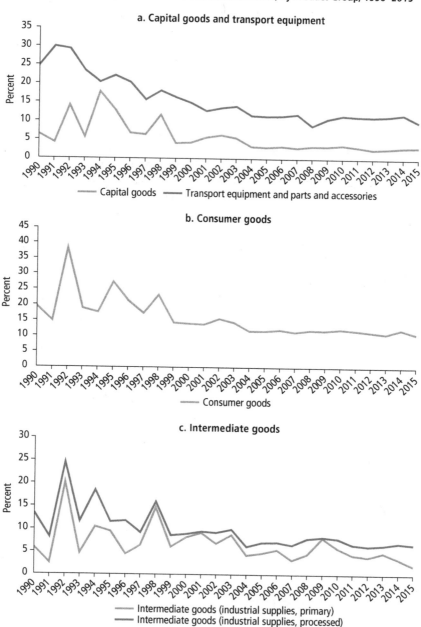

Source: World Bank calculations based on World Integrated Trade Solution data.

and reap the benefits of free trade to boost industrialization efforts in the region. The United Nations Economic Commission for Africa estimates that the agreement will boost intra-African trade by 52 percent by 2022 (Odijie 2018, 2019).

However, the AfCFTA will not automatically accelerate industrialization across Sub-Saharan Africa. The potential impact of the agreement on industrialization will depend on whether countries in the region embrace industrialization as a potential path to sustainable economic growth, realizing their comparative advantages and focusing on increasing their productive capabilities in the increasingly competitive global market, with a strategic focus on industrialization (Oqubay 2019).

Currently, the prime goal of the AfCFTA is to boost intraregional trade, with no program governing industrial policy in the region. A mechanism must be developed to deal with the lack of coordination that is likely to occur at the continental level to avoid creating winners and losers (Odijie 2018). A regional industrial policy that is based on supply-side strategies in addition to traditional demand-side strategies would be required. This strategy should include the creation of conditions to allow for scale economies and complementarities that can drive more production, processing, and higher-value exports from the region (Gereffi 2014).

Annex 5 to the Protocol on Trade in Goods of the AfCFTA includes detailed plans to remove and deal with the many NTBs impeding trade in Sub-Saharan Africa by establishing a reporting, monitoring, and elimination mechanism whereby the private sector can file a complaint related to NTBs. This process is expected to help the benefits of the free trade agreement materialize and improve the effectiveness of tariff liberalization efforts through the AfCFTA.

As detailed in the AfCFTA, these plans cover a wide range of restrictive practices other than tariffs that make trade difficult and costly within the region. The areas covered include but are not limited to customs clearance delays, restrictive licensing processes, certification challenges, uncoordinated transport-related regulation and corruption, technical barriers to trade, and sanitary and phytosanitary measures. The system is expected to ease reporting and problem-resolution related to NTBs by providing traders, freighters, firms, and other parties affected by NTBs a mechanism for reporting NTB-related issues to a specifically designed website and offline complaints procedure and for receiving information on NTB resolution processes. Each complaint filed on the NTB website is checked by the AfCFTA NTBs coordination unit to ascertain the validity of the complaint, accept or reject it, or ask for further clarification from the complainant. Once accepted, it is transmitted to the government of the responsible trading partner (national focal point) for a reaction and resolution within a concrete timeline (Erasmus 2019).

The large economies and the relatively industrialized economies in the region can institute policies to drive investments in technology and capital-intensive sectors. Small economies and economies with weak industrial bases can leverage low costs and proximity to large regional markets to build capacity in specialized GVC niches in the context of a regional production system (Gereffi 2014). Such a negotiated system would not only resolve the issue of coordination failures but also help build domestic industrial capacity according to each country's comparative advantage and productive capacity. For this system to be successful, the region should negotiate as a unit, as well as invest in connectivity and infrastructure (Odijie 2018; Oqubay 2019).

Infrastructure Development

Reducing Overall Trade Costs

The quality of infrastructure is a key factor in determining how GVC participation affects economic upgrading because infrastructure can influence the predictability, reliability, and timeliness of GVCs (WEF 2013). Many countries are unable to integrate into GVCs because low-quality infrastructure makes them unable to meet the requirements for timely production and delivery. For example, slow and unpredictable land transport has kept most of Sub-Saharan Africa out of GVCs for electronics and fruits and vegetables (Arvis, Marteau, and Raballand 2010; Christ and Ferrantino 2011).

Studies suggest that reducing trade barriers such as border administration, transport and communications infrastructure, and related services would have a greater impact on trade and growth of gross domestic product (GDP) than the complete elimination of tariffs (World Bank 2020). Transport costs in developing countries remain the main obstacle to entering, establishing, or moving up in GVCs (OECD and WTO 2013). For example, port congestion and access to rail and port services are critical factors for GVC competitiveness among countries in the Southern African Customs Union (Farole 2016).

Improving the quality of infrastructure and promoting international connectivity, therefore, would enhance forward and backward links within GVCs by securing the flow and lowering the costs of inputs and outputs, increasing speed, and minimizing uncertainty. Higher-quality infrastructure and better connectivity at the border would have a positive impact on GVC integration as well as on GVC upgrading. Policies pertaining to infrastructure investments and operations should be a critical part of any industrial policy strategy (Kummritz, Taglioni, and Winkler 2017).

Developing a Digital Ecosystem

The diffusion of advanced digital production technologies such as robotics and the emergence of new technologies such as artificial intelligence, the Internet of Things, additive manufacturing, and synthetic biology are radically changing the nature of manufacturing, blurring the boundaries between physical and digital production systems. These emerging technologies are expected to profoundly affect the future of manufacturing-led development in Africa (Hallward-Driemeier and Nayyar 2017). To transform and boost industrial growth, however, Africa needs to position itself to leverage these technologies, especially by overcoming the region's low information and communication technology (ICT) adoption and inadequate ICT skills base (Choi, Dutz, and Usman 2019).

Sub-Saharan Africa suffers from the digital divide because of limited expansion of ICT, which limits the associated gains in productivity, jobs, and competitiveness, and hence restricts the widespread adoption of ICT in manufacturing. As shown in figure 6.4, based on five pillars—national ICT strategy, business environment, infrastructure, financial capital, and ICT skills

Figure 6.4 Readiness to Leverage the Potential of the Internet

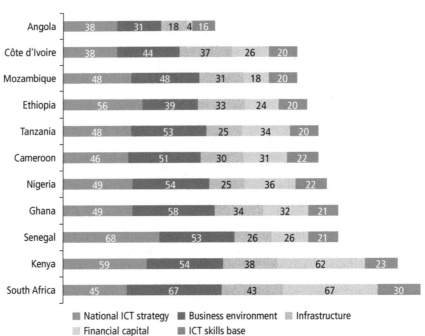

Source: McKinsey Global Institute 2013.
Note: Each variable is a composite index scored between 0 (not ready) and 100 (fully ready). ICT = information and communication technology.

base—most countries in the region are not ready to exploit the opportunities offered by the internet (McKinsey Global Institute 2013). The challenge is even more pronounced when considering their readiness as measured by their ICT skills base.

Thus, African countries should invest in building and expanding digital infrastructure.[1] Additionally, such efforts must involve developing complementary digital skills (through dynamic education policy and training programs), enforcing targeted reforms in ICT sector regulation, enabling firm and industry capabilities to facilitate the adoption of digital technologies, providing incentives for digital entrepreneurship, and promoting widespread adoption of digital technologies in public services.[2] Policy should also aim to address other supply-side constraints such as access to connectivity infrastructure and other complementary infrastructure, including electricity.

Policy interventions, therefore, will be required to build up strong enabling sectors in logistics, digital infrastructure, finance, and energy. Such interventions should improve the logistics sector and help provide a wide range of low-cost and high-quality services, expand the provision of reliable and affordable ICT services, facilitate access to finance through development of the banking sector and establishment of secondary markets, and target investment in power generation capacity as well as improve its affordability and accessibility, especially for business enterprises.

Competition Policy

Lessening or Eliminating Barriers to Entry for Domestic and Foreign Firms

The manufacturing experiences of Sub-Saharan African countries such as Côte d'Ivoire and Ethiopia suggest that young firms are the main drivers of job growth. This evidence makes entry and exit barriers central to defining the policy agenda for job creation and growth reform. In most of the region, restrictions on firm entry are pervasive. There is strong evidence that entry regulations hamper entry, especially in industries that naturally should have high entry (Klapper, Laeven, and Rajan 2004). Policies that ease the multitude of entry barriers to new firms could yield large gains by raising aggregate productivity, maintaining market discipline, and expanding job creation. Hence, policies that promote competition should be central to industrialization strategies in the region. The possibility of entry by itself provides a market selection mechanism and fosters greater competition between new entrants and existing firms as well as among the new entrants. Evidence from China and other East Asian economies shows that the creation and selection of new firms in the nonstate sector has been the most important source of productivity and output growth in the manufacturing sector.[3]

Eliminating regulatory distortions that restrict entry has been shown to be instrumental in many countries. In India, the elimination of compulsory industrial licensing, called the *license raj*, which regulated firm entry and imposed output capacity constraints, led to aggregate productivity gains. Most of the reallocation gains are attributed to new entrants in deregulated industries during the early postreform period and incumbent firms in the later period (Alfaro and Chari 2014). Regulatory reforms that make it easier to start a formal business are associated with increases in the number of newly registered firms and higher levels of employment and productivity. Conversely, economies with cumbersome regulations and administrative procedures for starting a business are associated with fewer legally registered firms, greater informality, a smaller tax base, and more opportunities for corruption and tax evasion compared with economies with more efficient regulations.

Easing Capital Requirements and Access to Credit

In several Sub-Saharan African economies, the capital requirement—money entrepreneurs must deposit to start a business—is still a major obstacle to starting a business (Djankov 2009). In 2013, 13 economies in the region had minimum capital requirements exceeding 200 percent of income per capita, reaching a high of 528 percent in one country (World Bank 2013). In economies with high minimum capital requirements, small and medium-sized firms have less access to bank financing (World Bank 2013). Hence, the reduction or elimination of capital requirements would reduce the costs of entry for new firms. In addition, if capital requirements are prohibitively high, potential entrants may be less inclined to formalize their enterprises.

Another constraint that potential entrants face is limited access to finance. Although access to finance is improving in some countries, manufacturing firms in the region indicated that factors such as the complex application procedure, unfavorable interest rates, and high collateral requirements are major bottlenecks to accessing finance for the operation of their businesses. The effects of these obstacles tend to be worse for domestically owned firms, small and medium enterprises, and nonexporting manufacturing firms. Lack of access to finance caused by distortions in allocation or overall financial underdevelopment is a major constraint to the entry of new firms, particularly smaller firms, and should be remedied.

Reforming the Ownership and Structure of State-Owned Enterprises

State-owned enterprises (SOEs) and other large firms with state connections often enjoy favors that may introduce market distortions that limit the prospects of entry for new firms.[4] An indirect policy approach consisting of reforming and restructuring SOEs could improve SOE performance while reducing the distortions that impose barriers to the entry of new firms and associated investments in new technologies. Access to credit, land, key infrastructure (for example, electricity), and foreign exchange to purchase imports may be allocated accordingly.

Local and central governments may also impose complicated licensing regulations that restrict entry. In many countries, industrial policies that are intended to support a few strategic sectors may create distortions that restrict entry and hence limit the gains from the selection that increases productivity and job creation. Policies should aim to reduce the costs of entry by easing regulatory barriers to entry and minimizing the distortions in allocation associated with state-owned and state-affiliated incumbent firms.

Education and Skills Enhancement

Coordinating and Aligning Industrial and Trade Policies with Education and Skills Enhancement Policies

Manufacturing firms in Sub-Saharan Africa are largely operating in the labor-intensive segments of GVCs. The benefits of specializing in these segments are limited, particularly in GVCs that use cheap labor and low levels of technology. Economies such as the Republic of Korea, Singapore, and Taiwan, China, reaped significant gains from assembly manufacturing by using it as a basis for building higher-level productive capabilities, including nationally controlled GVCs, as part of ambitious industrial policy strategies.

The existing evidence suggests that there is a strong correlation between international fragmentation of production and the skills endowments of countries, and that the mix of skills of workers (skills bundle) plays a critical role in countries' industrial specialization and integration into GVCs. Thus, although integrating into GVCs and reaping sizable benefits will require development of the skills that are necessary for higher-level tasks, policies focused only on selected, specific skills rather than bundles of skills may reduce the ability of countries to reap the benefits of GVC participation.

Investing in education and skills development is the starting point for helping the youth in developing countries take advantage of the opportunities for employment in GVCs (World Bank 2020). Presently, many Sub-Saharan African countries' education systems are not designed to provide the skills needed for GVC-related activities. Furthermore, the region faces the future of work with a weak human capital base, and there is a huge gap between the demand for skills by employers and the supply of skills (Choi, Dutz, and Usman 2019). Hence, skills-enhancement policies should aim to equip the potential workforce with a set of skills—such as transferability, adaptability, and problem-solving, as well as managerial skills—to improve the productivity of workers involved in GVC-related activities. Policies should also facilitate access to education at all levels by removing restrictive bottlenecks.

Policies that target the development of specific industries could lower a country's comparative advantage if workers' skills do not match the requirements of the industry. Thus, understanding and anticipating skills requirements in production would be necessary for countries to seize the opportunities that emerge as a result of specific comparative advantages.

Furthermore, for the majority of Sub-Saharan African countries, upgrading their position in the value chain and reaping the benefits thereof is currently a policy priority. Upgrading into higher value chains is associated with larger expected economic benefits, including high-wage employment and higher incomes. Currently, integration into GVCs and upgrading in the region have happened mostly in less knowledge-intensive manufacturing industries although there is some evidence of upgrading in knowledge-intensive manufacturing industries in some countries.

The skills of workers in Sub-Saharan Africa at present are weakly aligned with the requirements for participation in activities downstream of the value chain, which partly explains the region's low specialization in industries in the lower rungs of the value chain. Thus, whether Sub-Saharan African countries will upgrade into other sophisticated segments of the value chain would depend on implementation of policies that support and make such a transition possible.

Education and skills-development policies can significantly influence countries' industrial structures and specialization in international trade; and the coordination and alignment of industrial and trade policies with education and skills-enhancement policies would be needed to maximize the gains from integrating into GVCs (Grundke et al. 2017).

Facilitating the Transition from Training to Jobs

Education policies should focus on innovative curriculum and teaching strategies that include a strong work-based learning component and that build strong literacy, numeracy, and cognitive skills and management and communication strategies that align with the characteristics of industries' skills requirements (OECD 2017). Education policies in countries that are ready to upgrade into activities higher up the value chain in technologically advanced industries should also focus on building social, emotional, and adaptability skills to complement cognitive skills (OECD 2017).

Enhancing International Cooperation for Skills Mobility

Policies should make room for the use of foreign talent. Skilled migrants have been found to contribute positively to Sub-Saharan Africa's participation in manufacturing GVCs, especially in countries with acute shortages of skilled labor (Nadege and Jammeh 2019). It is therefore imperative to have policies and agreements that encourage and promote intraregional skills mobility as a way to facilitate integration into high-skill tasks in manufacturing GVCs. Policy strategies should ensure the presence of a careful and effective blend of skills-related policies, migration policies, and employment-protection policies and that these policies are aligned with industrial and trade policies at the country level. While pursuing these strategies, efforts should be made to remove any barriers and bottlenecks to further skills development, particularly given the changing nature of work (OECD 2017).

Promoting the Empowerment of Women in Manufacturing through Skills Improvement

Promoting inclusiveness and empowerment of women should be an integral part of industrial policy in Sub-Saharan African countries. Despite their socio-economic contributions, women represent only 38 percent of the manufacturing workforce in Africa (Yong 2017) and, for every US$1 made by men in manufacturing, services, and trade, women earn only 70 cents (Kabaya and Lusigi 2018). A set of policies adopted by the Ethiopian government underscores the potential role that governments can play to create employment opportunities for women in manufacturing (box 6.2).

BOX 6.2

Women in Manufacturing Jobs: The Role of Industrial Policy

Female labor force participation is high in Ethiopia, 77.8 percent as of 2013, although 36 percent of this is in the informal sector. The share of women in the agricultural sector decreased by 10.8 percent between 2005 and 2014. The service sector rather than manufacturing has been the largest beneficiary of this labor shift. As of 2014, female workers represented 33.3 percent of the workforce in the manufacturing sector (large and medium scale). About 78 percent of women employed in manufacturing in Ethiopia reported an improvement in income and 63 percent recorded an increase in family living standards. This steady increase has been achieved through targeted government policies. Through the second Growth and Transformation Plan (GTP II), the Ethiopian government aims to ensure that growth in the manufacturing sector is equitable and inclusive, and benefits youth, women, and all communities.

The plan envisages creating new job opportunities in textiles and garments, leather and leather products, food and beverages, and the pharmaceutical industry. Women are expected to fill 60 percent of the low- and medium-skill jobs, and 30 percent of the high-skill jobs. In addition, GTP II also aims to increase the participation of women in high leadership positions in manufacturing (UNDP 2018).

(continued next page)

Box 6.2 Women in Manufacturing Jobs: The Role of Industrial Policy (continued)

The government's focus on ensuring equitable and inclusive industrialization-led growth is important for several reasons. In Ethiopia, women who participate in the manufacturing sector are on average less educated, rural migrants (62 percent) who work predominantly in labor-intensive and low-skill, low-paying jobs in subsectors such as agro-processing, textiles and apparel, and leather and leather goods manufacturing, and earn much less (77 percent of what their male counterparts earn) even after adjusting for education and experience. These patterns are also observed in women's participation in value chains. The country's garment sector, for example, has a disproportionately high concentration of women in low-skill jobs and factory floor operations. Women constitute 60 percent of the production workforce in the cutting stage and 95 percent in the sewing stage, but only 15 percent of the workforce in the finishing stage.

By contrast, in high-skill jobs or traditionally male-dominated subsectors such as the chemical and metal engineering industries, women account for only 10 percent and 20 percent of high-skilled production workers, respectively. Even in emerging manufacturing subsectors such as information and communication technology manufacturing, where women's participation rate has been on the rise, they are still overrepresented in the lower-skill strata (UNDP 2018).

Women are also underrepresented in top leadership positions in manufacturing, with about 8 percent of director positions held by women across all manufacturing industries, rising to 13 percent when the sample includes small manufacturing firms. On average, 16 percent of large- and medium-scale manufacturing firms are owned by women; women-owned firms tend to be smaller and concentrated in low-productivity, low-technology, and low-growth industries.

A set of policies implemented by the Ethiopian government was instrumental in promoting inclusiveness and empowerment of women in manufacturing. The Ministry of Industry's Industrial Development Strategic Plan (2013–2025) focused on a policy shift from agriculture-led to industrial-led development, emphasizing the labor-intensive industrial sector to generate employment. Although the strategic plan is gender neutral, the prioritization of labor-intensive, women-dominated subsectors has contributed to increased employment opportunities for women in manufacturing and spurred female entrepreneurship. The adoption of both the Growth and Transformation Plan I (GTP I) between 2011 and 2015 and GTP II during 2016–20 as part of the industrial development plan had specific gender targets and stipulated policies that enhanced women's entry into these sectors. The strategy to boost industrial performance through the development of industrial parks contributed to the creation of employment opportunities for women in manufacturing. For example, the Hawassa Industrial Park, which is a hub for the textiles and garment industry, is expected to create 60,000 jobs, of which 90 percent are expected to benefit women. Additionally, through its National Employment Policy and Strategy, Ethiopia has implemented policies to increase women's participation in the labor market, particularly in the formal sector. The strategy also emphasizes providing support to improve the skills, productivity, and income of women as well as providing daycare centers in or near work premises so working mothers can safely leave their children during working hours (UNDP 2018).

Links between Domestic Firms and Multinationals: Foreign Direct Investment and Technology Transfer

Building Domestic Links with Multinationals and Exporters

Sub-Saharan African countries need to capitalize on the opportunities presented by the emergence of the region as a new frontier for global investment. The period between 1980 and 2000 saw some volatility in FDI inflows to Sub-Saharan Africa, with inward FDI increasing from US$248 million in 1980 to US$6.4 billion in 2000. FDI inflows to the region increased by nearly fivefold between 2000 and 2015, from a global share of 0.472 percent in 2000 to 2.190 percent in 2015 (US$44.547 billion), and fell to 1.878 percent in 2017 (US$28.117 billion).[5] FDI inflows still account for a low percentage of total global flows and a low share of the region's GDP (6.4 percent). GVCs are typically coordinated by transnational corporations (foreign direct investors), and their increased presence has contributed to the expansion of GVCs in the region (figure 6.5).

In countries such as Tanzania and Uganda, although the manufacturing sector has not always been the largest recipient of capital investment, it has

Figure 6.5 **Foreign Direct Investment and Manufacturing GVCs in Sub-Saharan Africa, 1990–2015**

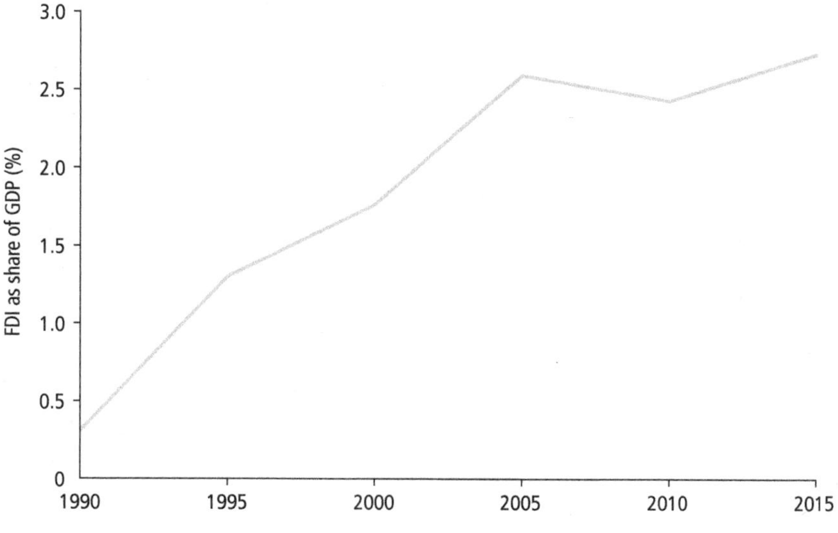

Source: World Bank calculations based on the World Bank World Development Indicators.
Note: FDI = foreign direct investment; GVC = global value chain.

generated the most FDI jobs (employment as a result of FDI). In Tanzania, the sector was the largest FDI job creator during 2008 and 2009, with an average of 36,303 jobs per year (43 percent of all FDI jobs created). In Uganda, the manufacturing FDI jobs created in 2012 accounted for 23 percent of full-time jobs and 79 percent of part-time jobs in the country. In Ethiopia, manufacturing FDI created 28 percent of all FDI jobs between 2008 and 2014. China, Germany, India, and the United Kingdom created the most job opportunities for Sub-Saharan Africa through greenfield projects between 2003 and 2014. Among investor groups, new partners (China and India) and intraregional partners (such as South Africa and Kenya) created jobs comparable to the number of jobs created by the region's traditional partners (Germany, the United Kingdom, and the United States) (Chen, Geiger, and Fu 2015).

Links to input industries must be built to attract FDI to transform manufacturing. For instance, Ethiopia, arguably a standout in the nascent stages of industrial transformation, has focused its industrial policy on reducing dependence on imported inputs in highly prioritized manufacturing industries—textiles and leather products (box 6.3). This policy stance helps generate better links to domestic supplier industries. Policies that promote the

---

BOX 6.3

Investment and Global Value Chain–Oriented Industrial Policy in Ethiopia

Since the early 2000s, Ethiopia has implemented an industrial policy strategy that aims to industrialize the country through global value chains. The country is attracting investment in its labor-intensive manufacturing industries, such as leather products and apparel, to assist its export promotion strategies. As part of its strategy, Ethiopia has put in place a range of financial incentives, including duty-free access to imported inputs and reforms to land leasing. These financial incentives are expected to boost exports. For instance, duty-free access to imported inputs is available only if final products are exported.

The strategy seems to be generating quick employment creation and increased export earnings. However, few links to domestic firms have been created. Export earnings have grown, but exports are dominated by foreign firms. For this strategy to work and for Ethiopia to successfully integrate domestic firms into global value chains, complementary policies should aim to make domestic manufacturing firms internationally competitive. Strategic policies should also be implemented, such as bargaining with foreign investors to create links and transfer technology to the domestic economy. This approach can take the form of creating explicit supplier programs and rewards for foreign companies that make extra efforts to help build the capacity of local suppliers.

Note: This box draws heavily on Hauge (2020).

building of vertically integrated industries have underpinned the industrial strategies of successful late industrializers. Therefore, industrial policy in the GVC era should emphasize increasing local content and technology transfer (Staritz, Plank, and Morris 2016).

Facilitating Knowledge Transfer via Foreign Direct Investment

A notable trend in the region pertains to the overwhelming majority of FDI flows that go into natural resources. Between 1998 and 2009, most of the flows into the top 10 FDI recipient countries in the region went into oil, gas, and mining projects. The primary sector has been the largest recipient of accumulated FDI into the region, although this predominance seems to be gradually changing. FDI has begun to flow into more diversified sectors in the region. In 2013, 63 percent of the total value of announced greenfield investment went to the services sector, 26 percent to manufacturing, and 11 percent to the primary sector (figure 6.6). Increasingly, traditional foreign investors have voluntarily withdrawn from resource-seeking FDI, and the primary beneficiary has been the services sector as these investors have shifted toward investments that target the emerging middle-class population with growing purchasing power. In addition, most modern services in Sub-Saharan Africa (ICT, telecommunications, insurance, banking, and so forth) are dominated by foreign multinational corporations (Broich and Szirmai 2014).

Figure 6.6 **Sectoral Distribution of Announced Greenfield Foreign Direct Investment Projects in Sub-Saharan Africa, 2004–13**

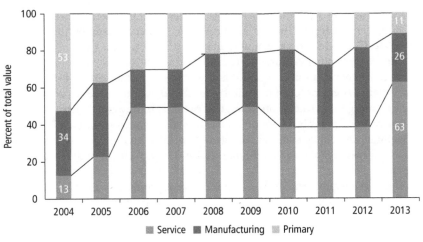

Source: Chen, Geiger, and Fu 2015.
Note: Calculations based on fDi Markets Database (www.fdimarkets.com).

Multinational corporations have strong incentives to promote knowledge transfers and to strengthen their domestic partners to enhance productivity along local value chains. This goal is particularly relevant for investors with intensive backward and forward links. Through FDI, domestic firms can benefit from new ideas, technology transfers, and spillovers from multinational corporations to stimulate productivity growth and expand the scale of their activities. Sub-Saharan Africa can leverage investments (foreign and domestic) to boost performance in GVCs, trade, and industrialization by (1) adopting investment policies that improve connectivity by modernizing communications, transport, and energy infrastructure while reforming services, which have become integral to global production and will deliver important benefits to developing countries through the supply chain; (2) adopting policies that unilaterally reduce investment barriers and improve the business climate; and (3) harmonizing and consolidating investment policy reforms at the regional and national levels to avoid undesirable fragmentation and overlaps of investment regimes.

Policy Framework: Integrate, Compete, Upgrade, and Enable

The set of policies that could be implemented to promote industrialization can be categorized into soft policies and hard policies. Soft policies aim to support the growth and productivity of all sectors in the economy, whereas hard policies target the development of traditional manufacturing, building sectors with some characteristics of manufacturing, and promoting indigenous entrepreneurship in small-scale manufacturing.[6] A suggested policy framework incorporating both soft policies and hard policies is characterized by four pillars: Integrate, Compete, Upgrade, and Enable, or ICUE (figure 6.7).

The *integrate* pillar captures policies that promote GVC participation as well as overall integration into regional and global economies through trade and investment. These policies include trade liberalization, trade diversification toward emerging market economies, and regional trade agreements.

The *compete* pillar is the set of policies aimed at reducing market distortions to facilitate the entry, survival, and growth of new establishments, and comprises reforms of SOEs and credit markets, and improvement of the investment climate.

The *upgrade* pillar encompasses policies that promote industrial and GVC upgrading and facilitate industrial shifts in employment shares and creation of value added. Industrial upgrading encompasses the rapid growth (in relative terms) and redistribution of employment and value added toward knowledge-intensive industries (for example, electrical and machinery and transport

Figure 6.7 Policy Framework: Integrate, Compete, Upgrade, and Enable

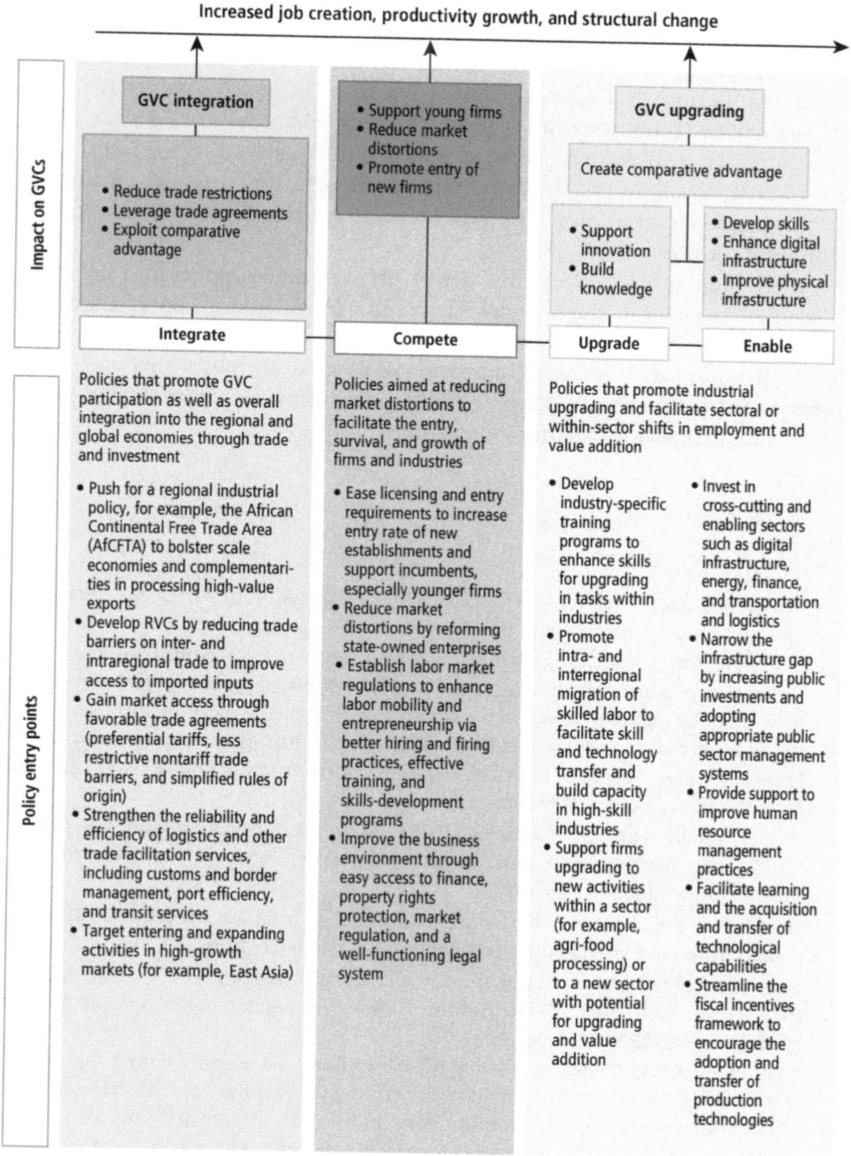

Increased job creation, productivity growth, and structural change

GVC integration

- Reduce trade restrictions
- Leverage trade agreements
- Exploit comparative advantage

- Support young firms
- Reduce market distortions
- Promote entry of new firms

GVC upgrading

Create comparative advantage

- Support innovation
- Build knowledge

- Develop skills
- Enhance digital infrastructure
- Improve physical infrastructure

Impact on GVCs

Integrate	Compete	Upgrade	Enable
Policies that promote GVC participation as well as overall integration into the regional and global economies through trade and investment	Policies aimed at reducing market distortions to facilitate the entry, survival, and growth of firms and industries	Policies that promote industrial upgrading and facilitate sectoral or within-sector shifts in employment and value addition	

Policy entry points

Integrate
- Push for a regional industrial policy, for example, the African Continental Free Trade Area (AfCFTA) to bolster scale economies and complementarities in processing high-value exports
- Develop RVCs by reducing trade barriers on inter- and intraregional trade to improve access to imported inputs
- Gain market access through favorable trade agreements (preferential tariffs, less restrictive nontariff trade barriers, and simplified rules of origin)
- Strengthen the reliability and efficiency of logistics and other trade facilitation services, including customs and border management, port efficiency, and transit services
- Target entering and expanding activities in high-growth markets (for example, East Asia)

Compete
- Ease licensing and entry requirements to increase entry rate of new establishments and support incumbents, especially younger firms
- Reduce market distortions by reforming state-owned enterprises
- Establish labor market regulations to enhance labor mobility and entrepreneurship via better hiring and firing practices, effective training, and skills-development programs
- Improve the business environment through easy access to finance, property rights protection, market regulation, and a well-functioning legal system

Upgrade
- Develop industry-specific training programs to enhance skills for upgrading in tasks within industries
- Promote intra- and interregional migration of skilled labor to facilitate skill and technology transfer and build capacity in high-skill industries
- Support firms upgrading to new activities within a sector (for example, agri-food processing) or to a new sector with potential for upgrading and value addition

Enable
- Invest in cross-cutting and enabling sectors such as digital infrastructure, energy, finance, and transportation and logistics
- Narrow the infrastructure gap by increasing public investments and adopting appropriate public sector management systems
- Provide support to improve human resource management practices
- Facilitate learning and the acquisition and transfer of technological capabilities
- Streamline the fiscal incentives framework to encourage the adoption and transfer of production technologies

Source: Original figure for this publication.
Note: GVC = global value chain; RVC = regional value chain.

equipment) and away from agriculture-based, labor-intensive industries (food and beverages, textiles and apparel, and wood and paper) and mining-based, capital-intensive industries (chemicals and non-metals and metals). GVC upgrading denotes the movement of workers into more sophisticated business functions in GVCs, such as when firms in an industry move from performing assembly activities to product design and redesign, logistics, after-sales services, and repairs. Policies that promote upgrading include those subsidizing research and development and innovation, supporting human resource management practices, and leveraging urbanizing and developing economic clusters.

Finally, the *enable* pillar is the set of policies that support and promote investment in enabling sectors, including digital infrastructure, energy, finance, transportation and logistics, and skills development. These sectors are cross-cutting in nature and capable of improving productive and absorptive capacities in agriculture and services, strengthening their links with manufacturing, and supporting inclusive and better job creation.

Notes

1. See Blimpo and Cosgrove-Davies (2019) on electrification in Africa as a necessary input for long-term economic transformation.
2. Scaling up the uptake of digital technology to transform the region's manufacturing sector requires investing in and promoting the birth and growth of tech entrepreneurs and the regional rollout of the Internet of Things. The recent rise of tech start-ups in mega cities across the region provides an optimistic picture. However, without large-scale investments in foundational digital infrastructure and skills, the region faces the risk of being left behind.
3. Brandt, Van Biesebroeck, and Zhang (2012) and Brandt, Kambourov, and Storesletten (2017) show that over 1998–2007 net entry accounted for more than two-thirds of total factor productivity growth.
4. Brandt, Van Biesebroeck, and Zhang (2012) find that, in China, the presence of state-owned firms gave rise to larger entry barriers for nonstate firms.
5. From the United Nations Conference on Trade and Development's UNCTADstat data set (accessed May 13, 2020), https://unctadstat.unctad.org/wds/TableViewer/tableView.aspx?ReportId=96740.
6. Such policies may include reforming the educational curriculum. For example, in a study on how a comprehensive teacher training program affects the delivery of a major entrepreneurship curriculum reform in Rwanda, Blimpo and Pugatch (2021) find that secondary school students who were exposed to the reform had increased participation in their own businesses and decreased employment in others.

References

Alfaro, L., and A. Chari. 2014. "Deregulation, Misallocation, and Size: Evidence from India." *Journal of Law and Economics* 57 (4): 897–936.

Arvis, J. F., J.-F. Marteau, and G. J. R. F. Raballand. 2010. *The Cost of Being Landlocked: Logistics Costs and Supply Chain Reliability*. Washington, DC: World Bank.

Balie, J., D. Del Prete, E. Magrini, P. Montalbano, and S. Nenci. 2018. "Does Trade Policy Impact Food and Agriculture Global Value Chain Participation?" *American Journal of Agricultural Economics* 101 (3): 773–89.

Blimpo, M. P., and T. Pugatch. 2021. "Entrepreneurship Education and Teacher Training in Rwanda." *Journal of Development Economics* 149: 102583.

Blimpo, M. P., and M. Cosgrove-Davies. 2019. *Electricity Access in Sub-Saharan Africa: Uptake, Reliability, and Complementary Factors for Economic Impact*. Africa Development Forum. Washington, DC: World Bank.

Brandt, L., G. Kambourov, and K. Storesletten. 2017. "Barriers to Entry and Regional Economic Growth in China." University of Toronto, Toronto, Canada.

Brandt, L., J. Van Biesebroeck, and Y. Zhang. 2012. "Creative Accounting or Creative Destruction? Firm-Level Productivity Growth in Chinese Manufacturing." *Journal of Development Economics* 97 (2): 339–51.

Broich, T., and A. Szirmai. 2014. "China's Embrace of Africa: An International Comparative Perspective." UNU–MERIT Working Paper Series 049, United Nations University–Maastricht Economic and Social Research Institute on Innovation and Technology, Maastricht, Netherlands.

Charles, M. B., R. Ryan, R. Oloruntoba, T. von der Heidt, and N. Ryan. 2009. "The EU-Africa Energy Partnership: Towards a Mutually Beneficial Renewable Transport Energy Alliance?" *Energy Policy* 37 (12): 5546–56.

Chen, G., M. Geiger, and M. Fu. 2015. *Manufacturing FDI in Sub-Saharan Africa: Trends, Determinants, and Impacts*. Washington, DC: World Bank.

Choi, J., M. Dutz, and Z. Usman. 2019. *The Future of Work in Africa: Harnessing the Potential of Digital Technologies for All*. Washington, DC: World Bank.

Christ, Nannette, and M. J. Ferrantino. 2011. "Land Transport for Export: The Effects of Cost, Time, and Uncertainty in Sub-Saharan Africa." *World Development* 39 (10): 1749–59.

Coulibaly, S., W. Kassa, and A. G. Zeufack. Forthcoming. *Africa in the New Trade Environment: Market Access in Troubled Times*. Washington, DC: World Bank.

Djankov, S. 2009. "The Regulation of Entry: A Survey." *World Bank Research Observer* 24 (2): 183–203.

Erasmus, G. 2019. "Dealing with Non-Tariff Barriers under AfCFTA: What Are the Prospects?" Trade Law Centre, Western Cape Region, South Africa.

Farole, T. 2016. "Factory Southern Africa? SACU in Global Value Chains." World Bank Group, Washington, DC.

Gereffi, G. 2014. "A Global Value Chain Perspective on Industrial Policy and Development in Emerging Markets." *Duke Journal of Comparative and International Law* 24: 433–58.

Grundke, R., J. S. Jamet, M. Kalamova, and M. Squicciarini. 2017. "Having the Right Mix: The Role of Skills Bundles for Comparative and Industry Performance in GVCs." OECD Science, Technology and Industry Working Paper 2017/03, Organisation for Economic Co-operation and Development, Paris.

Hallward-Driemeier, M., and G. Nayyar. 2017. *Trouble in the Making? The Future of Manufacturing-Led Development.* Washington, DC: World Bank.

Hauge, J. 2020. "Industrial Policy in the Era of Global Value-Chains: Towards a Developmentalist Framework on the Industrialization Experiences of South Korea and Taiwan." *World Economy* 43 (8): 2070–92.

Jank, M. J., G. Kutas, L. Fernando do Amaral, and A. M. Nasser. 2007. "EU and US Policies on Biofuels: Potential Impacts on Developing Countries." German Marshall Fund of the United States, Washington, DC.

Kabaya, O., and A. Lusigi. 2018. "African Employers for Gender Equality." UNDP Africa blog, November 26, 2018. https://www.africa.undp.org/content/rba/en/home /blog/2018/african-employers-for-gender-equality.html.

Kassa, W., and S. Coulibaly. 2019. "Revisiting the Trade Impact of the African Growth and Opportunity Act: A Synthetic Control Approach." Policy Research Working Paper 8993, World Bank, Washington, DC.

Kassa, W., and W. Owusu. Forthcoming. "Rules of Origin as Double-Edged Sword: Evidence from Textile GVC under AGOA." Policy Research Working Paper, World Bank, Washington, DC.

Klapper, L., L. Laeven, and R. Rajan. 2004. "Business Environment and Firm Entry: Evidence from International Data." Policy Research Working Paper 3232, World Bank, Washington, DC.

Kummritz, V., D. Taglioni, and D. Winkler. 2017. "Economic Upgrading through Global Value Chain Participation." Policy Research Working Paper 8007, World Bank, Washington, DC.

McKinsey Global Institute. 2013. "Lions Go Digital: The Internet's Transformative Potential in Africa." McKinsey and Company.

Nadege, D. Y., and K. Jammeh. 2019. "Determinants of Participation in Manufacturing GVCs in Africa: The Role of Skills and Skill Mobility." Policy Research Working Paper 8938, World Bank, Washington, DC.

Nguimkeu, P., and D. Abudu. 2019. "Public Policy and Country Integration to Manufacturing Global Value Chains: The Role of Trade and Competition Policies, Labor Market Regulation and Tax Incentives." World Bank, Washington, DC.

Odijie, E. M. 2018. "The Need for Industrial Policy Coordination in the African Continental Free Trade Area." *African Affairs* 118 (470): 182–93.

Odijie, E. M. 2019. "Free Trade Game Plan: Africa Should First Focus on Industrialization." *The National Interest* (blog), January 29, 2020. https://nationalinterest.org/blog/buzz /free-trade-game-plan-africa-should-first-focus-industrialization-117966.

OECD (Organisation for Economic Co-operation and Development). 2017. *OECD Skills Outlook 2017: Skills and Global Value Chains.* Paris: OECD Publishing.

OECD and WTO (Organisation for Economic Co-operation and Development and World Trade Organization). 2013. *Aid for Trade at a Glance 2013: Linking to Value Chains.* Paris: OECD Publishing.

Oqubay, A. 2019. "Why Industrialisation Is Vital for the African Continental Free Trade Agreement to Succeed." *ODI Insights* (blog), November 20, 2019. https://odi.org/en /insights/why-industrialisation-is-vital-for-the-african-continental-free-trade -agreement-to-succeed/.

Sector Working Group Secretariat. 2017. "Private Sector Development and Youth Employment Strategy (PSDYE) 2018–2024."

Schuenemann, F., and W. A. Kerr. 2019. "European Union Non-Tariff Barriers to Imports of African Biofuels." *Agrekon* 58: (4): 407–25.

Staritz, C., L. Plank, and M. Morris. 2016. "Global Value Chains, Industrial Policy and Sustainable Development: Ethiopia's Apparel Export Sector." Country Case Study, International Centre for Trade and Sustainable Development, Geneva.

UNDP (United Nations Development Programme). 2018. *A Study on Women in Manufacturing in Ethiopia: Opportunities, Challenges, and Strategic Interventions.* New York: UNDP.

Van Biesebroeck, J., and E. Zaurino. 2019. "Effects of Trade Liberalization on Textile and Apparel Exports from Sub-Sahara Africa." Policy Research Working Paper 8936, World Bank, Washington, DC.

WEF (World Economic Forum). 2013. *Enabling Trade: Valuing Growth Opportunities.* Geneva: WEF.

World Bank. 2013. "Why Are Minimum Capital Requirements a Concern for Entrepreneurs?" In *Doing Business 2014: Understanding Regulations for Small and Medium-Size Enterprises,* 41–45. Washington, DC: World Bank.

World Bank. 2020. *World Development Report 2020: Trading for Development in the Age of Global Value Chains.* Washington, DC: World Bank.

Yong, Li. 2017. "Africa's Industrialisation: Leaving No Woman Behind." *OECD Development Matters* (blog) April 25, 2017. https://oecd-development-matters .org/2017/04/25/africas-industrialisation-leaving-no-woman-behind/.